"The Rise and Fall of the Hawaiian Kingdom"™

(A Pictorial History)

A concise, pictorial history of Hawaii and its rulers from the birth of Kamehameha the Great to the establishment of the Territory of Hawaii in 1900.

Complied, Written, and Edited by:

Richard A. Wisniewski

Designed and Arranged by:

Herbert Goeas

Printed in Honolulu, Hawaii by:

Pacific Printing & Publishing, Inc.

•

Published & Distributed by:

Pacific Basin Enterprises
P.O. Box 8924
Honolulu, Hawaii 96830

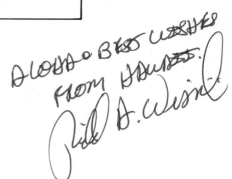

Table of Contents

Introduction

While many books have been written about the Hawaiian kingdom, few offer the reader a visual presentation of that unique part of Hawaii's past. This, then is my goal — to present a concise visual history of the Hawaiian kingdom from the circumstances that led to its formation to the events that caused its total destruction. This is the story of a continuing struggle for political power, first between rival Hawaiian chieftains, then between foreigners and Hawaiians. The foreigners, most of whom were Americans, increasingly sought to control and Americanize the islands while the native Hawaiians, faced with growing westernization of their lands and life-styles, strove to recapture the past. The involvement of these American traders and missionaries, and the involvement of their Hawaii-born children, in the internal and external affairs of the Hawaiian kingdom, drastically changed the political, social, religious and economic conditions in the islands and led to the annexation of these islands by the United States.

Since photography did not appear in Hawaii until the 1850's, the early chapters of this publication contain copies of drawings and paintings made by early artists who accompanied many of the foreign ships that visited the Hawaiian Islands. Many of the original drawings were submitted to European engravers who redrew them on copper plates in order to reproduce them for resale. In the process, these middlemen usually altered the appearance of the scene and the people in them, undoubtedly to make the finished product more saleable or more in tune to the engraver's personal tastes. Thus many of the Hawaiians depicted in the early chapters tend to have a noticeable European appearance to them.

To aid the reader in pronouncing Hawaiian words, he (or she) should give the vowels the following sounds:

a,	as the a in father		o,	as the o in no
e,	as the ey in they		u,	as the oo in too
i,	as the ee in see			

In addition, keep in mind that most vowels are pronounced separately, and that the full accent is usually placed on the second to the last vowel. The formation of the Hawaiian language is discussed in chapter three. The following sample word breakdowns should help you better understand the pronounciation of Hawaiian words:

Islands	People
Ha-wai'-i	Ka-me-ha-me'-ha (Founder of the Hawaiian Kingdom)
Mau'-i	Ka-a-hu-ma'-nu (One of Kamehameha's wives)
O-a'-hu	Ka-la-ni-o-pu'-u (King of the island of Hawaii)
Kau-ai'	Ka-la-ni-mo'-ku (Title of the chief counselor of the king)
Mo-lo-kai'	Ka-he-ki'-li (King of Maui)
La-nai'	Ka-u-mu-a-li'-i (King of Kauai)
Ni-i-hau'	Ke-o-pu-o-la'-ni (Mother of Kamehameha II and Kamehameha III)
Ka-ho-o-la'-we	Li-ho-li'-ho (Kamehameha II)
	Kau-i-ke-ao'-u-li (Kamehameha III)
	O-pu-ka-hai'-a (First Hawaiian covert)

THE AUTHOR

Dedicated to the
artists, historians and photographers
of yesterday
who helped capture and preserve
Hawaii's unique monarchial past
for this generation
and the generations to come.

Chapter 1

The Arrival of Captain James Cook

Born on October 27, 1728 in a two room clay cottage in the remote Yorkshire village of Marton-in-Cleveland, James Cook was the second of seven children. Growing up in a period when life was hard and money was scarce, Cook put to sea at an early age. His first years at sea were spent on colliers where he mastered the rigors of the Baltic and North Seas. In between voyages, he studied mathematics and navigation which would become so important to his future career. Enlisting in the Royal Navy as an ordinary seaman in 1755, Cook eventually received a commission and his first command through the help of influential friends and his own reputation as an outstanding navigator, marine surveyor and cartographer.

King George III, keenly interested in new ventures that would make new scientific discoveries and add to the expansion of his realm, lent his support to an expedition that would observe the Transit of Venus in the South Pacific in 1769. The Admiralty appointed Cook to command the *Endeavour Bark*, a former collier. Thus began Captain Cook's First of three Voyages of Discovery into the South Pacific, voyages which included polar exploration and a circumnavigation of the globe. He would be remembered as one of the world's greatest navigators and explorers.

Captain James Cook, Royal Navy   **State Archives**

John Webber   **State Archives**

John Webber (1752-1793) was the official artist on Cook's Third Voyage of Discovery. He accurately recorded memorable events, views of places and portraits of the people he encountered. His works were more widely dispersed than those of any other of Cook's artists.

In Webber's time, the only way to reproduce his drawings was to utilize the services of a professional engraver who redrew the scenes on copper plates. All too often, these middlemen could not resist the temptation to improve upon the drawings in their possession, perhaps in the hope of improving their salability. Invariably, unfamiliar subjects became more familiar, and the faces of people were softened beyond their actual appearance in order to become more charming, sophisticated and familiar for the European market.

Captain James Cook's Third Voyage into the Pacific was made in an attempt to find a Northeast Passage from the Pacific Ocean to the Atlantic Ocean. Cook's ship, *Resolution*, departed Plymouth, England on July 12, 1776. *Discovery*, commanded by Captain Charles Clerke, followed on August 1. Rendezvousing at Cape Town, South Africa, they replenished their supplies and put to sea on December 1. The squadron then proceeded to New Zealand and the Society Islands (Tahiti) for nearly a year of further observations. In December, 1777, the ships departed Bora Bora for the northward coast of America. On December 24, they discovered Christmas Island. Near the middle of January, 1778, several turtles were sighted and there were birds in the air — signs of land. On the morning of January 18, an island was sighted to the northeast and shortly thereafter, another to the west—first Oahu, then Kauai. The outside world had discovered the Hawaiian Islands.[1]

---

[1] References to other foreigners reaching these islands appear in Hawaiian legends. Also, it is claimed that the Spanish navigator Juan Gaetano may have "discovered" them in 1555. In both cases, however, no proof exists to satisfy historians.

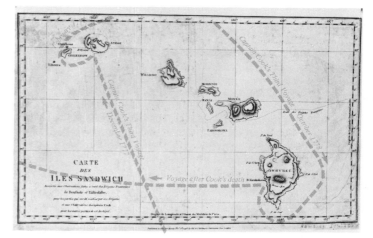

Early Map of the Sandwich (Hawaiian) Islands   State Archives

On the morning of January 19, 1778, Cook's ships took advantage of the prevailing winds and headed for the smaller of the two islands that they had discovered the preceding day. As they approached Kauai, a third island (Niihau) came into view. While Cook searched for an anchorage, a number of canoes ventured forth from Kauai. As the canoes came alongside the strange foreign ships, Cook was surprised to learn that the native men spoke in a language very similar to Tahitian. Several of Cook's veteran sailors, using a sort of pidgin-Tahitian dialect, proved to be tolerable interpreters. Some initial trading took place, and as the ships proceeded along the coast, more canoes ventured forth, this time bringing roasting pigs and potatoes instead of small fish as before. Seeking anything metal, the natives eagerly traded several small pigs for one sixpenny nail.

The following morning, January 20, Cook found an anchorage at Waimea on the western side of Kauai. The natives again approached the ships, and traded pigs, taro, potatoes and other foodstuffs for iron which they later formed into weapons. Daggers were especially prized. The natives had seen iron before, probably finding it on drift wood from wrecked ships. Several curious natives finally boarded the ships, their eyes flying from object to object in complete astonishment at the strange possessions of the foreigners.

Outrigger Canoes　　　　　　　**John Webber/Bishop Museum**

A landing party of three armed boats was sent ashore to look for a landing site and fresh water. Lt. Williamson, in command of the landing party, returned with news that a large fresh water pond had been discovered. Several hours later, Cook went ashore with an armed party to examine the water and test the disposition of the natives. Immediately upon landing, all the natives fell flat on their faces in adoration until they were prevailed upon to rise. Then they brought a number of small pigs and other foodstuffs and performed a ceremony complete with long prayers. As a sign of friendship, Cook gave them presents which he had brought from the ship. Satisfied, the party returned to the ship and made preparations to return the following morning to take on water. The next day, the natives assisted the men rolling the casks to and from the pool, eagerly performing any task asked of them.

Watering at Waimea, Kauai　　　**Painting by Roy Hewetson, Courtesy of Hawaiian Telephone Co.[1]**

[1]This acrylic painting appeared on the cover of Hawaiian Telephone Company's 1977-1978 telephone directory.

While the watering progressed, Cook, accompanied by surgeon's mate William Anderson and his artist John Webber, proceeded into the country up the valley. Everyone they met prostrated themselves on the ground until they passed. A number of natives followed them and one, who seemed to keep the rest in order, was chosen as a guide. Cook's intention was to examine several elevated objects, like pyramids, which had been visible from the ship's anchorage. Upon inspection of one, it proved to be a morai (temple) similar to others that he had seen in other South Pacific islands, especially Tahiti.

The morai's pyramid, made of sticks and small branches, measured about 20 feet high. Parts of it had been covered with a thin, light grey cloth perhaps in some religious or ceremonious purpose. Several erect carved boards stood near the pyramid and at their foot were square places enclosed with stones. Cook understood these to be graves. Cook gradually learned that three chiefs had been buried in this morai along with three human sacrifices, one for each chief.

A Morai, in Atooi (Kauai)　　　**John Webber/State Archives**

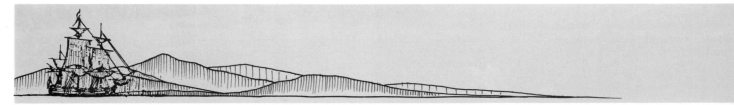

On one side of the morai was a house or shed which measured almost forty feet long. Inside, there appeared to be an altar, composed of an erect piece of carved wood with wooden figures on each side. In the middle of the house was an oblong area enclosed by stones. It was understood from the natives that this was the grave of seven chiefs. A similar oblong area outside the house contained the graves of seven human sacrifices.

After inspecting the morai, Cook returned to his ship about noon. Trading continued in a nearby village, where as before, iron nails and axes were exchanged for island produce. Cook and his men were continually impressed with the honesty, frankness and cheerful disposition of the natives.

Remaining only a few days at Kauai, Cook sailed on January 29 for Niihau. High surf prevented boats from going ashore, but it didn't stop the natives from coming to the ships to trade for iron. On the 30th, Lt. Gore, with an armed party of about 20 men in three boats, finally made the shore, but he and his party were unable to return because of rising surf. They remained on shore for two days and nights.

Despite strict orders from Cook forbidding physical contact between the native women and the sailors, the more than friendly attitude of the bare-breasted women proved too much for the sea-weary sailors to resist. As they had done on Kauai, the sailors devised various schemes to sneak the women on board, including dressing them up as men. On shore at Niihau,

The Inside of the House, in the Morai, in Atooi — John Webber/State Archives

the initial extreme reserve of the landing party only further excited the curiosity in the women, and according to Lt. Williamson, they used "every means in their power to provoke them to do that, which ye dread of punishment would have kept them from." Cook's strict precautions were impossible to enforce, and the introduction of venereal disease was made in the islands as it had been done in other parts of the Pacific.

An Inland View, in Atooi — John Webber/ Kamaaina Graphics

On February 1, Cook finally went ashore, landing with a ram goat and two ewes, a boar and a sow pig of English breed, plus seeds of melon, pumpkin and onion. In return, he received a large quantity of yams and salt plus additional fresh water.

Behind schedule, Cook sailed the next day for further explorations toward the north. As he left this island chain, Cook named them the Sandwich Islands in honor of his patron John Montagu, Earl of Sandwich and First Lord of the Admiralty.

Through the spring and summer months of 1778, Cook explored the western coast of North America and Alaska without finding the evasive sea route between the Pacific and Atlantic Oceans. His search took him through the Bering Strait and into the Arctic Ocean where ice packs, a shortage of food and the approach of winter made further exploration impossible. He decided to return to the sunshine and warmth of the Sandwich Islands where repairs could be affected, supplies easily obtained and further exploration of the islands would make better use of the winter months. He planned to return to the Arctic the following year.

John Montagu, Fourth Earl of Sandwich — State Archives

Cook had discovered the Hawaiian Islands unintentionally. He arrived during the makahiki season, a festive season in which taxes were collected, people rested from the labors of the harvest and war was forbidden. The Hawaiians, whose beliefs were confirmed by the kahunas (priests), believed Cook to be the reincarnation of one of their primary gods, Lono. Centuries before, Lono had introduced reforms in religion and government so as to bring justice to the people. He introduced competitive games as a substitute for warfare. Inspired by a divine vision, he sailed away promising to return someday. The symbols for Lono were white kapa banners hung from a cross-piece on which were hung feather streamers, fern and the skins and feathers of birds. Cook appeared from the sea, as Lono had promised to return. His ships had tall masts and white sails, very similar to the banners carried in the makahiki processions to signify the presence of Lono. Leisurely sailing around the islands, they took on the aura of a god.

The news of the strange visitors spread quickly to the other islands so that when Cook's ships again appeared in Hawaiian waters, this time in late November, 1778 off the coast of Maui, Cook was again greeted as the god Lono. Unknowingly, his squadron again arrived during the makahiki season. Cook's route around the islands was in a clockwise direction which followed the coastal procession of the natives in their celebration. Any lingering doubts were removed when Cook finally found an anchorage at Kealakekua Bay off the island of Hawaii (January, 1779). Just off the beach was the site of a heiau (temple) dedicated to Lono, and the area was the residence of a chief whose exploits were connnected with the myth of Lono.

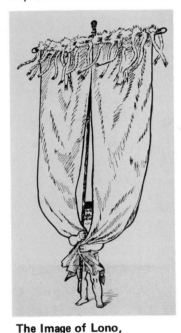

Upon departing from the cold climate of the Arctic, Cook intended to return to his original anchorage at Waimea, Kauai. His latitude and longitude being slightly off, he arrived on the morning of November 26, 1778 off the coast of a new, larger island with an "elevated saddle hill whose summit appeared above the clouds" according to Cook's diary. (He was referring to an extinct 10,000 foot volcano now called Haleakala — House of the Sun, on the island of Maui.) Strict regulations regarding discipline, the procuring of provisions and preventing the spread of venereal disease were laid down.

**The Image of Lono,
God of the Makahiki Season**

Upon sighting the foreign ships, the natives eagerly ventured forth to trade for iron. The following day, Kahekili, high chief of Maui, visited the *Discovery* and presented Captain Clerke with a red feather cloak. Several days later, as the ships were cruising along the east coast of Maui, Kalaniopuu, king of the island of Hawaii who was at war with the Maui chief, boarded the *Resolution* and presented Captain Cook with a beautiful feather cap and cloak, princely gifts on the part of the Hawaiians. The elderly Kalaniopuu, being sickly, remained only a short time. However, a portion of his party stayed overnight, including Kamehameha, a chief whose mana (power) was steadily rising.

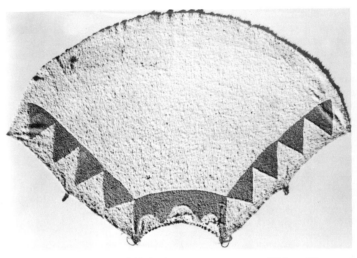

Feather Cloak of Chief Kalaniopuu   **Bishop Museum**

From late November until early January, 1779, Cook's ships sailed slowly around the east end of Maui and then Hawaii seeking a safe anchorage. Unfavorable winds, squalls and varied periods of calm, rain and high winds, prevented the squadron from venturing too close to the shore. Nevertheless, intermittant trading continued whenever the ships ventured near the shore. Finally, on January 17, 1779, Cook's ships found anchorage at Kealakekua Bay in the Kona district of Hawaii. Even before anchoring, great throngs of people surrounded the ships, manifesting their joy at Lono's return by singing and shouting. Lt. King's estimate put the number at not less than ten thousand.

The natives came in canoes, on surfboards or just swimming like huge schools of fish. Thousands lined the shore waiting to see Lono who had returned on a large island with trees, bringing gifts. They came to see the strangers who were reported to carry fire burning in their mouths (pipes); who could reach into their "skins" (jackets) and pull out objects; who could remove the tops of their heads (wigs) and wipe their foreheads with a cloth of such softness as had never been felt before (linen handkerchiefs); and some others who had heads with horns (officer's dress hats). Surely these had to be gods!

A View of Karakakooa (Kealakekua), in Owyhee (Hawaii)   **John Webber/ Kamaaina Graphics**

A number of high ranking chiefs boarded the *Resolution,* dressed in their splendid feather cloaks and helmets. Though most of the natives were scantily clothed, the chiefs had the right to wear brightly colored feather cloaks and helmets. In addition to being a mark of social position, these feather-covered garments were also worn by warriors of great ability, though only high ranking chiefs could wear the feathered helmets. Bright red and yellow feathers were used the most: red, because this color was associated with chiefs and gods; yellow, because of the scarcity of these feathers, as only a few feathers could be obtained from each bird. Professional bird hunters were employed to catch the birds, pluck the prized feathers, and then free the birds so that they would grow more feathers. One of the long cloaks might take generations to make. Captain Cook compared the feel and appearance of these garments to that of "the thickest and richest velvet."

The chiefs were men with strong, well-proportioned bodies. They were tall, six feet or more was common, and graceful. Their rule was absolute.

Hawaiian women dressed scantily, going around as close to nature as possible. They generally had only a piece of cloth wrapped around their waist. Leis of feathers or flowers decorated the heads and necks of high-born women. To be small, frail and fragile was not the Hawaiian idea of beauty. The chiefesses considered most beautiful were at least six feet tall and almost half again as wide. Religious laws (kapus) forbade women from eating certain foods such as bananas, coconuts and pork. In addition, they could not eat with their men. The penalty for disobedience of these kapus was death.

After a ceremony aboard the *Resolution* in which a piece of red cloth was placed over the shoulders of Cook, he went ashore with a landing party which included several of the chiefs. Upon landing, high ranking priests attached themselves to Cook and his party. Wherever they went, the people prostrated themselves, shouting "Orono" (Lono). The escorts took the party to an elaborate heiau where prayers and chants were repeatedly recited. Cook was again draped with a large piece of red cloth and offered a ceremonial pig. After additional ceremonies were performed, Cook was seated between two wooden idols. A procession of natives appeared carrying baked pig, breadfruit, poi, coconut and various vegetables. A rather potent concoction called awa was passed around, and one of the chiefs (Pareea) pulled pieces of the pig apart and hand fed the honored guests. Captain Cook, being fed by a priest named Koa, could not swallow a morsel of the "Putrid hog." Cook's reluctance was not diminished when the old chief chewed the meat for him and again tried to feed him. After a brief period of exchanging gifts, Cook hastily returned to the ship. All along the way, the people again prostrated themselves as Cook and his party passed.

A Man of the Sandwich Islands, with His Helmet   John Webber/ Kamaaina Graphics

A Young Woman of the Sandwich Islands   John Webber/ Kamaaina Graphics

An Offering before Capt. Cook, in the Sandwich Islands   John Webber/ Kamaaina Graphics

Tereoboo,[1] King of Owyhee, Bringing Presents to Capt. Cook   John Webber/ Kamaaina Graphics

Up until the 24th of January, events seemed to become routine. An observatory was set up on the shore. Everyday, the shore party received a supply of hogs and vegetables, and several canoes went to the ships loaded with provisions. No hint of payment was ever made. On the 24th, King Kalaniopuu returned and put a kapu on the bay so that no canoes ventured forth. On the 25th, he paid a private visit to the ships. The following day, the king set out from the village in three large canoes to pay a formal visit to the ships. The king and his chiefs were magnificently dressed in their rich feather cloaks and helmets and armed with long spears and daggers. Instead of boarding the ships, the canoes circled them and returned to the shore. Anticipating the king's move, Cook proceeded toward shore and they both arrived at about the same time. Inside the observation tent, the king removed his cloak and put it over Cook's shoulders. Then he put a feathered helmet on the captain's head. Other cloaks were laid out, and hogs and other foodstuffs were brought forth. The king exchanged names with Cook, a strong pledge of friendship. After the ceremony ended, Cook escorted the king and a number of his chiefs aboard the *Resolution* where they were presented with gifts of iron hatchets and other prized items. The trust between the two cultures was probably at its highest point.

---

[1] This chief was actually Kalaniopuu (also called Kaleiopuu) and because of the difficulty of understanding the Hawaiian language, different spellings appear in different journals depending on the acuteness of the listener's ear. There was no written Hawaiian language at this time, and as it was undergoing a consonant change, the *t* and *k, l* and *r* and other combinations were often interchanged to produce differences in spelling by the writers.

On the 28th of January, the natives, at the request of some of the ship's officers, put on a boxing exhibition. A large crowd of people had assembled. The combatants approached each other, stood at arms length and directed all blows to the face. No attempt was made to deflect the blows; rather they attempted to elude the impending blow by body movement or by retreating. Fighting in this unusual manner, the battles were quickly decided, for as soon as an opponent was knocked down, he was considered vanquished. Though the sailors were repeatedly encouraged to participate, they steadfastly refused, remembering well the blows they had previously received in a similar display in the Friendly Islands (Tonga Islands).

A Man of the Sandwich Islands Dancing   John Webber/ Kamaaina Graphics

Boxing Match before Capt. Cook   John Webber/State Archives

Other ceremonies and exhibitions continued, including fireworks displays by the ships. The foreign visitors were welcomed to inspect anything they wanted. Guides took them anywhere they wished to go. Native bearers even carried out heavy timber from within the forest. The ships were far from being short of provisions, and so trade was thrown open to everyone.

As February approached, several incidents occurred which undoubtedly made the natives question the god-like qualities of their visitors. The first was the death of William Watman, a seaman, who had been ailing for some time. The chiefs asked that he be buried on shore and they gave him a solemn ceremony in their heiau. This was followed by a brief service by Cook. The gods were mortal, although the attitude of the natives, for the moment at least, did not appear to change. The second event was the acquiring of logs and wooden idols from a heiau for use as firewood. The priest gave his approval, and a number of natives assisted in removing the desired wood. Finally, perhaps feeling the strain of the constant demands of the foreigners for food and other services, a number of the chiefs began inquiring as to when the foreigners might be leaving. Cook's two crews, totalling about 180 men, were devouring huge quantities of food in addition to storing vast quantities for their upcoming voyage. Perhaps already feeling the growing uneasiness, Cook made preparations to sail.

Learning of Cook's departure on the following day, King Kalaniopuu ordered a final collection of foodstuffs from the common people. Cook took as much as he had room for. The balance of the day was spent in getting all the ships' belongings back on board, including Lt. King who the natives had unsuccessfully tried to persuade to remain behind due to his exceptional politeness and consideration for the natives. Thus on the morning of February 4, the ships sailed out of the bay, followed by a large escort of canoes.

Cook planned to complete his survey of the island of Hawaii before visiting the other islands. Calm weather made their going slow. Then the weather gradually turned worse. The winds had risen to gale force, and on the morning of February 8, it was discovered that the foremast of the *Resolution* had been badly damaged. Unable to carry sail, it would have to be unstepped in a harbor. Reluctantly, Captain Cook decided to return to the nearest familiar harbor, Kealakekua Bay.

The squadron anchored in the bay on the 11th, almost exactly where they had anchored before. This time, the bay was deserted. The king was elsewhere. A kapu had been placed on the bay. The mast was unstepped and taken ashore under armed guard

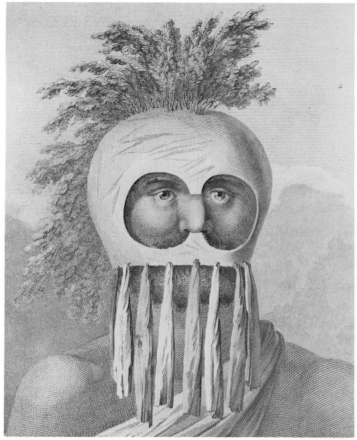

A Man of the Sandwich Islands, in a Mask
John Webber/ Kamaaina Graphics

for repairs on the 13th. The king returned the same morning, somewhat dismayed at their return. He must have been somewhat surprised to find the foremast and torn sails spread out on the beach. Nevertheless, a feeling of normalcy seemed to return.

A Canoe of the Sandwich Islands, the Rowers Masked

John Webber/Kamaaina Graphics

The Death of Captain Cook

John Webber/ Kamaaina Graphics

As in the past, the natives continued their petty thievery to obtain iron. On this day, the 13th, a watering party had almost been stoned. Almost at the same time, a native thief boarded the *Discovery* and made off with a pair of tongs and a chisel. Shots were fired. A boatload of sailors pursued the escaping canoe to shore, but the thief escaped. In attempting to seize the canoe, a scuffle broke out, and a chief named Palea was hit on the head with an oar. In reprisal, several sailors were beaten, but Palea managed to restore order.

During the night, a cutter from the *Discovery* was stolen. The following morning, Cook sent out armed boats to blockade the bay. With three boats, he led an armed party ashore in an attempt to take King Kalaniopuu hostage until the cutter was returned. Not knowing the full meaning of Cook's invitation to visit the *Resolution*, the king proceeded toward the beach, satisfying Cook that he had nothing to do with the theft. Before reaching the water, the king's wife and several chiefs caught up with him and pleaded with the king not to go any further. Confused, the king sat down. A great crowd had been gathering, and now it numbered several thousand, many armed with spears, clubs, daggers and stones.

A native messenger arrived, bearing the sad news that a chief had been killed attempting to cross the blockaded bay. The crowd grew angry and pressed close to the landing party. The marines formed a line at the water's edge. A dagger flashed. Cook fired a shot. The charge, either blank or loaded with small shot, did no apparent damage. The crowd started throwing stones, more daggers flashed, more shots were fired, and a general melee broke out. Cook, making his way toward the boats, was clubbed from behind. Before he could get back on his feet, he was stabbed in the back and clubbed again. Whether he drowned or was clubbed to death is uncertain.

Four marines were killed. The rest of the party managed to get to the waiting boats and escape. The dead had to be left behind. The Hawaiians took charge of the bodies, treating Cook's like one of their own chiefs.[1]

Cook died at the height of his career (51) never fully realizing the religious importance the natives had placed upon him as the reincarnation of their god Lono. Each of his two visits had coincided with the makahiki season, and his death in symbolic conflict occurred at the close of the makahiki season.

Sporadic fighting continued for a few days, with both sides making reprisals against the other. The mast and a number of sails were still on shore, and they were recovered during a brief truce under heavy guard. After about a week, peace was finally restored. Part of Cook's bones were begrudingly given up by the Hawaiians, and a funeral service was held on the 21st of February. The next evening, the squadron weighed anchor and left the bay. After a brief stop at Oahu, they returned to their original anchorage at Waimea, Kauai. Here and at Niihau they remained for about two weeks, taking on supplies. Finally, on March 15, 1779, the *Resolution* and the *Discovery* with Captain Clerke in charge sailed from the Sandwich Islands to continue their explorations to the north.

No foreign ships would visit the islands again until 1786.

The Apotheosis of Captain Cook   **Bishop Museum**

---

[1] The flesh was stripped from the bones, the palms and the intestines were kept, and the remains were consumed by fire. The bones were saved and worshipped.

Chapter 2

The Founding of the Hawaiian Kingdom

Kamehameha ("The Lonely One") was born in Kohala on the island of Hawaii on a stormy night probably in November of 1758.[1] Thunder, lightning and a strange light in the heavens with the tail feathers of a bird, according to legend, announced the birth of the baby who was to become a great chief. Kamehameha's father was Keoua Kupuapaikalani, chief of Kohala and a grandson of Keawe who once ruled over a powerful kingdom on the island of Hawaii. Kekuiapoiwa, Kamehameha's mother, was the daughter of a chief from Kona.

The infant was immediately taken away after birth and hidden to protect him from possible death at the hands of the warring clans. Old chief Alapai, fearing treachery from his rival (chief Kahekili of Maui) and obsessed with the idea that he had been the father of his niece's child, demanded the immediate death of the child, fearing that it would ultimately destroy his kingdom.

The child, originally named Paiea, spent five years hidden in a secluded valley called Waipio, a sanctuary to endangered Alii (royalty) for many centuries. Haunted with legends and possessing many holy sites, this valley was sparsely inhabited. The care and security provided the child clearly marked him as an Alii. When the death threat passed, the child was returned to the custody of his parents. King Alapai, now old and feeble, accepted Paiea and gave him the name Kamehameha ("The Lonely One"). At Kailua, the care and training reserved for the Alii continued for about seven more years.

At about the age of fourteen, Kamehameha's father died (perhaps by poisoning). King Kalaniopuu, Kamehameha's uncle and rightful heir to the kingdom of King Keawe, adopted Kamehameha at the dying request of his brother. Treated as a son, Kamehameha relocated to the district of Kau, domain of the fire-goddess Pele on the snow-rimmed slopes of Mauna Loa. Here a special breed of Hawaiians resided: proud, independent, religious and fierce in battle. Under the careful tutoring of a very great warrior, Kamehameha learned spear throwing and dodging, wrestling and the rudimentary tactics of warfare. Here also, his sexual stirrings were provided for with carefully selected young women. Through oral recitation, he memorized his genealogy clear back to the gods. Without a written language, he learned navigation, history, astronomy, religious ceremonies, prayers and kapus (tabus), and other vital information necessary to become an Alii-aimoku (a District Chief). Kamehameha's physical aptitudes became unmatched as did his ability at catching and dodging spears thrown at him.

---

[1] This is the probable date accepted by many historians. Another popular date is 1753. Dates as early as 1736 and as late as 1761 have been offered. Likewise, there is disagreement over the month, the place and even the parentage of Kamehameha. References to a strange light in the heavens at the time of his birth might refer to Halley's Comet which would have been visible in Hawaiian skies in November or December of 1758. Whether Keoua was his true father or chief Kahekili of Maui by tryst, is still uncertain. Nevertheless, Kamehameha was a highborn Alii (royalty).

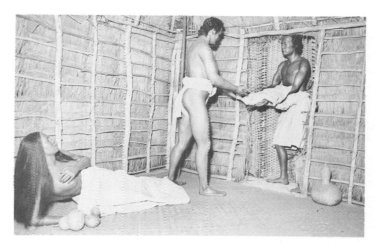

Scene Depicting the Birth of Kamehameha

Lahaina's Hawaiian Wax Museum/Photo by Author

The Valley of Waipio, from the Sand Hills on the Beach

William Ellis/ State Archives

Kamehameha during Spear Practice

Wood/State Archives

Kamehameha had his first taste of combat in a brief civil war fought after the death of King Alapai. The king's son was killed and Kalaniopuu now controlled both Districts of Kau and Kona. Kamehameha ingratiated himself to his uncle by representing the aging king in personal combat against a rival Hilo chief. Receiving many battle scars, Kamehameha's superior strength prevailed and he saved the honor of his king.

Later, King Kalaniopuu became ruler of the entire island of Hawaii and parts of East Maui. Continuous warfare, interrupted by brief periods of peace, became the norm with its accompanying death and destruction.

On January 17, 1779, Kamehameha accompanied his uncle, King Kalaniopuu, aboard the *Discovery*. This was his second meeting with the foreigners. Lt. James King, in describing one of the principal attendants of the King, said that the attendant "was Maiha-maiha (Kamehameha), whose hair was now plaisted over with a brown dirty sort of paste or powder, & which added to as savage a looking face as I ever saw, it however by no means seemed an emblem of his disposition, which was good natur'd & humorous, although his manner shewd somewhat of an overbearing spirit, & he seemed to be the principal director in this interview."

Kamehameha was undoubtedly very impressed with Cook's warriors and he desperately needed their guns, cannon and iron weapons. They would certainly add to his mana (power and prestige).

Captain Cook Meeting King Kalaniopuu

Lahaina's Hawaiian Wax Museum/Photo by Author

Ku (Kukailimoku), Hawaiian War God   Bishop Museum

After Captain Cook's departure, King Kalaniopuu resumed his efforts to conquer Maui. This new advance against Maui's King Kahekili proved disastrous, so much so that Kalaniopuu lost the eastern District of Hana which he had previously captured.

About a year after Cook's departure, Kalaniopuu, shrunken with age and rendered helpless by a lifetime of awa drinking, called together his chiefs and counselors to arrange for the disposal of his kingdom. At his death, the rule over the land would pass to his son, Kiwalao, the senior heir. Kamehameha would be second in the line of succession and would receive custody of Ku, the war god—a feathery image with a mouth full of sharp teeth.

Kamehameha by now was an experienced warrior—tall, strong and fearless. He moved with an aura of power and violence. Legends say that he further added to his mana (power and prestige) by claiming and keeping Captain Cook's hair. Returning to his home District of Kohala, Kamehameha bided his time. He was still there when his uncle died in 1782. Following the death of this important chief, his lands were redistributed. Kamehameha now took control of Ku, the war god.

Kiwalao took control of his father's kingdom by forming an alliance with his uncle (Keawemauhili) and his younger brother (Keoua). At a place called Mokuohai in mid-1782, they did battle with Kamehameha. Kiwalao was killed. Kamehameha now became a major contestor for power. But during the next four years, despite almost continuous warfare, neither side gained the advantage. The island of Hawaii remained divided into three kingdoms. In the meantime, Kahekili, ruler of Maui, had taken the island of Oahu from his foster-son. By 1786, it looked as though Kahekili was on his way in uniting all the islands under his own rule. He ruled the kingdom of Maui (which included Molokai and Lanai), he was now all powerful on Oahu, and he entered into an agreement with his half brother (Kaeokulani) on Kauai.

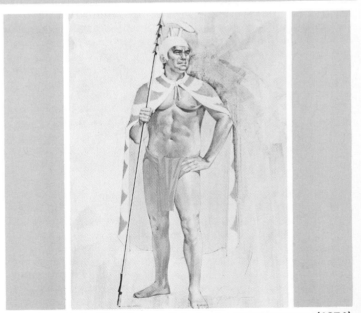

Kamehameha in His Prime   Painting by Roy Hewetson (1974)

For the most part, wars were fought along traditional lines. Sacrifices, prayers and individual combat between opposing champions often preceded the formal attack. Once the battle had commenced, spears and slings were used to break up organized formations, and hand-to-hand combat took over. Stones, wooden clubs, tripping weapons, daggers and even bare hands were employed so that brute strength often decided the final outcome.

For centuries, war on the individual islands and between the islands was the normal course of events. Despite its depopulation, oppression, destruction and loss of individual freedom, the race as a whole managed to survive. New weapons which might help tip the balance of power between the warring factions had been seen with the arrival of Cook. However, the amount of iron and iron daggers obtained was insignificant, especially since both sides possessed them. The few muskets left behind were literally useless due to a lack of ammunition and the knowledge to fire them.

As a result of Cook's discoveries along the northwest coast of America, a new fur trade developed between these hunting grounds and their market in Canton, China. Requiring a rendezvous point to replenish their exhausted supplies of fresh meat, fruits and vegetables, salt, firewood and fresh water, these traders began calling at the Sandwich Islands. In 1786, four foreign ships called: two British, commanded by Captains Portlock and Dixon, and two French naval vessels, commanded by the famous explorer Captain J.F.G. de La Perouse. Each year

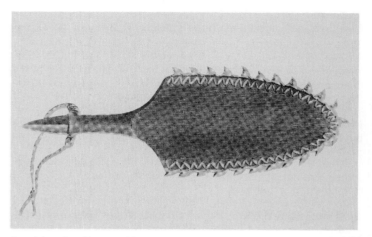

Combination Dagger-Club with Shark's Teeth   **State Archives**

thereafter, one or more foreign ships visited the islands.

Almost four years of relative peace prevailed. During this time, the Hawaiian chiefs supplied themselves with the new foreign weapons. When trading did not produce the desired weapons, other methods were resorted to, including thefts, direct attacks or ransoming anchors and boats for sought after weapons. The chiefs became masters of deceit and contradiction, blaming each other for the various incidents. Despite these incidents, the foreign ships continued to come in increasing numbers.

View of the Anchorage of the French Frigates Lying off Maui   **Blondela/ State Archives**

Chief Kaiana   **John Webber/Kamaaina Graphics**

An unexpected bonus that many of these early ships' captains discovered was man-power. Many young Hawaiians, lured by the adventure of foreign travel, were eager to sail. A number of Hawaiians literally traveled as tourists. They were either high ranking chiefs or personal servants of the ship's captain. One of these high chiefs was Kaiana of Kauai who accompanied Captain Meares to Canton, China in 1787 and later sailed to Oregon with Captain Douglas.

Upon his return to Hawaii near the end of 1788, Kaiana allied himself with Kamehameha. His foreign travel greatly enhanced his prestige, and for several years he became one of Kamehameha's principal officers and advisors. However, ambitions for power would later prompt Kaiana to switch sides and oppose Kamehameha in the Nuuanu Valley battle of 1795 in which Kaiana would be killed.

At the end of January, 1790, Simon Metcalfe, commander of the American merchantman *Eleanora,* sailed into Hawaiian waters and anchored off Honuaula, Maui (near Lahaina). Following an incident involving the theft of a boat and the death of a sailor on watch, Metcalfe bombarded the village and had his men set fire to its huts and heiaus. He soon learned from the terrified natives that the thieves had come from a village down the coast called Olowalu. Weighing anchor and moving down the coast to this village, Metcalfe took on fresh water and attempted to recover the missing boat and the body of the sailor. After recovering only a piece of the boat's keel and the thighbones of the sailor, Metcalfe and his officers plotted revenge. Enticing the trading canoes to come out again, he ordered the gunports dropped and opened fire mercilessly with the deck guns and the cannon below. The ocean turned blood red and the slaughter claimed more than a hundred natives killed plus many more wounded. The Olowalu Massacre went down in Hawaiian antiquities as the battle of "The spilled brains" (Kalolopahu), since many of the natives had been shot in the head.

From Maui, Simon Metcalfe sailed to the Kona coast of the island of Hawaii. Here he ran roughshod over a chief named Kameeiamoku who was prominent in Kamehameha's court. The chief, committing some breach of Metcalfe's discipline aboard the ship, was brutally struck with a rope, humiliated by an angry tirade and expelled from the ship. The chief swore revenge on the next ship to enter his territory. Ironically, the next ship was a small schooner named the *Fair American*, commanded by Metcalfe's son Thomas. Boarding the schooner on the pretext of trading, the foreigners were caught off guard and thrown overboard. Floundering in the water, they were beaten to death with clubs and paddles. A strong swimmer named Isaac Davis managed to escape the initial slaughter, only to be plucked from the sea by his attackers. His life was spared by the intervention of a lesser, more compassionate, chief.

In the meantime, Simon Metcalfe anchored in Kealakekua Bay, unaware of the events that took place elsewhere on Hawaii. Being at Kealakekua and learning of the events that had transpired, Kamehameha placed a kapu on the bay. Seeing no trading canoes, Metcalfe sent out a shore party. The ship's boatswain, an Englishman named John Young, wandered away from the shore party and was apprehended by Kamehameha's warriors. The balance of the shore party returned to the ship. After waiting several days, Metcalfe sailed away thinking Young had either deserted or was killed. Kamehameha, now controlling the northwestern half of the island of Hawaii, took possession of the captured schooner, *Fair American*, and placed Davis and Young under his protection.

Young and Davis quickly caught the keen eye of Kamehameha who needed skilled seamen for his newly acquired foreign vessel. Despite an unsuccessful escape attempt, the two foreign-

John Young (in 1818)   **A. Pellion/State Archives**

ers were well treated. Gradually adjusting to their fate, they taught Kamehameha's warriors how to use the cannons and muskets aboard the *Fair American*. They coached the king on foreign dress, life style and custom. They even taught him tricks in trading with the ever-increasing number of ships calling on the islands. Given wives, land and the equivalent status of chiefs, Davis and Young exerted tremendous influence on the ambitious king and later became his confidential advisors. With their help, Kamehameha equipped an army, Anglo-style, plus a navy that included an immense fleet of shallow draft and double-hulled canoes in addition to the cannon-equipped *Fair American*.

Learning that Kahekili, king of Maui, was away on Oahu trying to put down a full-fledged revolt, Kamehameha made plans for an ambitious amphibious assault on Maui. He consulted the kahunas, built new heiaus and received pledges of canoes, warriors and supplies from his chiefs. Kamehameha even won the friendship of a former enemy, Keawe, who still ruled almost a third of the island of Hawaii. This new ally sent him warriors and a fleet of canoes. Ready for conquest, Kamehameha sailed for Maui with his counselors, chiefs, younger relatives and his wife Kaahumanu and her servants. He had an enormous fleet of canoes plus a large brass cannon and his two foreign advisors, Davis and Young. The destination was Hana which had been lost when King Kalaniopuu was alive.

Kamehameha's fleet beached to the south of Hana. Legend says that the canoes blanketed the beach for a distance of nearly five miles. The defenders retreated except for a fort on the point of Hana. Kamehameha bypassed the fort and worked his way along the northern coast to assault the capital of Wailuku. Along the way, he picked up supplies and won support for his cause among many of the local chiefs. Kahekili's son (Kalani-

Olowalu Massacre Petroglyph   **Hawaii Visitors Bureau**

Iao Valley, Maui   **Hawaii Visitors Bureau**

kupule) ruled Maui while the king was away on Oahu. Hearing of the approaching army, he sent his most gifted warrior (Kapakahili) and a large army to meet Kamehameha. They met at a small hill called Puukoa. Here in hand-to-hand combat, Kamehameha slew the mighty warrior. In the heavy fighting, Kamehameha's forces were victorious with the help of fresh reinforcements.

Kamehameha now moved on to Wailuku for the major confrontation. Not only did he have the advantage of better position, more men and the cannon and muskets of the foreigners, he also had the psychological advantage of defeating the forces of the king's best warrior. Kamehameha had to work quickly, lest the king on Oahu learn of the initial defeat and send reinforcements. As Kamehameha's forces began arriving, the bay filled with war canoes. When the large brass cannon arrived with its specially constructed wheels and more than eighty attendants to move, load and fire it, Kamehameha was ready and the battle began. After two days of constant fighting, the defenders were pushed up against the narrow pass of the Iao Valley. The cannon was brought up and fired into the valley and the hills above it, routing the defenders. Kamehameha's forces pursued them and a great slaughter took place, so much so that the bodies filled the stream and stopped the flow of water. This battle received the name of "The damning of the waters" (Kapaniwai). Despite the large number of casualties, most of them were commoners and all the important chiefs escaped, many to Oahu or Molokai.

After his conquest of Maui, Kamehameha went to Molokai where he took into his care his step-mother's daughter (Keopuolani), a very high ranking Alii. Because Kaahumanu (his favorite wife) could not produce any children for Kamehameha, his niece would later become another of his wives and bear two princes who would follow Kamehameha to the throne.

While still on Molokai, Kamehameha sent his favorite wife's grandmother to Kauai in search of a renowned soothsayer who could provide divine guidance for Kamehameha. She found him at a stop in Waikiki. Being a cousin, he revealed to her that in order for Kamehameha to rule over all the islands, he must build a great heiau for the god Ku at Puukohola. If he did as the seer foresaw, he would gain the kingdom without suffering a scratch.

In the meantime, Kamehameha received the bad news that his rival on the island of Hawaii (Keoua) had killed his recent ally Keawe, ravaged Kamehameha's lands and treated his people badly. Returning home, Kamehameha engaged his rival in two bloody, inconclusive battles. Since neither side gained a victory, they both withdrew to their own territories.

Encouraged by the destruction of part of Keoua's forces by a sudden eruption of Kilauea in November of 1790, Kamehameha, guided by his kahunas, set out to build the prophesized heiau.

While the heiau at Puukohola was being built, intermittent warfare continued. At every stage of its construction, the kahunas performed special ceremonies. Workers by the thousands were employed. Even chiefs of high and low rank, including Kamehameha himself, carried stones for the walls and platforms. Upon completion, it resembled a fortress, having been assembled by using tens of thousands of boulders belched from the depths of the earth by the goddess Pele.

Kamehameha sent two emissaries to Keoua to arrange a meeting between the two kings in order that a peace settlement might be arranged. Against the advise of his advisors, Keoua accepted the invitation. On his way to the meeting, he stopped off to bathe, and sensing death, prepared himself. As Keoua's canoes approached the shore where Kamehameha was waiting, they were surrounded by canoes of Kamehameha's forces led by Keeaumoku, one of Kamehameha's top counselors. Keeaumoku threw a spear at the rival chief who caught it and threw it back. Musket fire opened up from the shore, the canoes moved in closer and a minor battle took place in which the rival chief and most of his attendants in the canoe were killed. Whether Kamehameha had planned this deed ahead of time or whether it was spontaneous is uncertain. With their king dead, the remain-

Warrior of the Sandwich Islands　　　**Arago/State Archives**

Heiau of Puukohola　　　**Bishop Museum**

Village Scene on the　　　**Thomas Heddington/**
Island of Hawaii　　　**Bishop Museum**

ing forces were permitted to live.

The body of the fallen king was taken to the heiau at Puukohola and offered as a sacrifice to the war god, Ku. The prophecy was fulfilled. Thus in 1791, the island of Hawaii came under the undisputed rule of Kamehameha.

The senseless power struggles and their resulting wars devastated the economy of the islands so much that Kamehameha rested for several years in order that recovery could take place. Thus a period of peace prevailed from 1791 to about the summer of 1794. During this period, the number of foreign ships visiting the islands continued to increase and the chiefs took advantage of this calm to acquire foreign weapons, skills and advisors. Many of the traders openly encouraged this rivalry, selling guns and ammunition to both sides.

During this period of calm, the visits of the British explorer Captain George Vancouver produced a number of significant events and undoubtedly helped maintain the uneasy truce between the rival chiefs. Vancouver's expedition had two main objectives: 1) to recover certain lands at Nootka Sound on the northwest coast of North America allegedly seized from British colonists by the Spanish; and 2) to complete the exploration of that coast originally begun by Captain Cook. Ordered to winter in the Sandwich Islands, Vancouver's squadron, the *Discovery* and the *Chatham*, called on Hawaii three times. A third cargo ship, the *Daedalus*, joined them twice with supplies. The first visit in March of 1792 was very short and didn't amount to very much. However, the second and third visits (February-March, 1793 and January-March, 1794) cemented the friendship between Vancouver and Kamehameha.

As a junior officer, Vancouver had accompanied Captain Cook on both of his visits to the Hawaiian Islands. Now as commander of an official exploring expedition, he was impressed with the locational value of the islands and sought to associate them with the British Empire. On his last two visits, Vancouver visited all the islands, meeting with all the important chiefs. He maintained friendly relations with these chiefs, especially with Kamehameha, whose superior position he recognized and whose friendship he cultivated. Vancouver continually preached peace and even tried, unsuccessfully, to conclude and ratify a peace treaty between the chiefs of the leeward islands and Kamehameha. He attempted to patch up many disputes between the rival chiefs, and he successfully reunited Kamehameha with his favorite wife (Kaahumanu) after a marital dispute involving a flirtation with high chief Kaiana.

Captain George Vancouver State Archives

Vancouver flatly refused to sell arms to anyone, opting instead to aid the people in establishing a stable economy. To this end, he introduced the first horned cattle into the islands, plus goats and geese, grapevines, orange and almond trees and several varieties of vegetable seeds. In 1793, Vancouver rigged a full set of sails on one of Kamehameha's large double canoes and presented him with a union jack and pennant. In 1794, Vancouver helped Kamehameha construct a foreign style vessel, supplying the ironwork, masts and needed sails. The vessel was named the *Britannia*.

Having been thoroughly ingratiated to Vancouver and undoubtedly wanting protection from his enemies, Kamehameha "ceded" the island of Hawaii to the British crown in late February, 1794, prior to Vancouver's final departure from the Hawaiian Islands. Rather than attempting to give away the land, Kamehameha may have done this act to secure aid and protection for his kingdom. In any event, the British government never acted on this cession.

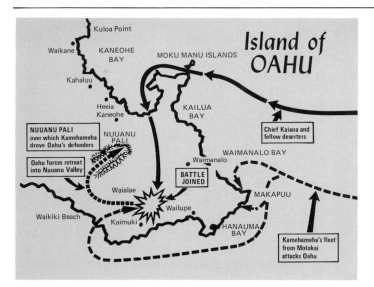

Map of Oahu

In the summer of 1794, several months after Vancouver's departure, the aged Maui King, Kahekili, died at Waikiki. His kingdom consisted of all the islands except Hawaii which was controlled by Kamehameha. (Kahekili indirectly controlled Kauai and Niihau through his brother, Kaeo.) Upon the king's death, this kingdom was divided up between his brother (Kaeo) and his son (Kalanikupule), although the native accounts do not agree as to the exact division. In any event, whether through jealousy or a dispute over succession, these two chiefs drifted into war with each other.

In November of 1794, Kaeo, aided by warriors from Waianae and Waialua, attacked Kalanikupule and attempted to conquer Oahu. His aim was to capture Waikiki which at that time was the center of government. Initially being successful, Kaeo's forces were later defeated when Kalanikupule obtained guns and ammunition from Captain William Brown[1] of the *Jackall* plus the volunteer services of about nine English sailors. In the final battle fought in the middle of December, Kaeo was killed. Arrogant with victory, Kalanikupule made plans to attack Kamehameha on the island of Hawaii.

The time was right for Kamehameha. Warned of the king's hostile intent, Kamehameha was already preparing a huge army and a fleet of canoes. Having assembled 16,000 men plus cannon, guns and the technical knowledge of Young and Davis, Kamehameha attacked Maui, destroying Lahaina and ravaging the western side of the island. Capturing Molokai with little resistance, he proceeded on to Oahu. On their way through the rough Molokai channel, chief Kaiana deserted with his army to join forces with Kalanikupule. Nevertheless, Kamehameha landed his well seasoned forces at Waikiki in April, 1795. In the Nuuanu Valley, the Oahu defenders made a stand. The ensuing battle was fierce, the defenders giving ground only after many chiefs and warriors had been killed. The survivors either fled into the mountains or were pushed over the steep cliffs of the valley to find death far below on the rocks. Others, fearing torture and sacrifice if captured, elected a quick death by jumping into the deep crevasse below.

---

[1] Captain William Brown is credited with being the first foreigner to enter Honolulu harbor, probably in 1792 or 1793. Honolulu means "Fair Haven."

Kalanikupule had managed to escape and it took several months to find him. Once found, the fugitive king was sacrificed to Ku, the war god, at a heiau at Moanalua. After Kamehameha's decisive victory, he remained on Oahu, completing the pacification of the islands and preparing his next campaign to acquire possession of Kauai and Niihau. In the spring of 1796, Kamehameha attempted an invasion of Kauai, but strong winds and high seas in the channel swamped many canoes and postponed the invasion attempt.

While still consolidating his kingdom on Oahu, Kamehameha was forced to return to Hawaii because of a rebellion started by Namakeha, Kaiana's brother. In preparing to leave, Kamehameha was advised to take the young chiefs with him lest they become power hungry in his absence. So leaving mostly trusted commoners in charge, Kamehameha returned to Hawaii in September, 1796 to re-establish his supremacy. The main battle took place at Hilo and Kamehameha's superior forces crushed the revolt. Namakeha, who managed to escape, was later captured and in January, 1797 was sacrificed to Ku.

Although Kauai remained a thorn in his side, this battle at Hilo would be the final battle for Kamehameha in his attempt to unite all the islands under his rule. Kamehameha remained on Hawaii for about six years administering his kingdom, rewarding his loyal followers with gifts of land and encouraging peaceful activities with his subjects as well as with the foreign ships which continued to call on the islands.

View of Nuuanu-Pali on Oahu   **State Archives**

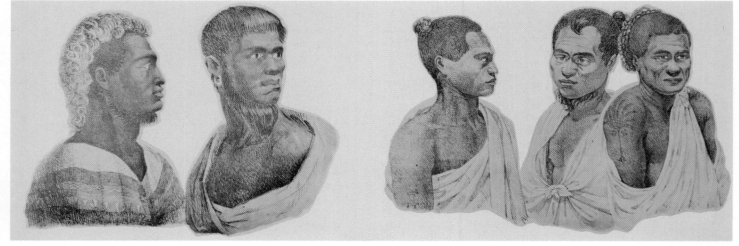
Inhabitants of the Sandwich Islands   **Choris/State Archives**

Kamehameha Reviewing   **Plaque on Kamehameha Statue/**
His *Peleleu* Fleet   **Photo by Dick Wisniewski**

During these years of peace, Kamehameha planned for the conquest of Kauai. He ordered his chiefs to construct *peleleu* war canoes. These canoes were actually two large single canoes lashed together and having a covered platform at the stern. Equipped with a mast and sails, they would be seaworthy enough to withstand the stormy channel between Kauai and Oahu. In addition to the *peleleu* fleet which numbered over eight hundred and took almost five years to assemble, Kamehameha also had his foreign carpenters build a squadron of small schooners. Through skillful trading, he acquired a large supply of cannons, muskets and ammunition.

Kamehameha and his armada moved to Maui in 1802, remained about a year, and then proceeded to Oahu, arriving in late 1803 or early 1804. About ready to launch his invasion on Kauai in the spring of 1804, a terrible pestilence appeared called "Okuu" by the natives. Spreading swiftly, it decimated the population and destroyed many prime chiefs and warriors of Kamehameha's army. The exact nature of the disease was never determined, but the possibilities of cholera, typhoid fever and the bubonic plague have been advanced. Kamehameha himself was stricken with the disease but managed to survive its death grip. The invasion of Kauai was postponed and the *peleleu* fleet never sailed, rotting instead in the hot sun.

During the pestilence, one of Kamehameha's top advisors (Keeaumoku) died. Prior to his death, he warned Kamehameha that only one person, namely Kamehameha's wife (Kaahumanu), might succeed in stirring up a rebellion against his government since she had many blood relatives who were chiefs. Heeding this dying man's advice, Kamehameha put a death kapu on any man who slept with her.

Despite his setbacks, Kamehameha was still intent on bringing Kauai into his kingdom. So he continued making plans and again began assembling a navy, this time patterned after the foreign ships. In 1805, he purchased the *Lelia Byrd*, a 175 ton vessel which became his flagship. By 1810, he had assembled more than thirty ships of various sizes at Waikiki Beach plus about a dozen more in Honolulu Harbor.

Between 1805 and 1810, a number of attempts at reaching a peace agreement between Kamehameha and the ruler of Kauai, now Kaumualii,[1] had been tried by both sides. Despite the fact that Kamehameha thought war could be avoided and Kauai could be annexed by peaceful means, distrust kept the Kauai king from coming to Oahu and meeting with Kamehameha. However, in 1810, an American trader named Captain Nathan Winship finally persuaded Kaumualii to go with him to Honolulu and arrange a truce. Meeting face to face, the two kings settled their differences; Kauai would be a tributary kingdom of Kamehameha's and Kaumualii would continue to rule over it. In return, the Kauai king would acknowledge Kamehameha as his sovereign, thereby making Kamehameha undisputed ruler and ensuring peace for the kingdom.

In the early years of Kamehameha's kingdom, he had a body of advisors who in effect acted as a council of state. Because of their power and assistance in aiding Kamehameha in his struggle for supremacy, these five chiefs[2] were almost always consulted before decisions on important matters could be made. As these chiefs died and their sons replaced them, their influence diminished and Kamehameha's authority became absolute.

Kamehameha appointed a young chief named Kalanimoku to act as his executive officer. The name was actually more of a title. This young chief adopted the name William Pitt, after his contemporary, the English prime minister. Kalanimoku acted in the capacities of prime minister, treasurer and advisor to the king in both government and business dealings.

An important new feature introduced by Kamehameha was the appointment of governors to be his representatives on each of the other islands (except Kauai). Because Kamehameha could only be on one island at a time, these governors were appointed on the basis of proven loyalty and executive ability rather than on chiefly rank. The only other administrative officials of any importance were the tax collectors who collected the large revenues required for the support of the king and his royal court, the army and the navy. Since there was no local coinage and foreign money was very scarce, tax payments took the form of produce and articles manufactured by the common people.

The kapu system was an all-important power that was traditional to all ruling kings and their kahunas. This system was the only law code the people had ever known. Its power of life and death held the nation together. Kapus touched every facet of Hawaiian life—religion, government, landholding, agriculture, fishing, sex, the eating of food, war, house and canoe construction and even play. These prohibitions and restrictions constantly reminded the people of the presence of the gods and since the Alii were believed to be descendants of the gods, many of the kapus referred to them. Inbreeding kept the bloodlines pure,

---

[1] Kaumualii was the son of Kaeo, the former king of Kauai who had been killed in an attempt to conquer Oahu.

[2] Four of these chiefs were from Kona—Keeaumoku, Kameeiamoku, Kamanawa and Keaweaheulu. The fifth was a renowned warrior named Kehuhaupio who had been Kamehameha's military tutor.

Early View of Waikiki   Burgess/State Archives

Kalanimoku ("Billy Pitt") in 1818   A. Pellion/State Archives

Method of Punishment   Jacques Arago/
in the Sandwich Islands   State Archives

thereby preserving the mana, the power and prestige, of the chiefs. The penalties for violating the kapus were severe—often death by clubbing, strangling, heiau sacrifice and other gruesome methods. Though these kapus were often oppressive for the common people and women of all classes, the people remained intensely loyal just as they had done for centuries.

Kamehameha continued to reside on Oahu until the summer of 1812 when he returned to the Kona District of Hawaii. Peace prevailed, and Kamehameha spent much of his time fishing, rebuilding heiaus and attending to agricultural production. Foreign trade continued to grow and Kamehameha took an active interest in it.

In founding the Hawaiian kingdom, Kamehameha did not create a new form of government. Instead, the government continued basically as it had before—a feudal system ruled by an autocrat. This time, however, there was one ruler with supreme authority. The lands were redistributed to the ruling chiefs, and their land holdings were scattered over several islands to lessen the danger of rebellion. To further minimize this danger, Kamehameha adopted the policy of keeping the ruling chiefs near him as much as possible and requiring them to travel with him when he went from place to place.

The consolidation of the Hawaiian Islands by Kamehameha into one kingdom was one of the greatest achievements in Hawaiian history. Three important factors contributed to this achievement: 1) the foreigners with their weapons, advice and physical aid; 2) the feudal Hawaiian society with its lack of distinct tribes having intense tribal loyalties; and probably the most important influence 3) the personality of Kamehameha.

High-born and trained to lead, Kamehameha possessed all the qualities of a strong leader. Powerful in physique, agile, fearless and possessing a strong mind, he easily inspired loyalty in his followers. Though ruthless in war, he was kind and forgiving when the need arose. He used new things and new ideas to promote his own interests. He appreciated the advantages offered by the foreigners and used them in his service. Yet he never fell into their power. Kamehameha's good judgment and strong will prevailed. Through constant vigilance and internal strength, he held his kingdom together until the last days of his life.

Following the custom of all great chiefs, Kamehameha took many wives during his lifetime. Seven of his wives were very high-ranking chiefesses who provided the offspring with a high degree of mana. These seven regal wives bore him twelve royal children. Kamehameha had twenty-one official wives plus a larger number of lovers and these may have produced as many as sixty offspring.

Kaahumanu, Kamehameha's favorite wife, was young, desirable, passionate and ambitious. Being high-spirited and independent, she caused Kamehameha much grief, yet she remained his true love and confidant. Despite her regal status, she bore him no children. The two royal sons that would later become kings (Liholiho ruled as Kamehameha II, and Kauikeaouli ruled as Kamehameha III) were born by another regal wive, Keopuolani, Kamehameha's niece. She was the highest ranking chiefess in the court, coming from the greatest families of Maui and Hawaii.

During the early part of the 1800's, Hawaii and Great Britain enjoyed a special relationship due to Kamehameha's policy of "cession." Great Britain, undoubtedly due to the great distance involved and her preoccupation with war, did not commit herself to anything more than maintaining cordial relations with the island kingdom. Nevertheless, this special relationship was recognized by other foreign vessels calling on the islands.

The Hawaiian flag came into existence during the period when the United States and Great Britain were at war (War of 1812). Captain George Vancouver during his warm and personal friendship with Kamehameha had presented him with a union jack. Later, after having helped Kamehameha construct the *Britannia*, the first foreign vessel built in the islands, Vancouver presented Kamehameha with the British flag. Shortly thereafter in late February, 1794, Kamehameha "ceded" the island of Hawaii to the protection of Great Britain, retaining the rights to regulate his own internal affairs. Several days later, the British flag was hoisted ashore. For almost twenty-two years, it flew over the king's residence protected by a battery of 16 carriage guns. Conflicting accounts abound concerning the design of the Hawaiian flag, some crediting Captain Alexander Adams while others credit Captain George Beckley. Both were friends of Kamehameha and he undoubtedly consulted with one or both

Kamehameha, King of the Sandwich Islands

Choris/State Archives

Queen Kaahumanu — Choris/State Archives

Hawaiian Flag — State Archives

of them. In any event, the number of alternating white, red, and blue stripes (eight) on the present flag represents the principal islands of Hawaii. The British union jack probably was included because of Hawaii's special relationship with the British.

The first Russian ships visited the Hawaiian islands in 1804, attempting to capitalize on the resources of the islands. However, the establishment of a Russian settlement in California eased the supply problems of the Russian American Company. This company, which consolidated Russian interests in the Aleutian Islands and Alaska, had an imperial charter which granted it a virtual monopoly on the fur and fishing trade in this region.

At the end of January, 1815, the *Bering*, an American trading ship recently acquired by the Russian American Company, was shipwrecked in a storm off Waimea, Kauai. Informed of the news, the Russian American Company obtained the services of a German doctor, Georg Anton Scheffer, to recover the lost cargo and attempt to establish a regular trade between the islands and the Russian settlements. Scheffer, posing as a naturalist, arrived in November and gained the favor of Kamehameha through his physician's skills. Against the advice of John Young, Kameha-

meha gave Scheffer the use of the royal storehouses at Honolulu. Fearing the wrath of the American traders, Scheffer made a brief stop at Honolulu and then proceeded to Kauai to conduct his salvage business with the Kauai king.

Scheffer quickly earned the favor of the Kauai king (Kaumualii) through his professional skills. Preying on the king's desire to be independent of Kamehameha, he involved the king in a treasonable plot against Kamehameha. By June of 1816, Scheffer succeeded in having the king place his kingdom under the protection of the Russian Emperor, obtained an exclusive right to the sandalwood trade and also the right to construct factories and plantations for agricultural products. In addition, he acquired the king's signature on agreements granting the company half of Oahu along with complete control of four of its harbors, even though Kamehameha was in complete charge of Oahu.

Port of Honolulu in 1816

Returning to Honolulu, Scheffer built a blockhouse, raised the Russian flag and supposedly made plans to build a fort. In the process he managed to arouse the ire of the natives by entering a heiau which had a kapu on it. Learning of these events, Kamehameha sent a delegation with orders to have the Russians leave—peacefully or by force. Lacking sufficient forces, the Russians departed, Scheffer returning to Kauai. Realizing the importance of the harbor, John Young and Kalanimoku ("Billy Pitt") oversaw the construction of the fort using coral blocks cut from the nearby reef. Captain Beckley became its first commandant.

In November, 1816, another Russian ship visited Hawaii—the *Rurick*, commanded by Lt. Otto von Kotzebue of the Russian Imperial Navy. Being on a peaceful mission, he managed to settle the uneasiness of the Hawaiians caused by Scheffer. With Kamehameha satisfied, Kotzebue and his crew were treated with generosity and good will. Sailing into Honolulu harbor in December, the *Rurick* became the first foreign vessel to exchange gun salutes with the new fort. Kotzebue visited the islands again in 1817. Louis Choris, an artist attached to Kotzebue's expedition, made several portraits of Kamehameha, one of only two artists to do so during his lifetime.

Meeting between Captain von Kotzebue and His Aides at Kamehameha's Court

On Kauai, Scheffer consolidated his alliance with the king. The following year, 1817, he built a fort at Waimea and raised the Russian flag. Under mounting pressure from Kamehameha and other foreign traders interested in the sandalwood trade, King Kaumualii finally changed his opinion of the doctor and ordered him and his men off the island. Resisting, Scheffer and the other Russians were driven out by force in May, 1817. Escaping to Oahu, Scheffer managed to work his way to China and from there to St. Petersburg. Back in Russia, Scheffer and the directors of the Russian American Company tried to persuade the government to pursue a more aggressive role. The czar refused to become involved and instructed the company to stick to peaceful activities with the islands.

The settlement at Honolulu consisted of coral stone buildings dominated by a fort, the king's palace and other buildings surrounded by hundreds of grass huts. Since Kamehameha had moved his palace from Waikiki to the sheltered harbor (though he spent most of his time on the island of Hawaii), Honolulu was fast becoming an important and regular port of call for foreign vessels.

The return visit of Kotzebue in 1817 and the visit of another Russian, Captain Golovnin in 1818 greatly eased the fears of the Hawaiians and offset much of the damage done by Scheffer.

View of the Port of Honolulu   **Choris/State Archives**

Kamehameha the Great (in 1818)   **Tikhanoff/Bishop Museum**

On April 15, 1819, the Spaniard Don Francisco de Paula Marin,[1] a trusted advisor and confidant of Kamehameha who possessed some medical knowledge, was summoned from Honolulu to proceed to Kailua, Hawaii to attend to the king who had been ill for some time. The religious and medical powers of the kahunas had not improved the condition of Kamehameha. Marin stayed with Kamehameha to his last days, but his services were ineffective. On the eighth day of May, 1819, Kamehameha the Great succumbed to his long illness.

As word of the king's death reached the people, a great grief fell upon them. As evidence of sorrow, those who lived in close association with the king augmented their sorrow by self-mutilation, such as knocking out one or more front teeth. But some of the more extreme examples of sorrow such as suicide, had gradually faded away as a result of the influence of the foreigners' culture. With the exception of human sacrifice, which Kamehameha had forbid on his deathbed, the old customs were observed for the departed king. At the appropriate time, the bones were carefully hidden and their location has never been revealed.

---

[1] Don Francisco de Paula Marin excelled in the fields of agriculture and commerce and is generally credited with planting the first pineapples on January 2, 1813.

The crossed kapu sticks announced the death of the great chief. Liholiho, Kamehameha's son and heir, fled to Kohala until Kailua could be ceremoniously cleansed. About a week later, he returned for his formal installation as king with the title of Kamehameha II. Wearing an English red suit with gold trim, a feather helmet and a feather cloak over his shoulders, Liholiho presented himself to the chiefs and commoners. Kaahumanu, the royal guardian and favorite wife of Kamehameha, presided over the ceremony, officially passing on to the new king the chiefs, the people, the guns and the land. In her final statement, she said ". . . we two shall share the rule over the land." The king consented, thereby becoming Kamehameha II.

In claiming to echo the last words of her deceased king and husband, Kaahumanu created for herself a new position in the government, that of kuhina nui. In effect, she became executive officer and would share in the rule of the land. Kalanimoku retained his position of "prime minister." Custody of the war god, Ku, went to Liholiho's cousin, Kekuaokalani, as Kamehameha the Great had instructed. Although the king was the highest officer in the land, the kuhina nui would be more active in administering the routine affairs of government. Whether Kamehameha had wanted her to have this new power or whether she usurped it, the fact remained that no one challenged her authority. The new king was young (about 22), had a reputation as a gambler and a playboy, and had an affliction for the foreigners' whiskey. With these shortcomings, Liholiho would need the guidance of a firm hand.

With the rule of the land now divided between Liholiho and Kaahumanu and the custody of the war god, Ku, no longer in possession of the person who also ruled the land, the prediction of a well-known German naturalist named Adelbert von Chamisso who had accompanied Kotzebue on his visits to the islands, seemed about to come true: "...after the death of the old hero, his kingdom, founded and kept together by force, will fall to pieces, the partition of it being already decided upon, and prepared."[1]

---

[1] This statement was made between 1816 and 1817, after Kamehameha the Great had formally proclaimed Liholiho as his successor and named a new custodian for the war god, Ku. One more event in the year of 1819, the abolition of the kapu system in November, would make that year stand out in Hawaiian history.

Temples Built for Kamehameha

Arago/State Archives

Chapter 3

A New Religion

Born in 1797, Kalani Kua Liholiho ("Heaven's Great Glowing") was raised during long years of peace. Because his mother (Keopuolani) was the highest-ranking chiefess in the land and his father was Kamehameha the Great, Liholiho was considered sacred. Reared away from military camps, he led a sheltered life. Adored and spoiled, he grew up in luxury. At the age of five, his father proclaimed him successor to the throne. Although coached in warfare, he commanded no troops, fought in no battles and never ruled over an island or district before becoming king. During childhood, the sacred prince was carried on the shoulders of his kahu (royal guardian) so that his precious feet might touch the earth only when necessary.

At the young age of twenty-two, he ascended the throne at a time when foreign influences, material possessions and new standards and ideas were propelling the Hawaiians into the modern western world. Unknown diseases were taking a large toll of the population. The demands for foodstuffs and sandalwood continued to increase as more and more foreign ships continued to call on the islands. Rum was being distilled on Oahu and dozens of foreigners had taken residence there, a number of them being deserters, loafers and vagrants. A new, jealous God loomed over the horizon and traditional values and practices were increasingly being questioned.

By the time of his coronation, Liholiho had acquired four high-born wives, each possessing adequate mana to continue the

Interior of a Chief's House (Liholiho) in the Sandwich Islands (1817) Choris/ State Archives

royal lineage. His third wife, Kamamalu, was his half sister and his favorite. Thrust into greatness under the shadow of his mighty father, Liholiho often escaped from reality by drinking, gambling and seeking other pleasures. Early in his reign, still unsure of his powers, he was unable to resist the pressure of the ruling chiefs for a share in the royal sandalwood monopoly.

The Baptism of the Prime Minister of the King Arago/ State Archives

In August of 1819, the French warship l'Uraine, commanded by Captain Louis de Freycinet, visited the islands with a company of French scientists and explorers. The prime minister "Billy Pitt" (Kalanimoku), learning from John Young that a Catholic Priest on board the French ship was a representative of the true God in heaven, had himself baptized by the priest as "pope" over the islands. Attending the ceremony were the king and several of his wives, Queen Kaahumanu and a number of high ranking chiefs. Assured of paradise, Kalanimoku went home to his seven wives and made a sacrifice to his gods.

Learning that Liholiho's cousin (Kekuaokalani, keeper of the war god, Ku) openly talked of overthrowing the royal power and slaughtering all Europeans living in the islands, John Young solicited the help of the French captain. In an official declaration made before an assemblage of ruling chiefs, Captain Freycinet pledged the friendship and protection of French ships to maintain the tranquility of the island kingdom.

Shortly after the inauguration of Kamehameha II (Liholiho), Queen Kaahumanu let the king know of her personal intention of bringing about the destruction of the kapu regarding the segregation of the sexes at meal time. Obtaining the allegiance of the queen mother, Keopuolani, who had such high mana that she was literally a royal prisoner, the two women put mounting pressure on the new king until he finally gave in. During the first week in November, 1819, a great feast was prepared in Kailua, Hawaii. Nearly all the leading chiefs and several foreigners were seated at two tables set in European fashion. One table seated the men, the other the women. For two days prior to the feast,

the king reinforced his reluctant decision by imbibing in rum while sailing off the coast of Kailua with his retainers.

Upon arriving at the feast, the king made several passes around both tables and then, without warning, sat at an empty chair at the women's table. Though perturbed and perhaps uncomfortable with his decision, he ate voraciously. A great joy settled over most of the guests; the eating kapu had been broken. When the meal was finished, Liholiho ordered the destruction of the heiaus and the burning of the idols.

The prime minister, Kalanimoku, supported the breaking of the kapus, as did the high priest (Hewahewa). But not all of the people agreed with the sudden issuance of the new orders. Rather than burning the idols, many of them were hidden and secretly worshipped. Kekuaokalani, keeper of the war god, and a sizeable number of followers, including, quite naturally, many priests, mounted an insurrection. Efforts at reconciliation failed and a battle was fought at Kuamoo, south of Kailua in late December. The king's army, led by Kalanimoku, easily crushed the revolt since they had superior numbers and the majority of the new weapons. In the fighting, Kekuaokalani was killed.

The overthrow of the kapu system had slowly been developing for many years, ever since the first arrival of the foreigners. These foreigners, for the most part, had a total disregard for the kapus and they continually insisted that they were wrong. Aboard ship, many of the kapus were flagrantly ignored when natives of both sexes came aboard. Foreigners openly violated the kapus ashore and went away unpunished. Natives who sailed off to foreign lands and returned told of constantly violating the kapus and suffering no apparent harm. News had recently reached the islands that the kapu system on Tahiti had been overturned. Thus, the pressures were mounting for its overthrow.

Yet until the death of Kamehameha the Great, who firmly believed in the kapu system and used it to acquire control of the kingdom, no one would have dared suggest such a radical change. But the modification of the mourning kapus at the death of Kamehameha, plus the cooperation of a majority of the ruling chiefs in agreeing to end the eating kapu initiated by Kaahumanu, were added steps in overthrowing the kapu system. The relations between the chiefs and the commoners remained more or less the same, but the chiefs were freed to try their skill in amassing and using their own political power to heights they could have never reached otherwise.

With the old kapus no longer officially enforced and formal religious ceremonies discontinued, the religious foundation of the nation had been eroded and a vacuum entered the social life of the Hawaiians. It is quite remarkable that while the old Hawaiian gods were being discarded, missionaries from New England were already at sea on their way to the islands firmly intent on persuading the ''heathens'' to embrace the teachings of Christianity. Furthermore, two American whaling ships from New Bedford, the *Balena* and the *Equator,* visited the islands in October, 1819, and took an off-shore whale which yielded over a hundred barrels of unexpected oil. These whaling ships would be the advance guard of a vast fleet that would soon descend upon the tiny island kingdom.

Born before the turn of the nineteenth century and raised near Kealakekua Bay, Opukahaia lost his parents during the period that wars ravaged the islands. While still a young boy, an American sea captain named Brintnall offered him passage to New Haven along with another native boy, Hopu. Lured by the great ships and the prospects of visiting a foreign land, he eagerly accepted. Taught some English by a Yale man aboard ship, the young lad arrived in New Haven in 1809. Ashore, he headed for Yale to seek additional instruction. Alone, friendless and not knowing how to acquire an education, he broke down in tears on the steps of one of the main buildings. Befriended by Rev. Edwin Dwight, a resident graduate, Obookiah (as they spelled it) perfected his English, and several years later he enrolled in the Foreign Mission School at Cornwall, Conn. when it opened. In the total class of twelve, seven were Hawaiians who had drifted into the area on various trading and whaling ships.

Inspired by evangelical revival and religious zeal, a number of European and American missionary societies had been formed in the late 1790's and early 1800's to spread the gospel throughout the world. It was hoped that the Foreign Mission School would provide a number of Christian messengers who would

House of Kalanimoku, Prime Minister of the King   Pellion/ State Archives

View of the King's Morai at Kealakekua, Island of Hawaii   Arago/ State Archives

Henry Opukahaia (Obookiah)   State Archives

return to their own people and spread the gospel. But Obookiah who had been so eager to return to the islands as a convert, would not be among them. He died of a fever in 1817, almost two years before the first mission was organized. Yet his death, and prior exemplary behavior, only encouraged the Protestant community. Aware of the increasing operations of New England traders in the Pacific, the American Board of Commissioners for Foreign Missions[1] organized a mission to the Hawaiian Islands in 1819. Four Hawaiians[2] would accompany the mission, headed by two ordained ministers.

[1] This board was an interdenominational body, composed mostly of Presbyterians and Congregationalists.

[2] The four Hawaiians were William Kanui, John Honolii, Thomas Hopu (Obookiah's shipboard companion) and George Kaumualii, son of the ruler of Kauai. All had adopted baptismal first names. All except George had been converted.

PIONEER COMPANY

Brig Thaddeus, 164 days from Boston. Arrived at Kailua, April 4, 1820. Landed at Honolulu, April 19, 1820.

Rev. Hiram Bingham Mrs. Sybil (Moseley) Bingham

Mr. Samuel Ruggles

Mrs. Nancy (Wells) Ruggles

Rev. Asa Thurston Mrs. Lucy (Goodale) Thurston

Capt. Daniel Chamberlain

Mrs. Mercy (Partridge) Whitney
Mrs. Jerusha (Burnett) Chamberlain

Mr. Samuel Whitney
Mr. Elisha Loomis

Dr. Thomas Holman Mrs. Lucia (Ruggles) Holman
Mrs. Maria Theresa (Sartwell) Loomis

Mrs. Holman Tomlinson

Pioneer Company of American Protestant Missionaries

State Archives

Before the mission could sail, wives had to be obtained for the six bachelors in the party. Within the space of two months, brides were found and marriages performed. The mission company consisted of two ordained ministers, Rev. Hiram Bingham and Rev. Asa Thurston; a physician, Dr. Thomas Holman; two teachers, Samuel Whitney and Samuel Ruggles; a printer, Elisha Loomis; a farmer, Daniel Chamberlain; plus their wives, Chamberlain's five children and the four Hawaiians. Clothed in self-righteousness and armed with the sword of the Prince of Peace, they were prepared for "bloodless war" with the savage sinners who they had to civilize and convert.

Departing Boston on the brig *Thaddeus* on October 23, 1819, they started their long voyage around Cape Horn and across the Pacific Ocean to the Hawaiian Islands eighteen thousand miles away. After five months of seasickness and cramped quarters, they sighted the snow-capped peaks of Mauna Kea on the island of Hawaii on March 30, 1820. Off Kohala, a small boat was lowered with several of the Hawaiians in it, including Thomas Hopu who had been born in the valley stretching before them. Upon their return, the mission learned of the events that had transpired earlier, including the death of Kamehameha, the abolition of the kapus, and the downfall of the idols. This was convincing evidence that God had prepared their way. On the following day, a number of natives came out in canoes to trade. The reaction of the missionaries, quoting from the journal of

A Woman of the   **Choris/**
Sandwich Islands[3]   **State Archives**

Hiram Bingham, was as follows: ". . . the appearance of destitution, degradation, and barbarism, among the chattering, and almost naked savages, whose heads and feet, and much of their sunburnt swarthy skins, were bare, was appalling. Some of our number, with gushing tears, turned away from the spectacle. Others with firmer nerve continued their gaze, but were ready to exclaim, 'Can these be human beings!'"

[3] This is a woman of high rank as indicated by the *lei niho palaoa* around her neck. This prized neckpiece consisted of a hooklike ornament carved from a whale's tooth and fastened to many lengths of braided human hair.

Several days later on April 4, the missionaries anchored off Kailua and proceeded ashore to present themselves to King Liholiho. Their attention was once again drawn to the multitude of nearly naked "heathen" of every age, sex and rank frolicking in the water, floating on surfboards or just lounging on the shore. Upon meeting the king, the missionaries introduced themselves and asked the king for his permission to remain in the islands for the purpose of teaching the people Christianity. Perhaps fearful of the followers of a new religion, the king took their request under consideration. Four days later, after much discussion with his advisors, the king allowed the missionaries to stay at Kailua for one year on a trial basis. The missionaries also wanted to establish a station at Honolulu and it took another four days before an affirmative decision was handed down on that request. By mutual agreement, Asa Thurston and Dr. Holman, together with their wives and two of the Hawaiians, would remain at Kailua while the balance of the mission company proceeded to Honolulu. Once settled at Honolulu, several of the missionaries accompanied George Kaumualii to Waimea, Kauai where his father was king. Thinking that his son had been lost or killed, the king was overjoyed upon his son's return and he eagerly assisted the missionaries in establishing a school.

The early months were difficult for the missionaries, yet they set to work with determination and energy. The plot of land allocated to the Honolulu mission was located about a half mile from the village of Honolulu. The area was hot and arid. Water had to be carried for almost a mile until a well could be dug.

The missionaries' chinaware had been smashed on the long voyage and their furniture was minimal. Life for them was primitive and hard as they labored under the layers of heavy clothing they had brought from New England.

Initially, outdoor sermons in rudimentary Hawaiian brought out several hundred curiosity seekers; yet so would the sight of the missionary women doing cooking or washing. Most natives found the constraint of clothing and the great effort of literacy unbearable. Until the chiefs could be converted to set an example, the commoners and lesser chiefs would never embrace this new and strange religion. Although the missionaries persisted, progress was slow. The king, for example, in order to convert, would have to give up four of his five wives and abstain from rum drinking; he would forgo neither! The early assistance given by the Hawaiian converts who had accompanied the mission from New England proved invaluable. They acted as interpreters and taught English to the natives; yet they were far from perfect. William Kanui later was excommunicated for becoming a drunkard.

Education was the top priority and small schools were established almost immediately at all three mission stations. Teaching English proved difficult and time-consuming, so the missionaries began to learn the Hawaiian language and attempted to reduce it into written form. But since the pronunciation varied from island to island and a number of letters were indistinguishable, the adoption of an alphabet came slow. It wasn't until the summer of 1826 that an alphabet was finally adopted.

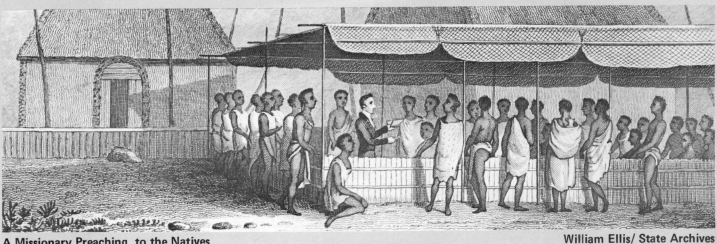

A Missionary Preaching to the Natives   **William Ellis/ State Archives**

The king's principal residence until the end of 1820 had been at Kailua, Hawaii. Recognizing the growing importance of Honolulu and the danger of the king's continued absence from there, Liholiho's chiefs and advisors persuaded the king to change his residence to Honolulu. The move was done gradually, in stages. In November, 1820, the king and his attendants sailed for Honolulu on the recently purchased yacht *Cleopatra's Barge*. This eighty-three foot yacht with lavish staterooms paneled in mahogany and inlaid with maple and other rare woods cost the king the equivalent of approximately $90,000 in sandalwood contracts which would be filled during this and the following year. The name of this yacht was changed to *Haaheo o Hawaii* (Pride of Hawaii). Despite the official change in residence, the king continued his habit of wandering from island to island with his chiefs and attendants.

The active trade in sandalwood began in 1811. Following the War of 1812, trade in the Pacific grew rapidly and became more competitive as European traders challenged the near monopoly held by the Americans. After the death of Kamehameha the Great, Liholiho begrudgingly shared the sandalwood trade with the ruling chiefs. Attempting to become rich, they forced the common people to cut and haul out of the woods huge quantities of sandalwood. The shrewd New England traders brought an unbelievable array of consumer goods including carriages,

Cleopatra's Barge   **George Ropes/Peabody Museum**

billiard tables, house frames and sailing ships. With the speculating fervor high, the chiefs bought nearly everything in sight. As the sandalwood became scarce, the chiefs signed promissory notes and continued buying, especially ships. The people spent so much time in cutting wood that cultivation was grossly neglected and the prices of vegetables and other foodstuffs soared.

In July, 1821, Liholiho journeyed to Kauai on an impluse to test the loyalty of Kauai's ruler, King Kaumualii. Receiving a royal welcome, Liholiho reaffirmed the treaty made between his late father, Kamehameha the Great, and the Kauai King. Several weeks later when Liholiho returned to Honolulu, he took Kaumualii along with him and in effect made him a royal prisoner of state. Kaahumanu, the kuhina nui, charmed by the handsome king's gentlemanly nature, married him in October. Shortly thereafter, she added a second husband to her court, Kaumualii's son (Kealiiahonui), thereby insuring the continued cooperation of the king and increasing her hold over the island of Kauai.

Shortly after her diplomatic triumph, Kaahumanu became ill. Nursed back to health by Sybil Bingham, she became much more receptive to the Christian religion. Since no one in the kingdom possessed as much authority as she did, her gradual acceptance of the new religion gave it official sanction. Kaahumanu's sympathy for the missionaries was instrumental in leading many chiefs into becoming converts. One of the chiefs who took an early interest in the new religion was Kaahumanu's brother, Cox Keeaumoku. He was among the first group of approximately sixty natives who attended Sunday service in mid-January, 1822. Later, he opened his own house for public services and for use as a temporary schoolhouse for himself and others.

Rev. William Ellis   **Hawaiian Mission Children's Society**

Liholiho carried on the policy of Kamehameha the Great in foreign relations in that he continued to regard the kingdom as being under the protection of the British Empire. In the spring of 1822, a small schooner, the *Prince Regent*, built in Sydney under the direction of the British government, arrived in Honolulu escorted by the *Mermaid* and her captain, J.R. Kent. The schooner was to be presented to Kamehameha the Great in accordance with Captain George Vancouver's promise. Learning of the great king's death, Captain Kent delivered the ship instead to Liholiho on May 1.

Rev. William Ellis, a passenger on the *Mermaid*, found himself and his fellow mission members temporarily detained in Honolulu due to a change in plans by Captain Kent. Ellis had spent the last six years in Tahiti engaged in missionary work for the London Missionary Society. At the urgent request of the American missionaries and many native chiefs, he remained in Hawaii for two years, interrupting his stay, briefly, to return to Tahiti to fetch his family. Because of his familiarity with the Tahitian language, which was so much like the Hawaiian, Ellis gained an early command of the Hawaiian language. Because of his knowledge and experience, his cooperation was especially helpful in completing the work of reducing the Hawaiian language into written form. He also composed the first Hawaiian hymns and wrote extensively on the social, cultural and religious practices of the Polynesian cultures.

The Old.	Corrected in English.	The New, or Hawaiian.
Tamaahmaah,	Kâh-mä'-hâh-mä-hâh,	Ka me' ha me' ha.
Terreioboo,	Kâh-lâh'-ny-o-poo'-oo,	Ka la' ni o pu' u.
Tamoree,	Kâh-oo'-moo âh-lee'-ee,	Ka u' mu a li' i.
Owhyhee,	Hâh-wŷe'-ee,	Ha wai' i.
Woahoo,	O-âh'-hoo,	O a' hu.
Attooi,	Cow'-eȳe',	Kau' ai'.
Hanaroorah,	Hōnō-loo'-loo,	Ho no lu' lu.

Examples Showing the Formation of the Hawaiian Language
Hiram Bingham

To the unacquainted, the spoken Hawaiian language appeared to be all one long word. Early attempts by foreigners to write down the names of various Hawaiian people and places resulted in different spellings. Realizing that education was the key to "winning" over the natives and that time was critical, the missionaries set to work to reduce the Hawaiian language to an easily understood and useable form. Eliminating all silent letters, and attempting to avoid arbitrary spellings, ambiguities, errors and inconsistencies, they assigned a certain character to a certain sound thereby deriving a true pronunciation in the Hawaiian language. The five vowels were the all-powerful nucleus (Ah, A, Ee, O, Oo — a, e, i, o, u) and when combined with the seven consonants (He, Ke, La, Mu, Nu, Pi, We — h, k, l, m, n, p, w) attempted to express every sound in the pure Hawaiian dialect. In order to preserve the identity of scripture names, additional consonants were adopted (b, d, f, g, r, s, t, v, & z), but these were soon modified and dropped completely in 1826, leaving the twelve basic letters to form the Hawaiian alphabet.

Printing in the language of the native people awakened a curiosity in the chiefs as well as the common people and gave a new impulse to the schools and the desire for education. Since the curriculum was very elementary, stressing the alphabet and reading, the natives found the lessons easy. Bright students were usually sent out on their own to establish additional schools once they had acquired a limited proficiency in reading.

Three Chiefs of   **Pellion/**
the Sandwich Islands[1]   **State Archives**

As the missionaries bridged the gap between ancient Hawaii and the 19th century, the natives were taught new crafts; they were warned of the evils of drink and prostitution; they were taught how to read and write; and they learned that they were being exploited by many merchants and sailors. As they learned the value of their products and as their desire for foreign goods increased, bartering took on a much more even-handed exchange and the prices of supplies rose significantly.

---

[1] Cox Keeaumoku, Governor of Maui and the son of Keeaumoku who was commander-in-chief of Kamehameha's forces in all his war campaigns, is in the center. One of his principal officers is on the right. The chief on the left, with the tatoo mourning the death of Kamehameha the Great, is Hoapili, guardian of the princess Nahienaena (Kamehameha's daughter) and husband of Keopuolani (Kamehameha's wife).

When the missionaries had made sufficient progress in reducing the Hawaiian language to written form, printing in Hawaii began in January, 1822. The missionaries had brought a printing press with them on their long voyage from New England plus several fonts of type. Mr. Loomis, a printer by trade, was spared from his religious duties so that he could set up the press and begin printing. On the afternoon of January 7, chief Keeaumoku, after receiving instructions on operating the press, eagerly applied the necessary strength to run off several impressions of the first printing in the Hawaiian Islands, a spelling lesson.

Now that the native people could see their own words in print, reading could be taught with considerable ease. The chiefs took more interest in education, and few commoners were among the early pupils. In fact, these early pupils were nearly all adults who pressed forward, demanding attention. The younger generations, lacking sufficient discipline, were often uncontrollable and chose to avoid the restraining nature of education. The earliest school buildings were nothing more than grass huts with a few mats laid over a dirt floor.

The educational work of the missionaries opened the minds and hearts of the natives to religious ideas. Yet few natives were admitted into the church because of the rigid standards imposed by the missionaries and their religion. Being Polynesians and not westerners, the Hawaiians did not fully grasp the concept of Christian sin. In order to establish the western ideals of right and wrong, the missionaries had to destroy the old Hawaiian standards. Only when these standards were destroyed could the concept of sin be realized and the need for a Christ become evident.

Preaching endlessly about the depravation and stupidity of the Hawaiian life-style, the missionaries shamed the Hawaiians into abandoning their ways and their hero ancestors. During the early years of missionary exposure, only a few natives were willing to endure this long, humiliating experience. The few that did, and many of the ones that followed in later years, paid a high price for eternal life; they lost their sense of individual worth and self-respect. Their future fate would be unhappy.

The second company of missionaries arrived in Honolulu on April 27, 1823. The reinforcements included Rev. & Mrs. Artemas Bishop, Dr. & Mrs. Abraham Blatchely, Mr. Levi Chamberlain, Mr. & Mrs. James Ely, Mr. & Mrs. Joseph Goodrich, Rev. & Mrs. William Richards, Rev. & Mrs. Charles S. Stewart, Miss Betsey Stockton, Stephen Popohe (a Tahitian), and three Hawaiians (Willam Kamooula, Richard Kalaioulu and Kupelii). Arriving on Sunday, the new missionaries were warmly received by their fellow comrades and the native chiefs. It was quickly decided that the labors of the new mission company would be best served on the islands of Hawaii and Maui.

On April 24, three days before the arrival of the second mission company, Liholiho, anticipating the feast of his accession to the throne of the Hawaiian Islands, began the annual festivities nearly two weeks ahead of time. Seated at the head of a table nearly 100 feet long, the king hosted an elaborate feast that had as its guests his five wives and about a hundred others including chiefs, favorites, several missionaries, sea captains and residents. Armed guards held at bay the thousands of spectators who crowded around to gaze at the splendor of the table and the magnificent appearance of several warriors parading around in their finest feathered warcloaks. Liholiho's sister, Nahienaena, was brought to the table in a four-wheeled carriage drawn by friends and servants. The king, bearing her on his back, introduced her as the daughter of Kamehameha the Great and then seated her beside her brother, Kauikeaouli, with whom she held equal rank. (The young prince was next in line for the throne.) The festival climaxed with formal processions in the final days and closed on the 8th of May, the anniversary of the death of Kamehameha the Great.

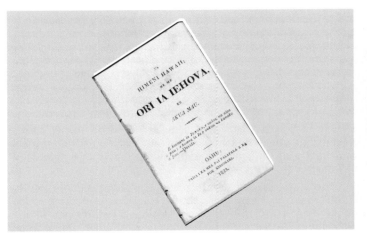

**First Hymnal Book Printed
at the Mission Press**

**Hawaiian Mission
Children's Society**

**Palace of Kalanimoku - Native Chapel -
Cottage of Mr. Ellis (in Honolulu)**

**William Ellis/
State Archives**

Princess Nahienaena

Robert Dampier/State Archives

The queen mother, Keopuolani, being in feeble health, moved to Waikiki in the spring of 1823. Here she showed unusual readiness to accept the scriptures preached by the missionaries. In May, accompanied by Rev. William Richards and Rev. Charles Stewart and their families, the queen mother sailed to Lahaina with her party of servants and relatives on *Cleopatra's Barge*. In Lahaina, a new mission post was established.

The queen mother's illness grew worse during the summer and she was now near death. On her deathbed, she asked the king to take care of the land and the people, protect the missionaries and walk the straight path. In her last hours, Rev. Ellis arrived at her side, and at the earnest request of the king and other chiefs at her side, baptized Keopuolani into the Christian faith. On the 16th of September, the queen mother expired. Except for loud and repeated wailing, the excesses of passion and other pagan practices which would have taken place at the death of a high ranking chief did not occur. The wailing lasted two days until the public Christian service commenced on the 18th. The queen mother, according to her last wishes, was buried in a coffin in the Christian tradition as a crowd numbering in the thousands looked on. The new religion was taking hold on the people.

Desiring to see his "friend" King George IV and get a look at the outside world, Liholiho planned a voyage to England. Perhaps fearing danger from the United States due to the large influx of American traders and missionaries, Liholiho may have wanted to obtain advice and assistance in governing and maintaining a better intercourse with the foreigners visiting or residing in the islands. Accompanied by his favorite wife (Kamamalu), Boki (Governor of Oahu) and his wife (Liliha), and a number of high ranking chiefs plus servants and interpreters, the king sailed November 27,1823 on the chartered British whaler *L'Aigle*.

In Liholiho's absence, his younger brother (Kauikeaouli) would succeed to the throne in the event of the king's death. Since this younger brother was only about nine years old, the post of regent was established. The queen dowager, Kaahumanu, would assume this post in addition to her duties as kuhina nui. Billy Pitt (Kalanimoku) would continue as prime minister.

After the king's departure, the older chiefs decided upon a more orderly and steadier policy in running the affairs of government. In proclamations issued by Kalanimoku and later by Kaahumanu, acting as regent in the absence of the king, a mini-code of laws was laid down based on the teachings of the missionaries. These verbal laws included observance of the Sabbath and prohibitions on murder, theft and fighting. With strong friends in power, the missionaries could see improvements in church and school attendance and more requests for books from the mission press.

The royal party arrived at Portsmouth, England in mid-May of 1824. Having no advance notice of their visit, the British government hastily assigned a guardian, the Honorable Frederick Gerald Byng. Conducted to London, the royal party received new wardrobes in an attempt to make them more presentable. Their dark skin color caused the Hawaiians some embarrassment in that they were ridiculed by the press and fashionable aristocrats. But generally, they received the most courteous treatment, seeing all the important buildings and places of interest, visiting theatres and occupying the royal boxes, attending receptions in their honor, etc.

Prior to attending an audience with King George set for June 21, the royal party was stricken with measles. Having never been exposed to the disease, their illness was serious. Queen Kamamalu died on the eight of July, her case complicated by pneumonia. There was little the attending physicians could do. Grief stricken, Liholiho sank into decline and passed away on the 14th. The other members of the royal party gradually recovered and Boki, as ranking chief, took charge. In September, Boki met with King George. In the discussions that followed, King George

Lamentations on the Death
of Queen Keopuolani
Roberts/
State Archives

Kamehameha II (Liholiho) Ἀ **John Hayter/State Archives**

Queen Kamamalu Ἀ **John Hayter/State Archives**

promised his protection from external forces and promised not to take possession of the islands. By appointing a consul to the islands, he recognized the independence of the Sandwich Islands.

The 46 gun frigate *H.M.S. Blonde* was dispatched to return the royal party back to the Sandwich Islands, including the bodies of the deceased king and queen. Commanded by the Right Honorable (George Anson) Lord Byron, the *Blonde* sailed from Portsmouth in late September, 1824. Byron had received secret instructions to assert British sovereignty over the islands in the form of a protectorate only in the event that another foreign power attempted to establish its sovereignty or to make an exclusive settlement in the island group.

On March 9, 1825, two whaling ships brought news of the king and queen's death in London. Because of the changing circumstances and the influence of the missionaries, the dis-order which often followed such important news scarcely took place. In Mid-April, Captain Richard Charlton, newly appointed British consul, arrived in Honolulu with the news that the bodies of the king and queen were being returned to the islands. On May 6, 1825, the *H.M.S. Blonde* arrived at Honolulu after making an initial stop at Hilo. On the morning of the 11th, the sumptuously decorated coffins were taken ashore for funeral ceremonies. The king's guard lined the road, armed with muskets and dressed in a bizarre mixture of native costume and English dress. Stopping at the church, a brief funeral service was conducted. Finally, the coffins were placed inside Kalanimoku's own house until a more suitable place could be constructed.

H.M.S. Blonde **off Cape Horn**   Robert Dampier/ State Archives

Kauikeaouli (Kamehameha III)   Robert Dampier/State Archives

On June 6, 1825, a national council was held to officially determine succession to the throne. In an unanimous decision, the dead king's younger brother, Kauikeaouli, would become king with the title of Kamehameha III. Because the new king was only twelve years old, Kalanimoku was appointed his special guardian. Kaahumanu continued as regent. In the meantime, the young king would be instructed by the missionaries in religion, writing and reading. This council also adopted an important policy concerning the reversion of lands. Henceforth, hereditary succession became law except in cases where the chief or landholder infringed on the laws; then they would revert back to the king. This policy, adopted by Kamehameha the Great, had been abandoned by Liholiho.

The Regency of Kaahumanu

As the crossroads of the North Pacific, Hawaii became an important way station for sailing ships. The fur trade between the northwest coast of America and China started about 1785 as a direct result of Captain Cook's Voyages of Discovery. Another main branch of trade was the sandalwood trade between Hawaii and China which often overlapped the later years of the fur trade. With the discovery of sperm whales off Hawaiian waters and off the coast of Japan in 1819 and 1820, the Hawaiian Islands became the principal replenishment port since Japanese ports were closed to foreign ships. In 1822, about sixty whaling ships called at the islands. By the end of the decade, they averaged more than one hundred and forty per year. These visits were concentrated in the spring and fall, crowding the harbors at Honolulu and Lahaina. As the liberty parties swarmed ashore, the streets filled with sailors intent on fulfilling their long-suppressed desires for rum, gambling and especially sexual pleasure. Fights were frequent and law enforcement was lax, especially in the early part of the decade.

By the mid-1820's, Honolulu had become a major distribution point. Cargos were broken up, some for local consumption, the balance joined together with other cargos for re-shipment to California, China or Europe. Horses became an important export item from California to Hawaii. Around 1830, Mexican cowboys began teaching local cowhands (paniolos) the art of cattle ranching. The local trade likewise increased as more foreigners took up residence in the islands. Also, the desires of the natives increased as the work of the missionaries raised their standard of living. In the decade of the 20's, a number of retail stores were established, including mercantile shops, boarding houses, billiard saloons, grog shops and even a bakery. A number of these early establishments went through many changes in ownership over the years and a few still exist today under different names.

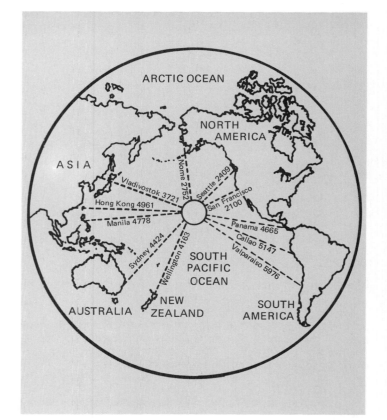

Hawaii-Crossroads of the Pacific

Before 1820, foreigners who acquired land and became residents of Hawaii were mostly of a humble status, commonly sailors. In matters of property, they conformed to the customs imposed upon them by the native rulers. This situation changed after 1820. As the number of foreigners increased, more and more of them were men of higher status in life: merchants, mechanics, missionaries and professional men. Having little respect for the native system, they began to deal with their property like they would do in their homelands. The native authorities, by treating the property of foreigners the same as they did for the natives, aroused much dissatisfaction. Before 1830, most of the differences between the native government and the foreigners concerned moral laws and sandalwood debts. After 1830, land and property rights became the main area of discontent.

In the decade of the 20's, the king maintained his right to control the residency of foreigners. Foreigners who held land did so at the pleasure of the king. But as more and more foreigners took up residence, including official representatives of foreign governments, the pendulum of change began to swing toward the foreigners as the native government, still groping its way into the western world, attempted to maintain a middle ground.

View near Honolulu, Oahu (1825)

Robert Dampier/ State Archives

The period between 1825 and 1840, the pre-constitutional period, was a critical period when the government began changing under the influence of foreign ideas and domestic politics influenced by the missionaries. A system of laws began to evolve. The growing interests of foreigners brought out the problem of their place and their rights in the community. Also, the question of Hawaiian independence was emerging and a solution would soon have to be found.

As early as March of 1822, two "Notices" were published in Honolulu. The first related to disturbances caused by seamen on shore liberty who if "found riotous or disturbing the peace" would be imprisoned in the fort until a fine of thirty dollars per offender was paid for their release. The second "Notice" called for the confinement and early expulsion from the islands of any residing foreigner found guilty of molesting strangers or in any way disturbing the peace.

Honolulu Fort (About 1837)   Belcher/State Archives

In the meantime, the excessive sandalwood debts amassed by the chiefs began to cause concern among the traders. These debts became so high (estimated to be about $200,000) that the traders complained to the United States government. In response, two American warships first the *Dolphin* and then the *Peacock*, visited the islands at different times during 1826 with instructions to investigate the situation and render aid to American commerce.

In negotiations with the chiefs, the officers in charge received acknowledgements of the debts and renewed pledges of repayment. In effect, these debts became Hawaii's national debt. Although special taxes were levied against the people, the debts were not fully paid. The dwindling sandalwood forests were repeatedly assaulted, so much so that the trade nearly came to an end in 1829. Yet despite signing new notes and conducting new sandalwood gathering campaigns in 1829, again induced by the presence of another American warship (the *Vincennes*), the debts were not fully paid until 1843!

Palace of Kamehameha III in 1826   **State Archives**

Hawaii's first "treaty" with a foreign government was signed on December 23, 1826. Intending to safeguard American commerce in the Pacific, the "articles of arrangement" became in effect a treaty of friendship between the United States and the island kingdom of Hawaii. Although the treaty was never ratified by the United States' government, it nevertheless was signed by a duly appointed representative named John C. Jones, Jr., Agent for Commerce and Seamen. The treaty provided for the admittance and protection of American ships in time of peace and war, regulated salvage cases, provided for the apprehension of deserters and protected the rights of American citizens in their lawful pursuits, including suing in island courts.

As the influence of the missionaries grew, churches were built on all of the larger Hawaiian Islands and the people were continually encouraged to attend services. In mid-1826, Kaahumanu and Rev. Bingham toured Oahu together with several hundred followers and instructed the natives in the rural areas about the Ten Commandments.

Yet the good works of the missionaries often ran head-on into the demands of the pleasure-bent whalers, nearly four-fifths of whom were also from New England. Courting royal favors, they often corrupted both chiefs and common people. Bringing no women with them, they preyed on the native women with the same eagerness and persistence as the whales they hunted.

A typical day for many visiting sailors consisted mostly of drinking, gambling and sleeping. During the spring and summer months when the whaling ships entered the port cities of Lahaina and Honolulu, the missionaries were particularly embarrassed when it came to "saving" the Hawaiian women from the boisterous sailors, especially when many of the young women really didn't want to be saved! The Hawaiian chiefs usually found themselves in the middle whenever strife arose; the foreign population and the sailors taking a pleasure-bent stand while the

The Queen at Waimea, Oahu, Recommending Christianity   Hiram Bingham/ State Archives

missionaries the opposite, puritan stand. A number of riots and armed demonstrations took place during the years 1825 through 1827, compelling the ruling chiefs to relax the enforcement of laws against promiscuous immorality.

Initially, the enforcement of any law depended on the mood of the local chief. The native population, accustomed to the repressive kapus, submitted without complaining very much to the enforcement of whatever laws existed. But the foreign population, fearful of intervention into their business profits or pleasures, complained loudly whenever certain laws were enforced against them. As the concept of uniform law began to be accepted, trial by jury (suggested by Lord Byron) was introduced after 1825 and the mode of execution was set at hanging. Yet enforcement remained lax, due partly to indifference and partly to the fact that no officials were specifically charged with the duty of enforcing the laws. However, this situation began to change toward the end of the decade.

In February, 1827, Kalanimoku died. God-fearing and strong-willed, he, along with his cousin Kaahumanu, held the nation together during the difficult years following the death of Kamehameha the Great. In addition, he had served as prime minister to Kamehameha during the twenty-four odd years of his reign. Rumors immediately began to circulate that Boki, Governor of Oahu and younger brother of Kalanimoku, was amassing an army in an attempt to overthrow Kaahumanu. But Boki, lacking the nerve to act and continually running into the strong will of the regent, probably never would have followed through even if the rumors were true.

Commercial enterprises were not entirely in the hands of foreigners. The natives also participated in a number of ways, although their scope was small when compared to that of the foreigners. A number of natives learned navigation and became masters of small, inter-island vessels. Among the chiefs, Boki was the boldest. After his return from England with the remains of the royal party, he associated with the British Consul, Richard Carlton, who encouraged Boki in his commercial enterprises and actually financed several of them. These activities included buying the entire cargo of a British ship and opening a retail store in 1827, opening a hotel, and sending trading expeditions to Alaska, Manila, Canton and Tahiti the following year. Although he even attempted to run a sugar plantation, most of Boki's ventures were not very successful.

Personal gain was only one of the reasons for Boki's various commercial ventures. As Governor of Oahu, he had an obligation to help pay the national debt which had been recently acknowledged by the chiefs in 1826. Yet Boki's ventures required heavy expenditures, causing him to sink deeper into debt and further delaying payments on the national debt. Another reason for Boki's ventures was his confrontations with the regent Kaahumanu and the Christian chiefs coached by Bingham. With his political ambitions blocked, life became unbearable for Boki.

Boki's last venture involved an expedition to the New Hebrides where sandalwood had been reported to exist in abundance. Two brigs, the *Kamehameha* and the *Becket,* sailed on December 2, 1829 with more than four hundred men including a number of foreigners. Although the sandalwood report proved to be true, Boki's venture turned out to be a failure. Both ships reached the island of Rotuma, north of Fiji, but from there Boki sailed ahead and his ship, the *Kamehameha*, vanished with all hands. The *Becket* later reached the New Hebrides and waited in vain for Boki's arrival. Unfriendly natives and the onset of disease forced the *Becket* to sail for Oahu. On the return voyage, starvation, disease and brutal seas devastated the crew. By the time they reached Honolulu on August 3, 1830, less than twenty survivors remained of the more than four hundred that initially set sail.

Liliha became acting governess after Boki left on his sandalwood expedition in late 1829. She continued the liberal policies of her husband, seldom enforcing laws, especially those objected to by the foreign community. She even granted licenses to rum sellers in direct violation of the law. Her laxity displeased many of the older and higher ranking chiefs. After learning of Boki's death, she returned to a more liberal life-style which infuriated

Kalanimoku, **Robert Dampier/**
Prime Minister of Hawaii **State Archives**

Boki and Liliha **John Hayter/Kamaaina Graphics**

Kuakini, Governor of Hawaii **William Ellis/State Archives**

the chiefs and caused them to plan her ouster. The chiefs, with the help of Liliha's father, dissolved an impending rebellion and forced Liliha to resign, whereupon she returned to Lahaina with her father. "Adams" Kuakini (Governor of the island of Hawaii and brother of Kaahumanu) was appointed acting Governor of Oahu in April, 1831.

Governor Kuakini, a huge man who weighed over three hundred pounds, commanded great respect among the common people. Being a recent convert, he now was in a position to compel the foreigners to heed the moral laws laid down by the missionaries. His vigorous enforcement of existing laws against gambling and liquor selling, backed up by armed guards patrolling the streets, caused violent protests by the foreign community. The enforcement became so effective that on Sundays the streets were literally deserted since music-making, dancing, games, carousing and even horseback riding were prohibited on the Sabbath. The tightening of the moral laws also put a strain on the Hawaiians. Many chants were outlawed, women could no longer swim in public places and the law against adultery was strictly enforced. Repeat offenders were sent to penal colonies; male offenders being sent to Kahoolawe while women offenders were banished to Lanai. Lesser offenders were forced to work on road building projects for varying time periods.

Father Alexis Bachelot   **State Archives**

Liliha's ouster cleared the way for the elimination of the Catholics from the islands. In France, a relatively new and zealous order, the Congregation of the Sacred Hearts of Jesus and Mary, had sailed from Bordeaux in November of 1826. Father Alexis Bachelot headed the mission which included three priests, a choir brother and two lay brothers. Several agricultural settlers also accompanied the expedition. Arriving in Honolulu on July 7, 1827, they were immediately ordered by Kaahumanu to leave on the same ship. Her order was not carried out since the captain, furious at not receiving payment for the cargo he brought to the islands, sailed away in a fit of anger. The Catholic mission, fearful of being expelled at an early date, maintained a low profile during their first year, devoting themselves to learning the language and obtaining a small parcel of land on which to construct a chapel. Five months after their arrival, Governor Boki granted them a small parcel of land for their chapel. The Catholics were able to stay in the islands through the support of Boki and a few other "rebel" chiefs. The support stemmed from Boki's desire to embarrass the Protestants and raise the ire of Kaahumanu with whom he was constantly at odds. The agricultural settlement became a failure and the settlers returned to France.

To the American Protestant missionaries, the Catholic presence constituted an invasion. Since Protestant Christianity by 1827 had literally become a state religion, anyone embracing the Catholic faith was considered insubordinate. Nevertheless, the Hawaiians discovered that Catholic Christianity had fewer restraints so irksome to the native spirit—they could smile, laugh, go swimming and even smoke. The initial successes of the Catholic mission posed serious problems for the ruling chiefs and the Protestant missionaries. But no action was taken by the chiefs until the summer of 1829 when a proclamation was issued in the streets prohibiting all natives from attending Catholic services.

When Boki departed on his ill-fated sandalwood venture, the Catholics lost their main ally. Shortly thereafter, in January, 1830, Kaahumanu personally forbid the priests from teaching the Catholic religion. With the same determination that she had used to eliminate the old Hawaiian gods, Kaahumanu commenced a reign of terror against the natives who embraced the new faith. Beatings, torture, prison sentences at hard labor and even exile were punishments doled out to those who persisted in their practice of the Catholic faith. While some Protestant missionaries protested these harsh sentences, others completely ignored the whole situation and pressed for the expulsion of the priests.

Kaahumanu ("The Feather Mantle") was about sixteen when she became Kamehameha the Great's wife. In full womanhood, she stood six feet tall and grew very portly, a mark of prestige among royalty. Following in her husband's footsteps, she became one of the most imposing native rulers of the Hawaiian kingdom. Possessing high rank and a dictatorial temper, she ruled her people with a firm hand. Since many of the leading chiefs in the land were related to her, Kaahumanu's edicts were seldom questioned. Her later years were filled with religious zeal and she remained a strong friend and protector of the Protestant missionaries.

In 1832, Kaahumanu became ill. Perhaps sensing death, she did not want to die in her Boston-style house in Honolulu. Rather, she was carried (in her bed) to another of her residences far up in the Manoa Valley—a small grass hut shaded with trees and surrounded by fragant maile, ilima and hibiscus blossoms. Following behind the regent were hundreds of natives chanting meles and reciting her genealogy clear back to the gods. While several missionaries and chiefs kept a vigil, Hiram Bingham presented the regent with a copy of the New Testament printed in Hawaiian. Just off the mission presses and bound in leather, the Bible had Kaahumanu's name stamped in gold on the cover. It gave her great pleasure in her final moments. The great queen breathed her last breath on June 5, 1832, at the age of approximately sixty-four. With the missionaries in full control, no wailings, mourning excesses or self-mutilations were allowed. Anything hinting of royal pomp and splendor was eliminated. The queen, having died a Christian, would have been pleased.

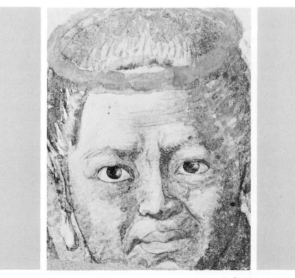

Kaahumanu, Regent of Hawaii   **Choris/Bishop Museum**

Chapter 5

Constitutional Government

Kamehameha III, second son of Queen Keopuolani and Kamehameha the Great, grew to manhood under the influence of Christian training and British-American opinion. Tall, reedy and handsome, he possessed the best physical attributes so characteristic of Hawaiian aristocracy. His shy, gentle nature and probing intellect gave little hint to the strong will hidden underneath. Like his brother, Liholiho, before him, Kamehameha III enjoyed drinking, gambling and female enticements, much to the dismay of the missionaries.

With Kaahumanu dead, the young king considered the regency ended and he sought to gain full control of the nation. Instead, he ran into the opposition of the council of chiefs who were reluctant to turn over the rule of the nation to an eighteen year-old youth of vacillating character. They insisted upon and received a joint safeguard in the form of another kuhina nui, Kinau. Kinau, a communicant in the mission church and a staunch Christian, was a daughter of Kamehameha the Great, one of the widows of Liholiho and a half sister of the young king. On July 5, 1832, the two rulers issued joint proclamations assuming their roles in governing the island kingdom. While the young king professed his superiority to rule, Kinau in effect assumed the role of regent much to the displeasure of the new king. Kinau also became Governor of Oahu, freeing Kuakini to

Kamehameha III (Kauikeaouli)   **State Archives**

return to the island of Hawaii and resume his duties there as governor.

With Kinau assuming the responsibilities of governing, Kamehameha III took to the pursuits of pleasure. The young king and his friends, encouraged by Liliha, declared guerrilla war on Christian morality. Beginning their "war" by drinking thirty-two barrels of spirits in a single week, they sought out church members and forced them to drink gin. They urged their friends to discard the Christian tabus and return to the hula, surfing, racing and gambling of the old days. The king sent a crier through the streets announcing the lifting of penalties against adultery and all other crimes except murder and theft. The king's example spread like a plague, emptying schools and churches. Unable to outshine the council of chiefs who were greatly influenced by the missionaries, the king tried to rally his people around the symbols of their own culture.

Dancing Scene in   **B. Lauvergne/**
the Sandwich Islands[1]   **State Archives**

On March 15, 1833, the king made a public announcement that he was assuming complete control of the government. While many of his friends were hoping that the king would appoint Liliha as the new kuhina nui, the king surprised everyone by reconfirming Kinau as kuhina nui (but not as regent), apparently to avoid the possibility of a civil war. Kinau and the other chiefs did not give in without a struggle. During the next two years, the government was in a rather ambiguous state of affairs as the king vacillated between complete independence and consenting to the wishes of the older chiefs. In the beginning of 1835, the king conceded defeat and reconciled himself with Kinau and left most of the responsibility of running the government in her hands. Kinau, in turn, continued to be thoroughly influenced by the Protestant missionaries.

Nahienaena, the king's sister, struggling with an old-world love entanglement with her brother on one hand and a new-world Christian conscience on the other hand, died at the age of twenty on December 30, 1836.

The king, chastened by the death of his beloved sister, now turned toward the good. He gave up drinking, shut down his distilleries and outlawed the importing of spirits. In February, 1837, Kamehameha III married Kalama in a great ceremony performed by Hiram Bingham. Although Kalama lacked high birth, the king hoped that she would provide him with an heir. Thereafter, the king moved to Lahaina for approximately two years. The ruling chiefs appointed William Richards as the king's instructor. Previously, Richards had translated 17 books of the Bible, 14 single-handedly. Because of his skill in the Hawaiian language among other reasons, the chiefs trusted him. He gradually became the king's confidential advisor, making him one of the most influential foreigners in the islands.

[1]The scene is a party given for the officers and crew of the French ship *La Bonite* in the fall of 1836.

In 1835, a Catholic brother named Columba Murphy visited Honolulu to determine the feasibility of starting up another mission. His report was optimistic and the following year Father Arsenius Walsh arrived. He was immediately ordered to leave, but the coincidental arrival of the French warship *La Bonita* on October 8th created a diversion in Walsh's favor. Already anchored in the harbor was the American warship *USS Peacock*, having returned from an Asian cruise. On October 24, the British man-of-war *Acteon* made her appearance.

These three ships' captains, in conferences with the king and the ruling chiefs, began questioning the right of the Hawaiian government to expel any foreigner and what rights a foreigner had in the kingdom. After a series of discussions,[1] it was agreed that the government still owned all of the land and that foreigners could use the land only at the king's pleasure. However, this did not give the king the right to destroy the property of the foreigners. Upon the intervention of Lord Edward Russell, the British captain, Father Walsh (a British citizen serving with a French missionary order) received permission to remain as long as he obeyed the laws of the land and did not spread his religion among the people.

Fathers Bachelot and Short reappeared in Honolulu in April, 1837, on the brig *Clementine*. They were soon recognized and the new Governor of Oahu, Kekuanaoa (Kinau's husband), ordered them to leave on the same ship. Affairs dragged on until the brig was ready to sail on May 20. Over the strong objections of the brig's owner, a Frenchman named Jules Dudoit who happened to be a British subject, and it's charter captain, an American named William French, Kinau had the two priests forcibly put on board. Dudoit immediately hauled down the British flag, abandoned the ship and took the flag to the British consul, Richard Charlton. Declaring that the flag had been violated by the Hawaiian government, Charlton publicly burned it in the street in protest. Dudoit vehemently maintained that his vessel had been seized and he held the government liable for any losses suffered by himself and William French.

An impasse remained until early July when two warships made a timely arrival at Honolulu: one British, the *Sulphur*; the other French, *La Venus*. Following a stormy interview with Kinau, Captain Belcher of the *Sulphur* sent a marine detachment to "recapture" the *Clementine*. The two priests were brought ashore and ceremoniously escorted to their former residence by the two captains, the consuls and a large crowd of spectators. Following the king's return to Honolulu on July 20, a number of long conferences were held in an attempt to settle the various questions involved. In the end, the two priests were permitted to remain temporarily until they could find passage on another vessel. The French were allowed to come and go freely and they would receive the same protection and advantages as the British had been afforded in the Russell Treaty the year before. The question of damages for the alleged "seizure" of the *Clementine* was left open to be settled at a future time.[2]

The warships sailed without further incidents. Father Short left Honolulu at the end of October. Father Bachelot departed on November 23 with Father Maigret who had just arrived. Less than two weeks out at sea, Bachelot died. On December 18, 1837, the king issued an ordinance completely rejecting the

View of Honolulu's Waterfront and Harbor in 1836

B. Lauvergne/ State Archives

Catholic religion. Native Catholics were increasingly harassed, jailed or forced into hard labor for their beliefs.

The British government never officially objected to the actions of the Hawaiian government in expelling British subjects. The French, however, defenders of Catholic missionary enterprises, pursued a different course. The reports reaching Paris suggested that the islands were pursuing an anti-French policy. The frigate *Artemise*, commanded by Captain Laplace, was ordered to visit Hawaii and teach the government respect for France and its priests. The 60-gun warship arrived in Honolulu on July 9, 1839 after fulfilling a similar mission at the Society Islands (Tahiti).[3] Threatening to level the city, Laplace issued a list of demands to the king. These included freedom of worship for Catholics with the same privileges granted to the Protestants; the grant of a parcel of land for a Catholic church to be administered by French priests; the immediate release of all Catholics

Assembly of Chiefs of the Sandwich Islands in Conference with the Captain of the *La Venus*

J. Masselot/ State Archives

---

[1] These discussions resulted in the signing of a form of treaty known as the Russell Treaty. Agreed upon and signed November 16, 1836, this treaty attempted to put British interests on a more secure footing.

[2] A settlement was reached in October, 1839, in which Dudoit and French each received $3,000.00 in full settlement of their claims. It is interesting to note that at this time, two United States warships, the *Columbia* and *John Adams*, were visiting Honolulu.

[3] A striking parallel existed between the events happening in Hawaii and Tahiti between 1835 and 1840 concerning the attempts of the Catholic missionaries to establish themselves in these two island groups. The main difference centered on the origin of the Protestant missionaries: in Hawaii, they were American; while in Tahiti, the missionaries were British.

imprisoned because of their religious beliefs; the depositing of $20,000 with the captain as a guarantee that these conditions would be carried out; and the firing of a twenty-one gun salute by the fort to the French flag, said salute being returned by the frigate.

With the threat of war looming, the government had little choice and gave in to the demands. Since the king was at Lahaina, the "Manifesto" was signed on his behalf by the kuhina nui and the Governor of Oahu. The king later ratified the treaty. The money was borrowed from Honolulu merchants.[1] In a show of force, Laplace came ashore the following Sunday with 120 marines and 60 seamen under arms to attend a mass celebrated by Father Walsh in one of the king's residences. Considering his work incomplete, the French captain then made additional demands on the tiny kingdom to protect the personal and commercial interests of French citizens. Two of these demands placed severe limitations on the king's sovereignty. One provided that French citizens could be tried only by a jury of foreigners proposed by the French consul and accepted by the Hawaiian government. The second demand in effect repealed the liquor law of 1838 since it guaranteed the importation of French merchandise, especially wines and brandies.

Once again the tiny island kingdom had to knuckle under to the demands of a foreign power. Being in an unfavorable position, the Americans, through their new commercial agent, Peter A. Brinsmade, demanded and received the same rights and privileges acquired by the British and French. It appeared that the Hawaiian government had only as much sovereignty as the major powers were willing to give it.

Mission Seminary at Lahainaluna (Maui)   Hiram Bingham/ State Archives

Scene on the Island of Oahu   J. Masselot/State Archives

---

[1] The $20,000 taken away by Captain Laplace in 1839 was restored to the Hawaiian government by a French admiral in 1846; the money was still packed, unopened, in the original boxes.

Father Louis Maigret (Mid-1830's)   State Archives

The main source of competent Protestant teachers came from the high school at Lahainaluna, a site about two miles up the hill where the air was cooler. Started by Rev. Lorrin Andrews in September, 1831, the school's main purpose was to train young men as assistant teachers of religion.

Hawaii's first newspaper, Lama Hawaii (The Hawaiian Luminary) was published at Lahainaluna beginning in February, 1834. With a second printing plant in operation, textbooks were printed for use by the high school and work continued on translating the Bible into the Hawaiian language. By May, 1839, the entire Bible had been translated and printed in Hawaiian, some parts of it being printed in the United States.

Several years after the founding of Lahainaluna school, it became a boarding school for boys aged eight to twenty in order to eliminate the tempting closeness of males and females. A separate boarding school for girls opened soon thereafter in Wailuku; close enough to get acquainted, but far enough away to eliminate sneak romances. In 1837, Lahainaluna boys' high school became a "Mission Seminary." Additional boarding schools were established in the decade of the thirties on each of the larger islands. Basically, the boarding schools for boys were intended as preparatory schools for the seminary at Lahainaluna, while the schools for girls were intended to train females who would become suitable wives for the future teachers and other educated and pious young men in the community.

Mission life in the mission stations, with the exception of Honolulu and possibly Lahaina, was a grueling, repetitious ordeal. Rising before daylight, the missionaries began their day with worship, followed by tutoring their children, running schools for teachers, attending a constant stream of visitors, conducting prayer meetings, making translations, preparing sermons, building new furniture, caring for cattle and fowl, farming, sewing, washing and attending to a host of other domestic chores.

Mission children (they were becoming more numerous with each new wave of missionaries) were generally shut off from Hawaiian life due to its frank and uninhibited acceptance of the body and its functions. Their education in the early years was provided by their parents or other missionaries. As they approached the "tender" years between six and eight, their parents sent them back to New England for a "proper" education, forcing them to endure the arduously long journey around Cape Horn.

Back in the "civilized" world, it was hoped that they would find "proper" mates. To avoid these long and tragic separations, the missionaries decided to erect a school for the education of their own children as well as the children of "pious foreign residents" who might be expected to settle permanently in the islands. The land at Punahou, initially destined to be a Hawaiian school for boys, was used for this purpose. The school formally opened in 1842 under the direction of Rev. Daniel Dole, a recent arrival to the islands.

Prior to the decision of using Punahou for the education of the missionary children, Governor Kekuanaoa of Oahu and other ruling chiefs had petitioned the missionaries to open a school for the education of their children. With the chiefs providing a building and financial support, the Chiefs' Children's School opened in 1839. Headed by Mr. and Mrs. Amos Cooke, who had recently arrived in 1837, this school catered almost exclusively to youngsters who had acknowledged claims to the throne. Amos and Juliette Cooke, assisted by John Ii and his wife Sarai, proceeded with their unique opportunity to shape the future destiny of the Hawaiian nation.[1]

Prior to 1837, the number of Hawaiians admitted into the church was very small. During the seventeen years that the missionaries had been in Hawaii, fewer than 1,300 received membership. Although church membership carried the official approval of the ruling chiefs, and despite the fact that the people came forward in ever increasing numbers to apply for membership, the missionaries maintained strict rules of discipline and applied very searching tests on the prospective candidates. Lacking a "deep feeling of sinfulness and unworthiness," most native candidates' applications for membership were put off.

Prodded by fraternal advice from the corresponding secretary (Dr. Rufus Anderson) of the American Board of Commissioners for Foreign missions and aided by the largest group of missionaries ever to arrive at one time, a "Great Revival" took place from June, 1837 to June, 1840. During this three year period, nearly 20,000 new members were taken into Hawaii's Protestant churches.[2] As the decade of the 1840's unfolded, Hawaii officially was considered a Christian nation. The king, although never becoming a church member, nevertheless included in the constitution of 1840 a declaration stating that all laws should be consistent with the spirit of God's law.

As the new decade approached, the Protestant missionaries began to feel a loosening of their influence on the course of events taking place in the Hawaiian kingdom. Although their influence continued to be strong, the actions of Captain Laplace in compelling the government to admit Catholics and French wines and brandies had successfully attacked the two policies which the missionaries considered most essential to the fullest success of their labors. In addition, a number of the mission's staunchest supporters in the government, including Kinau, died in 1839, and none of their successors were able to wield the same influence in the Hawaiian government.

Important shifts began taking place in the mission society. Forced by a sudden and drastic cut in funds from the Board in New England, the Hawaiian mission started favoring self-support through investments in sugar mills, or other work employing Hawaiian labor, thereby teaching industry to the natives while at the same time earning their own keep.

---

[1] All the future monarchs that followed Kamehameha III to the throne attended the Royal School as it was later called.

[2] A total of twelve mission companies were sent to the Hawaiian Islands spaced over a period of twenty-eight years, the first or pioneer company arriving on April 4, 1820 and the last or twelfth company arriving on February 26, 1848.

Hiram Bingham, who dominated the mission for twenty years, left Honolulu for New England on August 3, 1840 due to his wife's deteriorating ill health. As counselor and confidant to royalty and the ruling chiefs, Bingham's advice and aggressive personality greatly influenced the course of Hawaii's history. His last major undertaking, the new coral stone church at Kawaiahao which he designed, was still under construction when he departed.[3] While the native Christians did not want him to go, the foreign community couldn't wait to see him gone. Most foreigners considerd Bingham impossible to like, a meddling Puritan in black coat and tall hat, a plague. Despite receiving continued and sometimes violent abuse, Bingham endured limitless suffering in God's name. He spent his later years writing a 600 page autobiography of his experiences in the Sandwich Islands. Although he never gave up hope of someday returning to the islands, circumstances prevented it.

View of a Street in Honolulu[4]   **J. Masselot/State Archives**

New Native Church - Honolulu   **F. Olmsted/**
(Kawaiahao Church)   **State Archives**

---

[3] This was the fifth and current structure to bear the name Kawaiahao Church. Construction started in 1836 using coral blocks cut by natives from nearby reefs. It was completed in 1842. The previous structures were smaller and less permanent, being constructed from grassy materials which deteriorated under the influence of the elements.

[4] This drawing shows Kinau, the kuhina nui, leaving the First Bethel Church with her maids-of-honor in 1837.

As early as 1832, the missionaries felt a strong inclination to help the natives preserve their independence by teaching them to govern themselves as far as possible. Likewise, as the dealings with foreigners became more complex, the ruling chiefs turned to the missionaries for advice on matters of government since they had come to rely on them for advice on religious and moral matters. Initially, the missionaries had refused direct involvement because they felt it wasn't in their sphere of activity. But with the pressures for change building up in the ever growing foreign community, the missionaries felt that the most effective institutions of the mission lay in the orderly and peaceful development of Hawaii's political and economic life. With the ruling chiefs ignorant of world affairs, the danger always existed that some indiscreet action might prompt one of the major powers to seize the islands. In fact, Hiram Bingham in writing to the Board in 1837 noted more subtle dangers; he wrote that unless disinterested men were found who would advise the chiefs, "cunning speculators will ere long . . . give employment to the people as day labor, at a low rate, or introduce foreign labor to their exclusion, and put the products of the soil in their own pockets, thus keeping the aborigines poor, or hastening their extinction." Thus, he reasoned that the only way to prevent this situation from happening was to keep the real control of the political and economic institutions in the hands of the natives.

Significant changes started in 1838 when Rev. William Richards was appointed the king's "Chaplain, Teacher and Translator." It soon became clear that the government could not be changed to suit the foreigners until revolutionary changes were made in the relationships between the chiefs and the common people. Up to 1839, the powers of the national government were divided into three agencies: the king, the kuhina nui and the council of chiefs. The common people were still under complete subjection. The old feudal land system remained essentially intact as did the organization of government. Both of these conditions were unfavorable to the foreign residents and they constantly pressured the government for change. As the Hawaiian government attempted to settle the growing number of disputes between foreigners, it invariably offended one side or the other in rendering a decision. More and more, it seemed that the slightest provocation on the part of the government brought in one or more warships from the three great powers in the Pacific—England, France and the United States. Year by year, the Hawaiian government was less and less able to hold its own as the western world closed in on it. Consequently, the ruling chiefs were forced to reconstruct the government.

Changes began to take place rapidly. Following the king's adoption of a policy of religious tolerance (forced on him by the actions of the French Captain Laplace) in 1839, Kamehameha III followed this action with a declaration of rights for his subjects. This declaration recognized the rights of all men, chiefs and commoners, to "life, limb, the labor of his hands and productions of his mind." It also provided equal protection for both chiefs and commoners under the same laws. The declaration of rights, which may be called a Hawaiian Magna Carta, and the constitution which followed in 1840, were drafted with the help of a highly educated group of Hawaiians. These educated young Hawaiians included among others Daniel and John Ii, Timothy Haalilio, David Malo and Boaz Mahune, most of whom were educated at Lahainaluna. Many of those mentioned became companions and advisors to the king and the older chiefs. Greatly encouraged by the teachings of the missionaries, they favored a constitutional and representative government which would make changes favorable to the lower classes. In addition, they felt that change was necessary for the welfare and preservation of the Hawaiian nation.

David Malo, in a letter addressed to Kinau in 1837, predicted the wave of the future: "The ships of the white man have come, and smart people have arrived from the great countries which you have never seen before, they know our people are few in number and living in a small country; they will eat us up." Pressured by the educated young Hawaiians, the missionaries, the

foreign community and foreign commanders of warships, the king gave in to the principle of representative government. Through the summer of 1840, William Richards, the educated young Hawaiians and the ruling chiefs worked at drafting a written constitution.

A Street Scene in Honolulu (about 1840)   **State Archives**

David Malo   **State Archives**

Missionary Preaching Beneath a   **A.T. Agate[1] /**
Grove of Kukui Trees (in Kauai, 1840)   **State Archives**

In the early part of 1840, the missionaries gave up the administration of the common schools in favor of the government. The major share of responsibility for the education of Hawaii's youth now passed into the hands of independent organizations not associated with the mission. Later that same year, the constitution of 1840 was signed by the king and the kuhina nui on October 8. In addition to restating the existing political institutions and laws in effect throughout the country, the constitution's most momentous provision called for the creation of a

---

[1] Agate was an artist with Wilkes' Exploring Expedition.

"representative body" chosen by the people to become a part of the national legislature. For the first time in Hawaii's history, the political power of the government was shared by three distinct groups: the king (and kuhina nui), the ruling chiefs and the common people.

Events having international ramifications began to unfold in the early 1840's. The United States Exploring Expedition, commanded by Lt. Commander Charles Wilkes, arrived in the fall of 1840 and spent about six months in the islands. The expedition's two warships, the *Vincennes* and the *Peacock,* were supported by several smaller vessels and they were equipped to study all forms of natural life in addition to their primary task of exploring and mapping the islands. In this same year, Great Britain annexed New Zealand and France had several warships making their presence felt in the South Pacific. With its future security in question, the government of Hawaii began an attempt to have its independence recognized by the three great powers mentioned above.

Rev. William Richards   State Archives

Sir George Simpson, the North American governor for the Hudson's Bay Company, arrived in Honolulu in February, 1842. Becoming acquainted with the attempts thus far made at recognition, Simpson recommended that the government send a commissioner with full authority to negotiate treaties to the heads of each of the three great powers.[1] To this end, Simpson agreed to lend his personal support. As finally agreed upon, the mission consisted of Simpson, William Richards and Timothy Haalilio, the king's private secretary and a member of the Treasury Board. Richards and Haalilio went to Washington, arriving on December 5, 1842. Later, they would meet Simpson in London.

Through the intercession of several of Richard's friends in Washingtion, the Hawaii mission received advice and met various senators and representatives. Following numerous meetings with Secretary of State Webster, days of waiting and the exchange of much correspondence ensued. Finally on December 27, Richards and Haalilio met with President Tyler. In the discussion that followed, Richards hinted at placing the Hawaiian Islands under the protection of Great Britain in the event that the United States failed to recognize the independence of Hawaii. Subsequently, President Tyler forwarded the pertinent correspondence to Congress along with a message stating the importance of the

islands and the extent of American interests already there. The message went on to recommend the independent existence of the Hawaiian government and an appropriation for a consul to reside in the islands. In January, 1843, the Hawaii delegation received congressional approval on the president's pronouncement on Hawaii's independence without any formal treaty.

Dr. Gerrit P. Judd replaced William Richards prior to his departure for Washington. On May 15, 1842, Judd was appointed to the newly created government post of "Translator and Recorder." Early in August, news reached the islands that the French had seized the Marquesas Islands, and three months later, reports reached Honolulu that the French had established a protectorate in Tahiti. Many people began to wonder whether Hawaii might be next.

In late September, 1842, British Consul Richard Charlton abruptly left Honolulu bound for London to secure justice for British subjects and at the same time thwart the treaty efforts of Richards and Haalilio. Charlton had been feuding with the government over an alleged lease to a piece of land near the waterfront ever since 1826. Finding it hard to stay out of trouble and realizing that his requests for a British warship would not be honored, Charlton had decided to take his charges and those of several other British subjects directly to the British government.

Alexander Simpson, a relative of Sir George Simpson of the Hudson's Bay Company, had been appointed acting consul by Charlton. But the Hawaiian government refused to recognize the younger Simpson. A few weeks later, Simpson found himself defending Charlton in a law suit brought by an English firm based on a transaction that took place in 1833. Prosecuted in the Honolulu courts with a foreign jury, Charlton was found liable for almost $10,000 and his property was subsequently attached. Coloring the events that had transpired, Simpson sent a brief account of the affair to the British consul in Tepic, Mexico, suggesting the sending of a British warship to Honolulu to protect British interests.

The commander of the British squadron in the Pacific, Rear Admiral Richard Thomas, after reviewing the various communications presented to him, ordered Lord George Paulet, captain of the frigate *Carysfort*, to proceed to the Hawaiian and Society Islands.

Dr. Gerrit Parmele Judd   State Archives

---

[1] The heads of the three great powers were President John Tyler (United States), Queen Victoria (Great Britain) and King Louis Philippe (France).

Lord George Paulet   **State Archives**

The frigate *Carysfort* arrived in Honolulu on February 10, 1843. Acting consul Simpson immediately boarded and presented Lord Paulet letters and other documents relating to the various issues under disagreement. Simpson recommended no exchange of courtesies with the local authorities until he was recognized as acting consul. Following the advice of Simpson, Paulet incurred the wrath of the American and French consuls as well as that of many residents. As usual, the king was at Lahaina and had to be sent for before any action could be taken.

The king arrived a week later and received a letter from Paulet demanding a private audience. The king declined, offering instead to receive written communications through Dr. Judd, his confidential agent. Later, Paulet sent a second letter declining to deal with Judd, but enclosing certain demands which required compliance by four o'clock the following afternoon; otherwise "coercive steps to obtain these measures for my countrymen" would be taken. The demands were lengthy and involved the reversal of nearly all actions taken by the Hawaiian government thus far in the Charlton case, including the recognition of Simpson as acting consul.

The following morning, foreign residents were notified of the expected attack on the city. An English brig offered asylum to British residents. The normally quiet streets turned into an unusual spectacle as the foreign residents crowded the streets pushing and pulling carts filled with personal belongings on their way to the safety of the asylum ships. The king yielded under protest after lengthy discussions with his advisors, fearing that the British would use this episode as an excuse for seizing the islands. British honor had been appeased.

Simpson, backed fully by Lord Paulet and the guns of the *Carysfort*, took full advantage of the situation. Finally acknowledged as acting consul, Simpson forced the king into signing a 299 year lease on Charlton's land claim, insisted that previous court decisions be reversed and presented claims for indemnity amounting to more than $100,000. Daily conferences were held with the king and his advisors from the 20th through the 23rd of February, and both the king and Dr. Judd came to the same conclusion that the British were determined to take possession of the islands. With cession inevitable, the decision had to be made; cession to France and the United States or to Great Britain. Dr. Judd favored cession to Great Britain. The king and the chiefs agreed. Although they considered Charlton and Simpson their enemies, the government considered "England their FRIEND." The king would thrust himself into the arms of Great Britain.

Miriam Kekauluohi, Kuhina Nui[1]   **State Archives**

On the afternoon of February 25, the formal ceremony of a provisional cession to Great Britain was held within the fort. Kamehameha III made a short speech in Hawaiian and Dr. Judd translated it. "I have given away the life of the land," the king said, but he went on to declare that the government would take every possible means to restore the independence of the islands. Then the deed of cession was read, the Hawaiian flag was lowered and the British flag was hoisted as a twenty-one gun salute

was exchanged between the fort and the British frigate *Carysfort*. The ship's band then played "God Save the Queen" and "Isle of Beauty, Fare Thee Well."

Captain Paulet then read a proclamation which stated how the affairs of government would be carried out. The king, chiefs and other officers appointed by them would continue to govern the native population. A commission consisting of the king, Lord Paulet and two other British subjects would be concerned with relations with other powers (except negotiations with Great Britain) and with arrangements with foreign residents living in the islands. All other existing laws and revenue arrangements were to continue in force, the accounts being subject to inspection by the commission, pending receipt of communications from Great Britain. However, no sales, leases or transfers of land were to take place neither by action of the commission nor by natives to foreigners.

The islands were under the rule of the British commission for about five months. In the beginning, there were several weeks of relative harmony, but then the commission began to meddle in the affairs of the native government as Paulet began exerting his control. One of the British members had resigned due to ill health and Paulet had not replaced him. On May 11, Judd, acting as the king's representative, resigned and the king refused to appoint anyone else. The actions of the commission became progressively arbitrary and the events seemed to be heading for an open break when, on July 26, 1843, Rear Admiral Richard Thomas sailed into Honolulu Harbor in his flagship, *HMS Dublin*.

Admiral Thomas had immediately sailed from Valparaiso (Chile) for Honolulu as soon as he had received information on Paulet's actions. The day after his arrival, Admiral Thomas met with the king who this time happened to be in Honolulu. In

---

[1] Miriam Kekauluohi became kuhina nui following the death of Kinau in April, 1839. She was the daughter of a half-brother of Kamehameha the Great.

Rear Admiral Richard Thomas   **State Archives**

conferences held on the 27th and 28th with the king and Dr. Judd, it became apparent that Admiral Thomas intended to restore the independence of the islands, subject to securing certain agreements from the king. These agreements, somewhat in the form of a treaty, closely guarded the rights and privileges of British subjects in Hawaii and guaranteed them equality with the most favored foreigners. Since these articles were subject to whatever arrangements had or would be made in London, the king signed them, relying on the apparent good faith and friendly intentions of the admiral.

At formal ceremonies held on the morning of July 31, the Hawaiian flag was again raised over the tiny kingdom. The roar and reverberations of cannon fire from the *Carysfort, Dublin* and other English and American ships plus responding volleys from the fort and Punch Bowl battery announced Hawaii's independence. Later in the afternoon, a thanksgiving service was held at Kawaiahao Church in which the king was said to have proclaimed the words "Ua mau ke ea o ka aina i ka pono," the life of the land is perpetuated in righteousness.[1] Ten days of festivities and rejoicing followed.

Admiral Thomas, in restoring Hawaii's independence, acted upon his own initiative without any specific instructions from Great Britain. However, his actions were based on his knowledge of British policy and he acted with complete confidence, knowing that his actions would be approved (as they later were). Admiral Thomas took up residence on shore and remained for about six months until the new consul, William Miller arrived in February, 1844. During this time, the admiral attempted to ease the tensions caused by Paulet with his friendly and modest manner.[2]

William Richards and Timothy Haalilio arrived in London the early part of February, 1843, approximately the same time that the frigate *Carysfort* and Captain Paulet had arrived in Honolulu. The diplomatic mission encountered delays caused by the earlier arrival of Richard Charlton with his stack of complaints and charges against the Hawaiian government. Later, however, they received assurance that the independence of the islands would be recognized. This promise was formalized in a letter dated April 1, 1843.

Traveling to Paris, the Hawaiian diplomatic mission attempted to get a written declaration from France. In the meantime,

---

[1] This expresssion later became the motto of Hawaii.

[2] The site of the restoration ceremony later became a park called Thomas Square in commemoration of the admiral's part in Hawaii's history.

however, news had reached Europe that the Hawaiian Islands had been ceded to Lord Paulet, who represented Queen Victoria. Letters flew back and forth between London and Washington. Great Britain promptly disavowed Paulet's action and reiterated its determination to respect the independence of the Hawaiian Islands. In lengthy negotiations, most of the claims in dispute were settled in favor of the Hawaiian government or were postponed. However, Charlton's land claim was recognized by the British government, unless it could be proven that the original grant and claim were not genuine.[3]

By early October, the differences between Great Britain and Hawaii had been settled. News of Admiral Thomas' restoration of Hawaii's independence reached London and Paris shortly thereafter, clearing the way for a mutual agreement between Great Britain and France. On November 28, 1843, a joint declaration was signed in London recognizing Hawaii's independence. The United States, although asked to join in this declaration, declined, referring to treaty delays via the Senate, the government's independent foreign policy and its previously issued statement on the subject.[4]

Residence of General Miller,   **Paul Emmert/**
British Consul   **State Archives**

Now that Hawaii had been recognized by the three major powers, it began to adopt a firmer hand in dealing with the foreign community. In addition, the government began altering its course of action so as to strengthen itself and give it dignity. Ironically, to achieve these new ambitions, a number of foreigners were appointed to responsible positions in the government. These foreigners were all required to take an oath of allegiance to the king beginning in 1844. Likewise, foreigners desiring to marry native Hawaiians were also required to take the oath. Furthermore, a law enacted in August, 1843 put foreigners at a disadvantage concerning land holdings since it prohibited the gift of land to any foreigners by the government and by the natives.

The king's advisors, in order to give dignity to the monarchy, began withdrawing the king from the easy-going social relations he had previously maintained with foreigners and began surrounding the throne with pomp and royal etiquette. Hoping to make the king's administration more respectable in the eyes of both foreigners and natives, the government adopted the rules

---

[3] Richard Charlton returned to Honolulu in May, 1844 only to face legal difficulties. He finally sold his property and left the islands in 1846 while litigation over his lands and leases continued in the courts. He died in England near the end of 1852.

[4] Although the three great powers had recognized Hawaii's independence, treaty relations were still not on an equitable basis. The United States didn't make a treaty; France still considered the Laplace Treaty of 1839 in effect; and Great Britain, while drafting a new treaty, did so without consulting the Hawaiian government—it merely sent the document to the islands for signature.

Kamehameha III and His Wife Kalama[1]

August Plum / State Archives

of precedence and etiquette which the great powers had adopted at the Congress of Vienna in 1815. In addition, the king received a new title, *Ka Moi* ("The King").

Lacking the knowledge and experience to deal with the growing complexity of governmental affairs, the native chiefs were mostly excluded from the important positions that were being created in an attempt to catch up with western civilization. Even lesser positions such as pilots, harbor masters, collectors of custom duties and constables were mostly filled by naturalized foreigners. Dr. Judd had resigned from the mission shortly after being appointed to the Treasury Board and as the government's translator and recorder in 1842. He gradually rose in status to become the most conspicuous and influential member of the Hawaiian government. In November, 1843, he was appointed by the king to be secretary of state for foreign affairs. On March 9, 1844, the king appointed John Ricord attorney general for the kingdom. Arriving only two weeks earlier, Ricord was the only lawyer in the islands. Judd, overburdened with duties and responsibilities, initiated the appointment partly to ease his own burdens and partly out of fear that Ricord might be employed against him in the near future, since the more responsibilities he took on, the more enemies he made in the foreign community.

Prior to 1844, the legislature met in Lahaina. No session was held in 1844. After 1844, the sessions were held in Honolulu and the laws became more elaborate and precise in their phraseology. The growing foreign influence in Hawaii's government became obvious since the newly enacted laws were first written in English and then translated into Hawaiian. The reverse had been true when the legislature met in Lahaina.

First Iolani Palace[2]

State Archives

---

[1] This drawing was made in 1846. The royal couple's two children both died in infancy.

[2] Initially, the king's palace was known as Hale Alii (House of the Chief). Later it became known formally as Iolani Palace (Palace of the Bird of Heaven).

When the seat of government officially moved to Honolulu in July, 1844, the king shortly thereafter took up residence in a large coral-block house that had recently been built by Governor Kekuanaoa for his daughter Princess Victoria Kamamalu. Being the finest building in Honolulu at the time, the king exercised his regal prerogative and moved in. Diplomatically, Governor Kekuanaoa turned the house over to the king for his new palace. On February 6, 1845, the king gave his first European-style soirée at which he received the diplomatic and consular corps, officers from a United States warship, members of his cabinet, missionaries and prominent merchants and foreigners of the community. This grand court function was followed by a series of receptions during the following weeks in order to allow the various classes of people to pay homage to their king.

Despite Honolulu society's crisscrossed maze of alliances and feuding factions, one person stood out at the center of controversy—Dr. Gerrit P. Judd. Confident, fluent in the Hawaiian language, well-educated and rigidly honest, "King Bingham," as Judd referred to himself in 1845, had acquired the unquestioning trust of the king and the leading chiefs. Keenly aware of the government's weakness in matters of physical force (it lacked both a standing army and navy), Judd sought to maintain the sovereignty of the kingdom through his own high moral power. In his determined efforts to strengthen the government, Judd had his hands in nearly every phase of its activities irregardless of his title at the time.

Robert Crichton Wyllie

State Archives

Overworked to the point of suffering giddy spells, ringing in the ears and the loss of sight in his left eye due to a cataract, Judd recommended Robert Crichton Wyllie to succeed him in his post as minister of foreign relations. Wyllie received his appointment on March 26, 1845. Judd, instead of retiring, remained as head of the cabinet and several days later assumed the newly created post of minister of the interior.

Wyllie, a native of Scotland who had been educated as a doctor, came to Honolulu from Mexico in company with British Consul General William Miller in 1844. Later that same year, Wyllie served as British pro-consul when General Miller sailed to the South Pacific on an inspection tour of the islands under his jurisdiction. Miller returned the following March, and shortly thereafter, Wyllie accepted Judd's offer as minister of foreign relations in the Hawaiian government. Despite becoming alienated from Judd several years later, Wyllie continued in his post for twenty years.[3] He was one of the most influential members of the cabinet, second only to Judd, and was a staunch supporter of the monarchy and its structured society. A perpetual bachelor, Wyllie's life-style was almost exactly opposite that of the missionary Judd.

---

[3] Born in 1798, Wyllie died on October 19, 1865 while still serving in Hawaii's government.

Mataio Kekuanaoa, Governor of Oahu[1]   **State Archives**

As more complex legal disputes and questions began to arise in the tiny kingdom, mostly at Honolulu, the need for special courts such as probate, admiralty and chancery became obvious. With the advice and assistance of John Ricord, the recently appointed attorney general, Governor Kekuanaoa, as Judge of Oahu, assumed jurisdiction for these cases. Ricord provided these new courts with a body of law patterned after the common and civil laws as administered by Great Britain and the United States, since these two countries had the greatest percentage of foreigners living in the islands. With the abundance of law suits continually being generated between various factions of the foreign community, Governor Kekuanaoa's abilities were taxed beyond his limit. Lacking legal training and possessing only a limited knowledge of English, the governor was assisted by Dr. Judd and shortly thereafter by Ricord. Possessing the most legal knowledge and being the only lawyer in the islands, Ricord became the dominating figure in Oahu's judicial system. Since no one could challenge his legal opinions, this resulted in a great uneasiness and distrust of the courts on the part of many foreigners.

In September, 1845, Governor Kekuanaoa appointed Rev. Lorrin Andrews to act on his behalf in all cases involving foreigners. Andrews had previously been the principal of the high school at Lahainaluna. The following year, 1846, the judiciary was expanded, pending a more formal reorganization which was already under consideration. In December, a young American lawyer named William Little Lee, who had arrived in Honolulu only a few weeks before, was appointed as another judge to work with Andrews. John Ricord left the islands in the spring of 1847, leaving the problem of drafting the civil and criminal codes to Judge Lee.

John Young II (Keoni Ana)   **State Archives**

[1] Kekuanaoa was the husband of Kinau, the former kuhina nui, and the father of Prince Alexander Liholiho (later Kamehameha IV) and Prince Lot Kamehameha (later Kamehameha V).

The legislative session of 1845 became one of the most important in the kingdom's history because its suggestions and recommendations for new laws and changes to existing laws led to the passage of three organic acts which laid the foundation for the Hawaiian government for years to come. The first of these acts organized the "Executive Ministry." Passed in October, 1845, it took effect in March of the following year and provided for the king to appoint five ministers to take charge of the five executive departments of the government (interior, finance, foreign relations, public instruction and attorney general). The kuhina nui, now John Young II,[2] assumed the duties of minister of the interior. This first organic act also formally established the privy council which had previously been in existence as the old council of chiefs. Strengthened and modified, the privy council now consisted of the five ministers, the four governors and such other members as the king would appoint. On April 13, 1846, the king formally announced the remaining minister appointments; Wyllie as minister of foreign relations, Judd as minister of finance, Richards as minister of public instruction and Ricord as attorney general.

The second organic act was passed in April, 1846 and became effective later in the year. It detailed the functions of the five executive departments and, more importantly, created a board of commissioners to settle the issue of land titles. If the claim was found to be valid, then an award was made defining the character of title and the boundaries of the land. This award had the same characteristics as a royal patent, although the government retained a commutation right in the land. By paying a commutation fee, usually equal to one-third the value of unimproved land, the owner could obtain fee simple title to the land.[3]

John Papa Ii   **State Archives**

The third organic act became effective in January, 1848. It reorganized the judiciary department, providing for circuit and district courts to bring justice to all parts of the kingdom. In addition, a superior court was also created which acted as the supreme court in everything except name. The act further defined the jurisdiction of these various courts, provided for a condensed code of procedure and set down the method for jury selection. William L. Lee, John Ii, and Lorrin Andrews were appointed to the superior court, Lee serving as chief justice.

[2] John Young II (Keoni Ana), son of Kamehameha the Great's military advisor, was appointed Governor of Maui and the new kuhina nui on June 10, 1845, following the death of the preceding kuhina nui, Kekauluohi. Being part Hawaiian by a Hawaiian woman from a family of chiefs, John Young II was well liked by the native people and was a favorite of the king.

[3] This commutation fee was later reduced to one-fourth the value of the unimproved land in 1847.

A revolution in the landholding system loomed over the horizon. The ruling chiefs were satisfied with the status quo since they controlled the land and this control gave them their power over the commoners who worked the land and paid dearly to do so. Even foreigners who did business in the islands held their property at the pleasure of the chiefs. The interests of the chiefs and the foreigners were in almost continual conflict and the land issue intensified every year. As pressure for change mounted, the chiefs sensed the decline in their own power and their resistance toward a change in the land system weakened. The missionaries, well aware of the sharp decrease in the native population, strongly supported a land revolution since they felt that the natives needed the incentive of land ownership to lift them to a higher level of civilization. Yet this supposed benefit to the commoners would be at the expense of the chiefs.

The creation of the land commission[1] set the wheels of change in motion. But before the commission could make awards, the question of how to divide the lands had to be settled. The commission reached the conclusion that vested interests in the land belonged to the government (the king), the landlord and the tenant. The legislature, after much discussion, defined the rights of each of these three groups and provided procedures by which tenants might acquire land. However, no solution for actually dividing the land between the king and the landlords was reached. For nearly two years, the king and the chiefs labored in vain in an attempt to make a division. Lists were compiled of the lands and the landlords and much disagreement followed concerning which lands belonged to the king.

**William Little Lee (left) and
Charles Reed Bishop (right)**   **Bishop Museum**

Finally in December, 1847, a plan suggested by Judge Lee was adopted. It set forth seven rules to guide the division about to be undertaken. A committee consisting of John Young, Dr. Judd, J. Piikoi and Governor Kekuanaoa was appointed and the way for the "Great Mahele" was cleared. After a month of preliminary planning, the committee began the arduous task of dividing the lands between the king and the chiefs. Each of the 245 landlords came forward to have his claim recognized. A separate division was made with each one, allocating a portion of the land to the king. The "Mahele Book" recorded each transaction in two parts; one page listing the lands belonging to the king and the opposite page listing the lands belonging to the landlord. Except for the king's interest, all claimants had to present their claims to the land commission to be given awards. Noncompliance meant forfeiture. Since many of the chiefs failed to act during the prescribed time limit, subsequent amendments to the law extending the deadline were passed, the last in 1892!

---

[1] The land commission initially consisted of two foreigners (William Richards and John Ricord) and three Hawaiians (J.Y. Kanehoa, John Ii and Z. Kaauwai).

Kamehameha III (About 1850)   **State Archives**

After the land division, the government, as a separate entity, had an interest in the lands of both the king and the chiefs. This interest could be commuted away by the payment of the required fees, or in lieu of payment, surrendering a portion of the lands to the government. Shortly after the final division was made with the last chief, the king divided his lands into two parts: the small part became "Crown Lands"[2] and were his own private lands; the other, larger, part became government lands set apart forever for the chiefs and the people. Following the initial division, the king owned approximately half of the lands in the entire kingdom.

Although the common people had not been forgotten, no specific fraction of the lands had been set aside for them in the general settlement. Yet by and large, most common people weren't too concerned whether or not they received land in fee simple, perhaps because they were fearful of the new and unfamiliar system. While businessmen, missionaries, heirs of deceased foreigners and the humblest of men came forward to present their claims to the land commission, few native Hawaiians made any claims. Considered "indolent" and "improvident" by most foreigners, the Hawaiians had a philosophy of life which puzzled the foreigners who were raised to be industrious and to acquire property. Blaming the feudal land system of the past and the climate to a lesser degree, the missionaries and some foreigners started a movement to improve the condition of the natives by giving them land in fee simple and then freeing them from the labor tax.

After much discussion in the privy council and the cabinet, Judge Lee was requested to prepare a plan for apportioning a certain percentage of government lands, in fee simple, to every native family throughout the kingdom. In 1850, after legislative confirmation, all native tenants were granted kuleanas (fee simple titles to plots of land), without commutation, to the lands occupied and cultivated by them, except for houselots in Honolulu, Hilo and Lahaina. The only condition was that the claims had to be presented to the land commission for recognition. Also, additional government lands were set aside for sale to natives who had not received sufficient lands. Selling the land at $ .50 an acre, the government provided these remaining commoners with their kuleanas and wiped away the last remnants of the old feudal land system.

---

[2] After much controversy and many years, "Crown Lands" later referred to lands atttached to the crown itself and not the wearer of the crown. They would become distinct from government lands and from private lands owned by the king as an individual.

Although most of the kuleana lands were valuable for agricultural purposes, they amounted to only about 30,000 acres compared to roughly three million acres divided more or less equally between the government and the chiefs and another one million acres of crown lands. Since the limits of a kuleana had never been defined, they varied greatly in size. Districts were surveyed by different people and boundaries frequently overlapped. It would take another fifty years to straighten out the confusion; yet the land commission awards and the "Mahele Book" formed the basis on which nearly all land titles have rested from that time to the present.

Thus the acts of 1850 completed the change in Hawaii's land system. Foreigners and natives alike could buy and sell land. A great buying and selling frenzy followed in the years ahead, sparked by great advances in commerce and agriculture. Yet while many foreigners bought land, many natives sold land. The concept of the kuleana never took hold. Accustomed to living as a feudal tenant, trained to respect and honor superiors and submitting to all sorts of directives without complaint, the native was hardly in a position to accept and fully understand the sudden liberty thrust upon him. But he did understand the freedom to sell the land, and sell he did! During the ensuing fifty years, foreigners would acquire so much land that they would hold four times the amount held by the natives and the chiefs combined.

Custom House   **State Archives**

Although Hawaii's independence had been recognized for a number of years and a constitutional government had been established, the kingdom's security and domestic tranquillity continued to vacillate depending on the current rumors making the rounds. Being a small weak nation, Hawaii had to submit to the demands imposed upon her by the three great powers. Greater equality became a reality when the United States signed a new treaty in December, 1849. Likewise, a new treaty with Great Britain, generally following the American treaty, was signed in 1851. But France stood alone, refusing to make any real concessions. The Laplace Treaty of 1839 had been revised in Paris in 1846 and a new French Consul, Guillaume Patrice Dillon, had been sent to Honolulu to insist on its ratification. Arriving in early February, 1848, Dillon presented the new treaty to the king along with a large framed portrait of the French King (Louis Philippe). The new treaty was ratified by the king and the legislature even though it still contained the restrictive provisions of the 1839 treaty. Since existing treaties with other countries contained most favored nation clauses, they allowed citizens of other nations to claim the benefits provided by the French treaty as long as France refused to give them up.

In short order after his arrival, Dillon managed to turn many small complaints and demands into full scale diplomatic issues. His actions became so objectionable that the king and his advisors decided to deal directly with the French government and to seek the recall of Dillon. James J. Jarves (editor of the

government newspaper *Polynesian*) was appointed "Special Commissioner" to the three great powers and he was instructed to proceed to Paris and present the government's case directly to the French. Dillon subsequently appealed to the French navy in the Pacific for help.

Interior of Honolulu's Fort   **State Archives**

Two French frigates arrived in Honolulu in mid-August, 1849, commanded by Rear Admiral Legoarant de Tromelin who was in charge of all French naval forces in the Pacific. Prodded by Dillon, the admiral quickly presented the king with an ultimatum which contained ten demands for alleviating the alleged grievances of French citizens.

Surprisingly, the Hawaiian government refused to yield to the admiral's demands. Furious, the admiral sent an armed party ashore which took possession of the fort, government offices and the custom house. They also seized the king's yacht *Kamehameha* and detained all ships flying the Hawaiian flag, backing up their actions by the guns of the two warships. The Hawaiian flag, however, continued to fly on shore.

Several long discussions followed in the days ahead with Dr. Judd and Judge Lee representing the king. Despite proposals and counterproposals, no settlement was reached. The main issue was the duty on French brandy and other liquors; the current duty was $5.00 per gallon, almost 500 percent of its invoiced value. While these conferences proceeded, the French soldiers on shore dismantled the fort, spiked and damaged the guns, poured powder into the sea and released the prisoners inside the fort.

A settlement was never reached. On August 30, the admiral declared the Laplace treaty in effect again and he confiscated the king's schooner *Kamehameha*. On the 5th of September, Admiral de Tromelin and his squadron sailed. Likewise, Dillon and his family departed, sailing to France via San Francisco.

Smarting from the French actions, the Hawaiian government appointed Dr. Judd as another commissioner to assist Jarves in protesting the actions of the French and in appealing to the governments of the United States and Great Britain for assistance. Dr. Judd left Honolulu on September 11, 1849 in company with two young Hawaiian princes, Alexander Liholiho and his elder brother Lot Kamehameha. Making stops in San Francisco, Panama, Jamaica, New York and London, Judd and his party arrived in Paris in early 1850. The French government refused to negotiate with Judd. Since a stalemate had developed, Dr. Judd and the two Hawaiian princes returned to London. Further attempts to have the British and later the United States intervene diplomatically failed to produce a settlement. Consequently, Judd and his party returned to Honolulu, arriving on September 9, 1850.

The Hawaiian government averted another crisis with French warships in early 1851, and conditions remained unfavorable

Dr. Gerrit P. Judd with Prince Lot Kamehameha (left) and Prince Alexander Liholiho (right) in Paris, 1850 State Archives

for a number of years. After 1853, difficulties with France greatly subsided. In retrospect, it is interesting to note that while relations with France caused grave concern for the Hawaiian government, actual French involvement in the islands' economy was minimal. Few French merchant and whaling ships visited the islands, the number of French citizens residing in the kingdom was very small and nearly all the liquor imported into the islands was brought in and drunk by the British and the Americans.

Southeastern Honolulu and Waikiki in the early 1850's State Archives

While the Hawaiian authorities sought to smooth over the difficulties with France, other outside forces were at work preparing to generate new difficulties for the island kingdom. Rumors of California adventurers intent on overthrowing the Hawaiian government abounded in 1851 and 1852. A group of about 150 restless young men did arrive in Honolulu in November 1851, and they were thought to be the vanguard of a still larger group to come. Having received advance warning, the privy council increased the number of foreign policemen and plans were drawn up to establish a large standing army. The expected violence never occurred, although clashes with policemen took place inspired by excessive drinking. Whether the presence of American and British warships in the harbor aborted their plans or whether these young men actually had any plans

to overthrow the government was never determined. Several of them had inquired into various business opportunities and most of them returned to California in a short time. The few who remained were arrested and convicted on trumped-up evidence supplied by a discontented shipmate.

Annexation rumors also abounded, inspired by United States expansion in Texas, Oregon, California and New Mexico. This expansion prompted many Americans to firmly believe that it was the "manifest destiny" of the United States to spread itself throughout North America and its adjacent islands. The expansion of trade with China and the prospects for trading with Japan increased the importance of the islands to the United States. In addition, the strategic importance of Pearl Harbor as a naval rendezvous and commercial port had been recognized. The population of the islands kept changing in favor of foreigners and part-Hawaiians as the pure native population kept decreasing. Finally, the agricultural development of the islands, tied closely to the west coast of the United States for its market, produced a small but influential group of businessmen whose sentiment for annexation grew out of their desires for a duty-free market in which to sell their products.

Smallpox Hospital at Waikiki State Archives

The annexation movement in Honolulu was interrupted by a smallpox epidemic which broke out in May of 1853. As the epidemic spread, crude hospitals were hastily constructed at both ends of the city in an attempt to isolate and treat the disease. Infected houses were burned and many natives were vaccinated. Others, fearing western medical practices, refused help. Despite valiant attempts at containment, the smallpox epidemic spread rapidly during July and August. Its victims were mostly native Hawaiians who suffered a very high mortality rate from the disease. By October, Honolulu reported no new cases, but the disease continued to linger in the rural areas. Near the end of January, 1854, no new cases had been reported and the commissioners reported a total of 6,405 cases and 2,485 deaths.

During the height of the epidemic, public meetings were held in an effort to adopt more stringent measures to combat the disease so that the port would be safe for the fall arrival of the whaling fleet. These meetings gave a faction of foreigners an opportunity to launch an attack on Dr. Judd (minister of finance) and Richard Armstrong (minister of education). Being opposed to Judd's strong influence in the king's cabinet and his and Armstrong's strong opposition to the sale of spirits, this group led a long and intense struggle in which each side mustered all the support it could possibly find. Judd and Armstrong were accused of negligence in handling the early stages of the smallpox epidemic and a resolution was passed calling for their dismissal.

Honolulu Looking Seaward (About 1855)   **State Archives**

Prince Alexander Liholiho, who had become a member of the privy council in the early part of 1852, had thrown all his influence against Judd and the annexation movement which Judd had firmly advocated. Since the king had no surviving children, he had adopted Liholiho as his son and had proclaimed him heir to the throne on April 7, 1853. Possessing a brilliant mind, ambitious and concerned for his country's independence, the twenty year old prince held great influence with the king and the king increasingly relied on his judgment. Exposed to color prejudice in the United States on his trip to Paris with Dr.

Judd and his brother, Prince Lot Kamehameha, Prince Alexander had become staunchly anti-American. Raised and educated under the restraining influences of the missionaries and their daily prayer meetings, long sermons and daily exhortations, he hardened his heart into disliking the mission and yearned to taste the rewards of supreme power. Uniting with several other chiefs who equally opposed annexation, the prince was able to eventually persuade the king, who had been drinking excessively in recent years, to demand Judd's resignation.

Annexation talk continued both in the United States and Hawaii. David L. Gregg, the new commissioner of the United States for Hawaii, arrived in mid-December, 1853 and within a few weeks he became convinced that the Hawaiian government would soon seek annexation. With reports of insurrection abounding, the king signed an order on February 6, 1854 directing minister Wyllie to ascertain the views of the United States on the annexation issue and also the terms and conditions upon which annexation could take place. This order was in preparation of meeting any sudden danger which might arise and threaten the existence or independence of the kingdom. Pending word from Washington, Wyllie and Gregg began negotiations. Toward the end of May, 1854, Gregg received the necessary powers to negotiate and sign a treaty of annexation. With France and Great Britain about to enter the Crimean War, siding with Turkey and opposing Russia, the United States saw an opportunity to pursue a vigorous expansion policy.

Negotiations proceeded slowly since the various ministers and council members had to be consulted and satisfied. In addition, the negotiations had to be held in secret because of the tug-of-war taking place between opponents and proponents of annexation. The British and French consuls, learning of the negotiations, protested vehemently to the king and the council chiefs, expounding on the social and political evils existing in the United States, including slavery, racial prejudice, hatred of aristocracy, etc. During this delicate period, an unusually large number of American, British and French warships called on the islands, only adding to the tensions and uncertainties.

On December 15, 1854, Kamehameha III died at the age of 41. Although he had been in poor health for a year or more, the illness which ended his life lasted less than a week. With him died any hopes for annexation. Judge Lee and Prince Alexander had made it a point to absent themselves from Honolulu as much as possible in order to prolong the treaty negotiations. Since all drafts of the treaty were sent to Judge Lee, his travels and subsequent tardiness in sending back the drafts had bought the necessary time to stall the treaty. In addition, by including the clause that the islands would become a state and Hawaii's citizens would acquire all the rights and privileges of American citizens, Lee was confident that the Senate would never ratify such a treaty.

Prince Alexander and minister Wyllie fully cooperated with Judge Lee. Furthermore, the young prince knew that his consent was required before any decision was made. Within hours of the king's death, Governor Kekuanaoa led a company of soldiers into the streets of Honolulu announcing the death of the old king and the accession of the new king. One of the king's first official acts was to terminate the annexation negotiations.

**Kamehameha III About A
Year Before His Death**   **State Archives**

Chapter 6

A Changing Economy

The funeral for Kamehameha III, last son of Kamehameha the Great, was held on January 10, 1855 with pomp and pageantry, tears and chants befitting the noblest of Hawaiian kings. On the following day, Alexander Liholiho, the adopted son of the former king, took the oath of office in his formal inauguration as Kamehameha IV. During the ceremony, held before an immense crowd of both natives and foreigners in Kawaiahao Church, the new king gave his coronation address first in Hawaiian, then in English. He swore to uphold the constitution, increase civilization and its good virtues, and sought to preserve the independence of his kingdom. His nearly three years of serving as a member of the privy council had provided Liholiho with valuable political experience, and he stood ready to accept the serious responsibilities of his high position. His trip to England in 1849 and 1850 had instilled in him a great admiration for English institutions and his ideas and tastes were more European than Hawaiian. In this regard, Kamehameha IV firmly believed in the aristocracy's right and duty to rule over the lower classes.

The new king's cabinet remained essentially the same as the previous cabinet under Kamehameha III since Liholiho reappointed all of the previous ministers. While John Young II continued as minister of the interior, his position as kuhina nui was not renewed. Instead, the king appointed his sister, Princess Victoria Kamamalu. Prince Lot, the king's brother, was appointed a general commanding the armed forces. Prince Lot also became an important member of the government, taking part in deliberations of the cabinet, the privy council and the House of Nobles.

Kamehameha IV had ascended the throne as a bachelor, one month short of turning twenty-one. Shortly after coming to power, he was encouraged by his faithful advisor, Robert Wyllie, to marry in order to give stability to the crown and to continue the monarchy under a native dynasty. Fortunately, the king's desire to continue the Kamehameha line coincided with his desires for his childhood sweetheart, Emma Naea Rooke. Emma had been adopted in infancy by an English doctor, T.C.B. Rooke, and his wife who was a sister of Emma's mother. Emma was a granddaughter of John Young and a great-granddaughter of Keliimaikai, Kamehameha the Great's younger brother. Educated by a private tutor at the Royal School, Emma spoke fluent English. She received a refined upbringing, and her natural gifts of amiability and cordiality made her well liked.

The royal wedding took place in Kawaiahao Church on June 19, 1856 and was one of the grandest affairs to take place in the kingdom up to that date. It inspired a number of social functions during the ensuing months, including a grand ball hosted by the Chinese merchants of Honolulu. Less than two years later, a royal prince was born on May 20, 1858, rekindling the hopes of the Hawaiian race. With the consent of the privy council, the little prince received the title of "His Royal Highness the Prince of Hawaii" and was formally christened Albert Edward Kauikeaouli Leiopapa a Kamehameha. The young prince became an instant and intimate part of the royal couple's private life and he was taken nearly everywhere they went, whether by coach, wagon or ship.

Kamehameha IV (Alexander Liholiho) in 1855   **State Archives**

Queen Emma[1]   **State Archives**

---

[1] Under the patronage of Queen Emma, a temporary hospital and dispensary for needy Hawaiians opened in August of 1859. Known as "Queen's Hospital," a permanent structure was completed the following year.

Officially declared a city in 1850, Honolulu continued to expand. The population of the city numbered about ten thousand, nearly twenty percent of whom were foreign residents. The 1853 census showed a total population of 73,138, a decrease of over 35,000 from the 1835 census. As each year passed, Honolulu took on a greater resemblence to a New England seaport. Many new residences and businesses were constructed of stone or of lumber brought in from the Pacific northwest. Warehouses, a shipyard, a courthouse, a market building for trading produce, hotels, billiard saloons and countless other business and government buildings lined the streets as the city expanded in various directions. Imposing residences of chiefs, foreign consuls, government officials, sea captains, businessmen and missionaries dotted the beautiful Nuuanu Valley just north of the city.

A hand-operated fire engine first appeared in 1847, and the first volunteer fire company was formally organized in 1850. An 1849 treaty between Hawaii and the United States put mail service on an official basis near the end of 1850 and a post office was established. This post office issued stamps of two, five and thirteen cents value.[1] Possessing the best protected harbor in the islands, Honolulu attracted the trading ships and gradually became the commercial center of the kingdom. As the size and number of ships increased, improvements were made to the harbor. Dredging was begun to clear out and deepen the harbor. The old Fort was torn down in 1857 to make room for more water-front and warehouse space. Gas lighting appeared in 1859.

Exterior of Honolulu Fort
(About 1853)   Paul Emmert/
                                                   State Archives

View of Honolulu (Mid-1850's)   **State Archives**

The prosperity of the islands since the decade of the 1820's had been tied directly to the whaling industry. Although progress had been made in the agricultural industries of sugar, coffee and livestock, these industries continued to be plagued by shortages of capital and labor, and a suitable market evaded them due to high tariffs in the United States. Annexation would have eliminated the tariff issue, and in fact, it appeared to be only signatures away prior to the death of Kamehameha III. The new king, desirous of maintaining the kingdom's independence, quickly put an end to annexation negotiations and sought instead to substitute a treaty of reciprocity with the United States.

In order to obtain a reciprocity treaty with the United States and also to obtain guarantees of independence for the island kingdom, Judge William L. Lee was sent on an official mission to Washington in 1855. Following several months of discussions and negotiations, the draft of a reciprocity treaty was drawn up. In addition, the United States government reiterated its views concerning the independence of the islands and agreed to station a portion of its naval force at or near the Hawaiian Islands for the purpose of protecting American interests in that area. But a powerful opposition developed in the United States Senate, and the reciprocity treaty never went into effect.

Whaling continued to dominate the economy of the Hawaiian kingdom in the decade of the 1850's even though fears were being raised about the eventual withdrawal of the whaling fleet. These fears were well-founded, based on several poor years and temporary shrinkages in the size of the whaling fleet. But overall, whaling continued at high levels. The period between 1843 and 1860 has often been called the "golden age" of whaling in Hawaii's history. Three peak years stood out: 1846, 1853 and 1859. The astounding increase in the number of whaling ships visiting the islands (a high of 596 in 1846) was caused by the successive discoveries of new whaling grounds off the coast of North America near Alaska and in the region around the Arctic Ocean. These new discoveries resulted from the search for new whaling grounds as one area after another became fished out.

---

[1] These stamps were commonly called "Missionary" stamps and are highly prized by today's stamp collectors. The name originates from the fact that the primary users of these early stamps were the missionaries.

Whaling Scene (1840's)   **Lahaina's Hawaiian Wax Museum/**
                               Photo by Author

The huge mammals were relentlessly pursued into new and more distant parts of the ocean. These great distances necessitated longer voyages (four years became fairly common) and the cost of whaling soared as a result. As the average catch of oil became smaller and smaller, the price of whale oil rose higher and higher. This in turn stimulated the search for other kinds of lubricants and lighting sources. Natural gas, coal oil, kerosene and crude or partially refined petroleum began to replace whale oil in the late 1850's and early 1860's.

In the 1850's, whale oil and whale bone often were trans-shipped via other merchant ships bound for the home ports of the various whaling ships. This procedure saved costs and enabled the whaling ships to stay out longer in their quest for more whales. The islands were so dependent on the whaling fleet that the government encouraged their visits and gave them preferential treatment in terms of harbor and transit dues. Nearly every form of business enterprise in the cities depended in one way or another on the semi-annual visits of the whaling fleet. The government also benefited directly through the collection of various harbor fees as well as the imposition of fines by the police courts. Native policemen, paid a percentage of the imposed fines, were eager to enforce the various laws involving disturbing the peace, drunkenness, "furious riding," etc.

While competition from the growing petroleum industry was making inroads, the Civil War cut the active whaling fleet in half and nearly ruined the New England fleet. Many whaling ships were converted to the merchant fleet while others were sold or simply waited out the war in their home ports. Two Confederate cruisers, *Shenandoah* and *Alabama*, eagerly sought out Union whalers in the Pacific, seizing cargoes and burning the ships. Approximately forty-six ships were destroyed in this manner, including the *Harvest*, a merchant ship owned by a Honolulu firm, manned by native seamen and flying the Hawaiian flag.

Following the Civil War, the whaling industry recovered somewhat, but another disaster soon befell the fleet. During the fall of 1871, thirty-three whaleships (including several of Hawaiian registry) were trapped in the Arctic ice floes north of the Bering Strait. The crews were saved, but the ships and their cargoes were a total loss. Five years later, a similar disaster claimed a dozen more ships and about fifty crewmen. By this time, whaling had dropped to second place in the economic life of the Hawaiian Islands and came to an end in 1880. Fortunately for the Hawaiian economy, the decline of whaling occurred gradually, enabling businessmen to seek alternate opportunities. Agriculture, particularly the sugar industry, spurred by rapid population growth in California and Oregon, progressively replaced the whaling industry as Hawaii's main source of income.

Along with the development of the whaling industry came an expansion of merchant shipping to and from the islands. In effect, transportation at reasonably short intervals was available to nearly all parts of the civilized world. Regular lines of transportation between Hawaii and the United States (Pacific and Atlantic ports), Great Britain and her colonies, and Germany developed as trading interests from these countries established their Pacific headquarters in Honolulu. The development and settlement of California and the Oregon territory shifted much of Hawaii's trade from Atlantic ports to Pacific ports, with San Francisco becoming more and more important until she finally surpassed all the rest. The American Civil War greatly increased the hazards of moving merchandise around Cape Horn to eastern ports and consequently accelerated the shift to Pacific ports. Transcontinental rail service further eroded the importance of making Atlantic ports.

Early attempts at steamship travel between the islands generally were unsuccessful until 1860 when the steamer *Kilauea* began a long career in inter-island service. Prior to the 1860's, small coastal vessels plied the waters between the islands and the voyages were long and often rough. Generally, a passenger had to have a very good reason to induce himself to bear the hard-

Whaling off the Coast of Hawaii State Archives

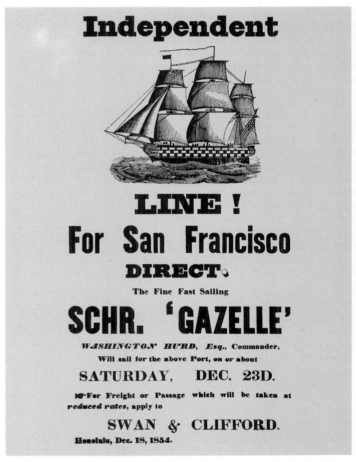

Display Advertisement (1854)[1] State Archives

ships and discomforts of these voyages. Most vessels lacked any navigational aids and lifesaving equipment. The captains were often incompetent, shipwrecks were common as were near disasters. It was not unheard of for a vessel to get lost in an attempt to travel from one island to another. With schedules irregular at best, a round trip to the island of Hawaii from Honolulu might take a month!

---

[1] Although the schooner depicted in this ad is rather eye-catching, it had little resemblance to the actual freight and passenger schooner making the voyage.

Two events which took place in 1859 had a profound influence on the establishment of the Episcopal Church in Hawaii. The first of these events was the long and serious illness of Robert Wyllie, minister of foreign relations. Wyllie's long ordeal renewed his interest in religion and he longed to establish an Episcopal chapel in Honolulu. The second event involved the king and his private secretary, a young American named Henry A. Neilson. In August, the king and queen, their young son and a large royal party left Honolulu for a royal holiday on the islands of Hawaii and Maui. While on Maui (or perhaps even earlier), malicious gossip had reached the king that his secretary was having an affair with the queen. Brooding over the matter, King Alexander spent several days at sea, drinking heavily and deliberating his course of action. On the evening of September 11th, he came ashore and sought out Neilson. Without uttering a sound, the king walked up to Neilson and shot him in the chest at close range. Miraculously the wound, though serious, was not fatal and there were several physicians nearby who quickly attended to Neilson's wound.

Neilson lived for two and a half years, although the wound undoubtedly contributed to his early death. The king's position shielded him from any prosecution and no legal notice was ever taken of the incident. Nevertheless, Kamehameha IV was filled with remorse and later inquiries into the affair proved his suspicions to be groundless. Strengthened by Wyllie and Queen Emma, Kamehameha IV set the wheels in motion to establish an Episcopal Church in Hawaii. Actually, the king's interest in this church had been implanted years before when he had witnessed their services while in England. Now he firmly believed that their doctrines and rituals were more compatible with his monarchy.

Since the constitution placed all religions on an equal footing, no government revenues could be used to fund the new church. Instead, the king offered to donate a site for the new church and to provide an annual salary of $1,000 for a qualified clergyman. In London, the Reverend Thomas Nettleship Staley was designated as bishop to head the new missionary diocese in Hawaii. Bishop Staley sailed for Hawaii with his family on August 17, 1862. The Hawaiian royal couple eagerly awaited the bishop's arrival because they intended his first official act to be the baptism of their young son, the Prince of Hawaii. Queen Victoria of England had agreed to be the child's godmother by proxy and had ordered a costly silver christening cup for her distant godson.

The silver cup arrived ahead of Bishop Staley in the care of Mr. and Mrs. William W.F. Synge, the new British consul general to Hawaii and his wife. Mrs. Synge had been designated by Queen Victoria to act as her proxy at the baptism. Their ship arrived on August 22, 1862. The following morning, before landing, Synge was informed that the Prince of Hawaii had come down with a mysterious disease. Some called it "brain fever";[1] in any event, the attending physicians could do nothing. A hurried baptism was performed by Rev. Clark of Kawaiahao Church according to the rites of the Church of England. The little prince clung to life for several days in a hopeless state. He succumbed to his disease on August 27, 1862, at the tender age of four, leaving his parents and the Hawaiian community in a state of intense sorrow and desolation.

---

[1] In attempting to cool off his son from an uncontrollable fit of passion, the king held his son's head under a spout of cold running water. Whether this cold water immersion had anything to do with the resulting disease is unclear. But in any event, the king blamed himself for the young prince's death.

Prince Albert was the last offspring born to a reigning Hawaiian monarch.

Henry A. Neilson (Private Secretary to Kamehameha IV) Bishop Museum

Albert Edward Kauikeaouli, The Prince of Hawaii State Archives

Bishop Thomas Nettleship Staley State Archives

Bishop Staley and his party arrived in October, 1862. A sermon preached on Sunday, October 19th, formally inaugurated the mission. Queen Emma was baptized a few days later. The royal couple was confirmed as members of the newly chartered Hawaiian Reformed Catholic Church at the end of November. Robert Wyllie and several other members of the king's cabinet joined shortly thereafter, followed by a number of high ranking chiefs in the months ahead.

Many Americans felt that the introduction of the Anglican Church into the Hawaiian kingdom was motivated by the British Government in an attempt to strengthen their influence and position in the islands, with the ultimate goal being to add them to the British Empire. It was true, however, that the king and his advisors sought out the presence of the Anglican Church and they were convinced that the presence of the new church would have a profound effect on preserving and strengthening the monarchy. Needless to say, the American Protestant missionaries were not pleased with the presence of the new church. Their influence on the monarchy and Hawaiian affairs had been greatly weakened by the accession of Kamehameha IV to the throne, and the new church's continued presence would only further erode any gains made in the past.

Despite the support of the monarchy, the Hawaiian Reformed Catholic Church failed to achieve the great success its founders had hoped for. While it did give much attention to education, the new church met stiff competition from the two other religious groups[1] which were already well established in the islands. These groups were the Hawaiian Evangelical Association which consisted of both native and foreign clergymen of the Congregational and Presbyterian Orders (the American Protestant missionaries), and the Roman Catholic Church. In addition to the wide differences in religious ideology and forms of worship, the Reformed Catholic Church was plagued by internal dissension and handicapped by a lack of adequate monetary support. Bishop Staley resigned in 1870, and the name of the church organization was later changed to the Anglican Church in Hawaii.

Following the death of his young son, Kamehameha IV kept himself out of the public eye as much as possible. Grief over the death of his son, guilt over the shooting and later death of his private secretary, and chronic asthma all began to take their toll on the reigning monarch. He became bad-tempered and moody; he ate less and drank more; and his asthma attacks increased both in frequency and severity to the point where he could scarcely breathe. The final attack came on the morning of November 30, 1863 with Queen Emma at his side desperately trying to breathe life into her choking, dying husband. Her valiant efforts failed, and the twenty-nine year old king joined his Hawaiian ancestors.

The sudden, unexpected death of Kamehameha IV left the kingdom without any formal successor since the royal couple had no living children. In the absence of a direct heir, the king's brother, Prince Lot Kamehameha, was considered to be the rightful heir to the throne. During the afternoon of November 30, a document was drawn up by the kuhina nui[2] and approved by the privy council proclaiming Prince Lot as king of the Hawaiian Islands with the title and style of Kamehameha V.

Kamehameha IV in Later Life State Archives

---

[1] A third religious organization on the Hawaiian scene was the Mormon Mission which arrived in December of 1850.

[2] The kuhina nui, Princess Victoria Kamamalu, in proclaiming the dead king's brother heir to the throne, removed any doubts about her ideas of succession and thereby eliminated the possibility of a regency being established until such time as the legislature elected a new king.

View of Honolulu Looking Inland

The Last Kamehameha

Lot Kamehameha, in assuming his role as king of the Hawaiian Islands in 1863, refused to be publicly inaugurated and likewise refused to take the oath to maintain the Constitution of 1852. He believed that Hawaii's sovereigns had the right to change the constitution at will since it had been a grant from the king (Kamehameha III). While the political ideas of the new reigning monarch were very similar to those of his deceased brother, there were marked differences between the two men. Kamehameha IV had been well-proportioned and elegant in appearance. He displayed high culture and social graces, and many of his court functions were patterned after those of the British. Lot, being large and heavy, resembled the founder of the dynasty (Kamehameha the Great) and was more Hawaiian in his point of view. Although both brothers had been educated at the Royal School and had traveled extensively, Lot cast aside the snobbery and gentlemanly manners of his predecessor, preferring instead many of the customs of the old ways. Strong-willed and unexcitable, Lot appeared to possess great energy, perseverance and strength of will.

Shortly after ascending the throne, Kamehameha V assembled his cabinet, gathering around him trusted men who would serve the new king throughout most of his reign. Robert Wyllie continued to serve as minister of foreign relations and advised the king on making the other appointments. Charles de Varigny, a Frenchman who was acting French consul following Perrin's death in 1862, became minister of finance. Charles G. Hopkins (editor of the newspaper *Polynesian*) became minister of the interior, and Charles C. Harris, an American lawyer and long-time resident of the islands, was appointed attorney general. The king's true father, Mataio Kekuanaoa (Governor of Oahu), assumed the position of kuhina nui, replacing the king's sister (Princess Victoria Kamamalu). Dr. Ferdinand W. Hutchison was appointed court physician; in 1865 he became minister of the interior, replacing Hopkins. Chief Justice Elisha H. Allen continued in his post as head of the supreme court.

After lengthy discussions with his cabinet members, Kamehameha V signed a royal proclamation in May, 1864 calling for publicly-elected delegates of the people to meet with him and the nobles in a constitutional convention on July 7, 1864. It was the king's desire to propose a new constitution more favorable to the crown rather than to propose new amendments to the old constitution. The convention started on the date originally proposed and consisted of three separate entities: the king, the fifteen nobles and twenty-six duly elected delegates of the people.

The convention's business continued reasonably smoothly until August 8th when the sixty-second article came up. This article dealt with limiting voters to those residents who could pass a literacy test and who possessed property or had an income qualification. While no serious objection was raised to the literacy test, the issue of property or an income qualification caused serious and long debate. Attempts at compromise were made on August 12th and 13th, but the convention remained deadlocked. The king took the initiative and abruptly dismissed the convention. In his closing message he bluntly stated: ". . . I make known today that the Constitution of 1852 is abrogated. I will give you a Constitution."

Kamehameha V (Lot Kamehameha) in Military Uniform   **State Archives**

The King Addressing the Legislature   **A. Daudenarde/ Bishop Museum**

On August 20, 1864, Kamehameha V signed his new constitution into law and the same day took an oath to maintain it. This new constitution was based upon the draft previously submitted to the convention, with a number of modifications being made. While the old constitution had 105 articles, the new constitution contained only 80. Over twenty articles were deleted and several others were combined. Although numerous changes were made, the significant changes were few in number. The new constitution abolished the office of kuhina nui, greatly curtailed the powers of the privy council, increased the powers and privileges of the king, and strengthened the administrative powers of the king's cabinet. The new constitution greatly strengthened the monarchy, providing the king and his cabinet with the dominating influence in the government.

The appointment of Frenchman Charles de Varigny to the king's cabinet convinced many Americans in Hawaii that the new king had adopted an anti-American policy. Actually, the foreign policy of Lot Kamehameha remained much the same as it had been under the previous reign of the king's brother. The prime objective of this foreign policy continued to be the safeguarding of the kingdom's independence. Feelings of mistrust between Americans, Frenchmen and Britishers living in the islands continued to grow and were strengthened by France's and Great Britain's unfriendly stance toward the United States during the Civil War. Even Queen Emma's visit to England in 1865 and 1866, made to overcome her grief at the death of her husband and also to benefit the Episcopal Mission in Hawaii which she greatly favored, was looked upon by many Americans as another attempt to more closely link the Hawaiian Islands to Great Britain. Following Kamehameha V's advice, Queen Emma visited the United States in August of 1866 in an attempt to lessen the fears of Americans living in Hawaii. This visit gave the United States an opportunity to convey to the Hawaiian authorities its recently adopted position of friendship and conciliation toward the islands. In addition to being welcomed in New York and meeting with President Johnson in Washington, Queen Emma was returned to Honolulu in regal style aboard the American warship *Vanderbilt*, flagship of Rear Admiral H.K. Thatcher.

Following the Civil War, the Navy's enlarged Pacific Squadron was divided into the North Pacific Squadron and the South Pacific Squadron. Falling within the operating area of the North Pacific Squadron, the Hawaiian Islands were frequently visited by various units of this command. The *USS Lackawanna*, commanded by Captain William Reynolds, was assigned to the islands for an indefinite stay. She arrived in Honolulu on February 9, 1867. In addition to strengthening America's position in the islands, the *Lackawanna* was also under orders to protect American interests. Undoubtedly, the presence of an American warship would have a calming effect should a serious political crisis develop upon the expected early death of the ailing king.

The arrival in July, 1866 of General Edward M. McCook to the islands as the new minister resident[1] revived the drive for a reciprocity treaty. Meeting with the sugar planters and influential businessmen, he quickly became a strong advocate of reciprocity. Journeying to Washington in late November, McCook successfully interested the president, Secretary of State Seward and various members of Congress to consider a reciprocity treaty. On February 1, 1867, the president signed a formal document authorizing McCook to negotiate and sign a reciprocity treaty with the government of the Hawaiian Islands. With the help of Hawaii's minister of finance, Charles C. Harris, McCook drew up and signed a treaty of reciprocity while the two men were in San Francisco in May of 1867. After much debate in Honolulu, the treaty was approved and ratified by the king on September 30. But in Washington, the treaty managed to linger in the senate for three years during five congressional sessions! In and out of the committee on foreign relations, the treaty was debated again and again. A vote was finally taken on June 1, 1870, but the necessary two-thirds majority was not achieved and the treaty was defeated.

While a reciprocity treaty would have greatly benefited the sugar industry in Hawaii, the industry nevertheless continued to grow. The turn-around in sugar exports occurred in 1856, and in each year thereafter, the amount of sugar exported continued a long steady climb from 555,000 pounds in 1856 to over 23 million pounds in 1873. The most phenomenal growth took place during the years 1861 through 1866, reflecting the artificial stimulus created by the American Civil War. In 1861,

---

[1] Minister resident was the term used to describe the American diplomatic representative in Hawaii. It began being used in 1863 when the United States raised the rank from commissioner to minister resident.

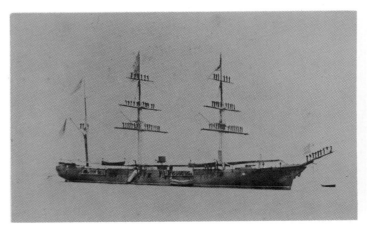

USS Lackawanna **off Honolulu in 1867 with Her Crew Manning the Yards**   **Official Navy Photo**

Charles C. Harris   **State Archives**

Wailuku Sugar Factory in 1867   **State Archives**

over 2½ million pounds of sugar were exported to the United States, leaping to over 17½ million pounds in 1866. During this remarkable growth, the number of plantations and mills nearly tripled. By war's end, sugar had replaced whaling as the island's economic mainstay.

Prior to the turn-around year of 1856, many small growers went bankrupt and a number of consolidations took place. These larger plantations became more productive and the industry's outlook improved as exports began flowing again to California and Oregon as these areas continued to expand. In addition to improvements in machinery, mills and production methods, the introduction of irrigation stabilized production and made possible sugar growing in areas otherwise ignored. Manuring the fields started in the early 1860's and steam power gradually replaced water and animal power. On the business side of the sugar industry, business houses in Honolulu began to furnish much of the capital needed by the plantations and they also served as agents. This system allowed many smaller plantations to obtain financial assistance without borrowing at high interest rates from banks in the United States. Following the Civil War, the progress of the sugar industry slowed due to fluctuating prices in the San Francisco market as well as an over-supply of sugar. Between 1867 and 1872, there was little increase in the number of plantations and in the acreage planted.

While a large number of Hawaiian males worked on sugar plantations, the continued growth of these plantations in the 1850's and 1860's required more and more laborers. Yet few additional natives were available. Many had emigrated to California or joined the whaling fleet. Others preferred to become farmers on their recently acquired lands. Also, the native population continued to decline, and a series of epidemics in the early fifties took thousands of lives, nearly all native Hawaiians. Despite a number of attempts to bring in natives from various islands of Polynesia and Micronesia to help restock the Hawaiian race, only about 200 of these natives were persuaded to immigrate to Hawaii.

In 1850, the Hawaiian legislature passed a law which provided the basis for contract labor and set penalties for its enforcement. In 1852, approximately 300 Chinese coolies arrived. Under contract for five years, they received $3 a month plus food, clothing, housing and transportation from China. The continued labor shortage led to the establishment of the Bureau of Immigration in December, 1864. The bureau supervised the importation of foreign laborers, regulated their contracts and encouraged the introduction of free immigrants from abroad. While a number of Asian countries were considered for supplying contract labor for the plantations, China offered the most available supply. In the fall of 1865, a total of 522 Chinese coolies arrived in the islands.

Chinese Coolies Working in a Sugar Cane Field State Archives

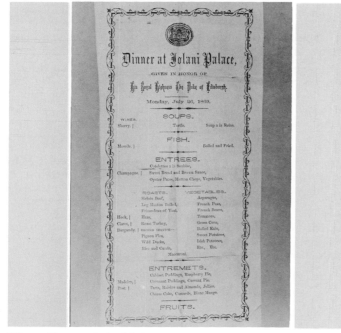

Dinner Menu at Iolani Palace— July 26, 1869 State Archives

The Hawaiian Hotel State Archives

The growth of steamship travel between Hawaii and the west coast of America, Australia and New Zealand caused a large increase in the number of visitors to the islands. These visitors included Mark Twain who came to Hawaii in March, 1866 aboard the *Ajax* as a correspondent for the Sacramento Union. Intending to stay only one month, Twain, traveling under his real name, Samuel Clemens, stayed four months and in the process wrote twenty-five letters to the Union describing with caustic humor and wit his experiences and impressions of Hawaii. Queen Victoria of Great Britain sent her second son, Alfred Ernest Albert, Duke of Edinburgh, to Hawaii on a state visit in 1869. Being the first foreign prince to visit the islands, he was accorded a formal state dinner announced by the menu shown above.

The arrival and departure of Mark Twain, the Duke of Edinburgh and others including envoys, politicians, merchants and opportunists created the need for hotel accomodations to lodge similar visitors in the years ahead. Since no private individuals were willing or capable of undertaking such an enterprise, the king felt that the government should undertake such a project. Although talk of building a first class hotel in Honolulu had surfaced as early as 1865, construction wasn't started until May of 1871. The Hawaiian Hotel, located on the corner of Hotel and Richards streets, formally opened with a subscription ball on February 29, 1872.[1]

[1] The term subscription ball referred to the fact that private individuals subscribed to Hotel Bonds and received a proportion of the rents received in lieu of interest. The name of the hotel later was changed to the Royal Hawaiian Hotel. In the course of time, it passed into private hands, and during World War I, it was converted into the present Armed Forces YMCA.

The Hawaiian Hotel was only one of a number of ambitious building programs initiated by Kamehameha V in an effort to present a credible and pleasing face to the governments of the world whose representatives continually visited his kingdom. Another major undertaking was the construction of Aliiolani Hale ("House of the Chief Unto Heavens"). Initially planned to be a new royal palace, various circumstances, including insufficient finances, delayed the project and its initial purpose was dropped in favor of a more useful one. The cornerstone was laid in February, 1872, and the building was completed in 1874.

Buildings of lesser scope included Iolani Barracks to house the royal household guards, a new prison, the Royal Mausoleum, new schoolhouses and warehouses, an insane asylum, a quarantine building to process the flood of immigrants, and other government structures. These heavy expenditures put a severe strain on the resources of the tiny kingdom. Since not all of these projects could be financed from general revenues, the government resorted to borrowing with great difficulty and at high interest rates (12% on most loans and up to 18% on others). As a result of this excessive borrowing, Hawaii's national debt stood at over $355,000 on March 31, 1874!

Aliiolani Hale
(Government Office Building)　　　　　　**State Archives**

Since Kamehameha V preferred to remain a bachelor, many of his ministers and the public were constantly worried about a successor. In 1864, Lot proclaimed his sister, Princess Victoria Kamamalu as heir-presumptive. But she died on May 26, 1866, again raising the question of succession. The king's ministers frequently proposed marriage to various eligible female aliis, including Queen Emma (the king's sister-in-law), fearing that the uncertainty of succession played into the hands of those factions favoring annexation. While the king was in love with his deceased brother's wife, there seemed to be too many obstacles in the way, including religious objections and Emma's devotion to the memory of her first husband.

Throughout the remainder of his reign, Lot Kamehameha remained stubborn and refused to name a successor. In his later years, he became even more obese and his heavy frame made it difficult for him to move about. In time, he could no longer ride a horse and thereafter spent most of his time indoors. Abandoning physical activity, Lot soon took to his bed. He steadily grew weaker and on December 11, 1872, a final effort was put forth to have the king appoint a successor. Reluctantly, he named High Chiefess Bernice Pauahi (wife of Charles R. Bishop, a prominent banker), but she refused, suggesting instead the king's half-sister, Ruth Keelikolani, and then Queen Emma. But the king passed on these suggestions, and before the matter could be brought up for discussion again, Lot Kamehameha died while preparations were underway for his birthday celebration. The Kamehameha line thus came to an abrupt end.

Lot Kamehameha in His Later Years　　　　**State Archives**

Chapter 8

The People Elect a New Monarch

The death of Kamehameha V threw the Hawaiian nation into a monarchical crisis. Under the provisions of the Constitution of 1864, the king had the right to name a successor when no direct heir existed. This choice was subject to the approval of the House of Nobles. But since no successor had been named, this decision passed to the legislature. The king's cabinet promptly scheduled a meeting of the legislature for January 8, 1873. Four alii soon stood out as possible candidates for the throne. They were William Charles Lunalilo, Ruth Keelikolani, David Kalakaua and Bernice Pauahi.

Contenders for the Throne

State Archives (All Photos)

1) William Lunalilo, a cousin of the deceased king, had the best natural claim to the throne since he was a grandson of a half-brother of Kamehameha the Great. Well-educated, Lunalilo was very popular with the people and his popularity grew as each day passed. While the dead king had felt that his subjects would accept Lunalilo's appointment as his successor, Lot Kamehameha had considered Lunalilo unfit for the position. Well aware of Lunalilo's political naivety, his frivolity and his excessive drinking habits, Lot had refused to name him.

2) Ruth Keelikolani, half-sister to the deceased king, was the favorite candidate among many of the chiefs because of her strict adherence to the "old" Hawaiian ways. Six feet tall and weighing over four hundred pounds, Ruth ruled as governess of the island of Hawaii. Remaining aloof to the teachings and influences of the missionaries, Ruth refused to speak the English language although she could if she wanted. Through inheritance and occasional business dealings, she had acquired vast tracts of land on all of the islands. But Ruth's genealogy was much too controversial and few people considered her as suitable for the position of ruling monarch.

3) David Kalakaua's blood line came from the fierce and independent chiefs of Kona who had supported Kamehameha the Great in his successful quest of uniting all the islands under one ruler. Educated at the Chiefs' Children's School, Kalakaua was well-educated and spoke English fluently. Possessing polished manners, he was considered a gentleman; yet he freely mingled in the general society. His long years in the Hawaiian legislature had sharpened his political skills. But the deceased king had refused to name Kalakaua as his successor because Lot considered him a "fool."

4) Bernice Pauahi, a great grand-daughter of Kamehameha the Great, remained in the running primarily because the late king had specifically designated her prior to his death. The king's cabinet felt duty-bound to present Bernice to the legislature as the late king's formal nominee. But Bernice, married to Charles R. Bishop who had started the first bank in the islands, remained steadfast in her refusal to accept the throne.

The overwhelming popular support for Lunalilo soon brought the number of candidates down to two: Lunalilo and Kalakaua. Resisting the demands of many enthusiastic supporters that he go to the palace and proclaim himself king, Lunalilo instead issued a manifesto on December 16 in which he proclaimed himself as the rightful heir to the throne. He offered to submit his claim to a vote by the people in a special election to be held on January 1, 1873. Pledging only to restore the Constitution of 1852, Lunalilo sought a peaceful and legal path to the throne. On December 28, Kalakaua issued his platform in anticipation of the upcoming election.

On January 1, a large number of male subjects in the kingdom went to the polls and voted almost unanimously for Lunalilo. The results were then submitted to the legislature. Meeting at noon on January 3, the legislature set to the task of electing a new king. A motion was made and passed to have each member of the legislature sign his name on the back of his ballot. This was a stroke of good fortune for Lunalilo's supporters who wanted to know how each member voted. Except for one abstention, all the ballots were cast for Lunalilo. On the following day, January 9, Lunalilo proceeded to Kawaiahao Church and made two short speeches: one to the legislature and the other to the general populace. In this latter speech, Lunalilo appealed to all Hawaiians to make every effort to reverse the continuing decline in the native population.

While the new king possessed a superior intelligence and was well read in English literature, he had little experience in practical matters and literally no experience in financial affairs since his guardians had seen to his affairs for many years. Despite having been a member of the Privy Council and the House of Nobles, Lunalilo had acquired almost no experience in public administration. Well aware of his weaknesses, Lunalilo quickly put together a cabinet consisting of men of high character and ability who would add strength to his new government. With the exception of a Scotsman, all the new cabinet ministers were Americans. Charles R. Bishop, the banker, became minister of foreign affairs. Edwin O. Hall, a local businessman previously associated with the American Protestant Mission in a lay capacity, took over as minister of the interior. Robert Stirling, a Scotsman who represented the British view, continued in his recent appointment under Kamehameha V as minister of finance. A. Francis Judd, the young lawyer son of Dr. Gerrit P. Judd, became attorney general. The king then sent a message to the legislature recommending a number of amendments which if enacted, would nullify numerous changes made in the Constitution of 1864. Unlike his predecessor, Lunalilo sought a more democratic approach to changing the constitution.

Several weeks after Lunalilo ascended the throne, customhouse figures were released showing that the quantity of sugar exported in 1872 had fallen off by nearly five million pounds. In addition to the smaller crop, the average price received had been lower than it had been for many years. The depressed state of the sugar industry naturally spilled over into other segments of the business community, and once again the old solutions of reciprocity and annexation began making the rounds in private as well as public conversations.

The arrival of a second American warship in less than two weeks, the *USS California*, added fuel to the reciprocity and annexation movement especially when it was learned that an admiral and two generals were aboard. The *California,* which arrived on January 15 and was the flagship of Admiral A.M. Pennock, had been scheduled to escort Kamehameha V to San Francisco for his planned trip to Europe. However, prior to departing San Francisco, word arrived of the king's death. Rather than cancel the scheduled visit, the Secretary of the Navy changed the purpose of the visit from one of international courtesy to one of increasing American influence and favor in the Hawaiian Islands. The two generals, John M. Schofield and B.S. Alexander, were ostensibly on a vacation trip. Actually,

Kawaiahao Church on Inaugural Day   **Bishop Museum**

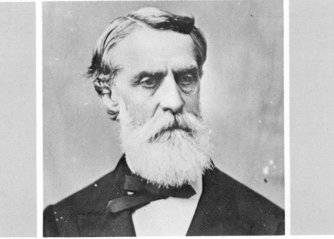

Charles Reed Bishop   **State Archives**

Honolulu Harbor in 1873   **State Archives**

they were on a confidential mission to ascertain the defense capabilities of the various ports and commercial facilities in the islands. Aided by Bishop and other local authorities, the two generals remained in the islands for about two months gathering information. In their report (which wasn't made public for twenty years), they stressed the strategic importance of Pearl Harbor and its potential as a naval base as well as other commercial purposes. The report also commented on the fact that it was the only large natural harbor in the islands and that development would cost a great deal of money since a large coral reef blocked the entrance channel.

Most modern authorities estimate the population of Hawaii at the time of Captain Cook's arrival to the islands at between 200,000 and 300,000. The higher figure is frequently used since a few of the early visitors to the islands, including Captain Clerke who came with Cook, estimated figures in excess of 300,000. In any event, the population started decreasing rapidly and continued its long decline for almost a century. It wasn't until the arrival of the American Protestant Missionaries that actual censuses were conducted. The Hawaiian government conducted its first complete census in 1850. An estimated low point of 53,900 was reached early in 1876. From that point on, growth was rapid owing to the large in-migration of foreigners and organized immigration of laborers for the plantations.

Many reasons have been put forth for the sharp decline in the native Hawaiian population. The early visitors brought gonorrhea and syphilis which caused sterility and stillbirths. Since diseases were literally unknown in early Hawaii, the early natives had no natural immunity. Later visitors brought in a vast array of diseases including cholera (1804), influenza (1820's), mumps (1839), measles and whooping cough (1848-1849) and smallpox (1853). Spreading in epidemic proportions, these diseases decimated the Hawaiian population which didn't have any built-in resistance to these diseases. Territorial wars, including Kamehameha the Great's unification drive, caused untold battlefield deaths and produced famine in a number of areas. Also, fertility was low and infant mortality, partially caused by infanticide, was exceptionally high. Finally, exploitation by native chiefs and foreigners alike plus despondency in many individuals caused additional deaths.

In the decade of the 1870's, leprosy became a serious threat to the population of Hawaii. Called *Mai Pake* (Chinese disease) by the natives, leprosy had been around for almost thirty years. Mildly contagious and slow in developing, it began making noticeable inroads in the 1860's, especially among the natives. Leprosy usually involves the nerves, skin, and eyes. Left untreated, it causes the bones in the hands and feet to shrink, leaving them deformed and subject to injury. The disease also weakens the immune system.

In 1865, the Board of Health received authority to enforce segregation of individuals stricken with the disease. Also during the same year, the board established a main isolation settlement on the north side of the island of Molokai. By 1872, almost 600 people had been sent to the settlement. During this period, friends and relatives of the afflicted were allowed to live in the settlement and care for them. Housed in the few residences of the former land owners, these people were expected to continue cultivating the existing crops and, in effect, become self-sufficient. But this goal was not realized and conditions rapidly deteriorated. In the early years, there was no resident doctor nor any hospital facilities nor any provisions made to treat the patients.

In early 1873, an investigation revealed that many infected individuals were living among healthy members of the general population. Following the advise of Dr. George Trousseau, a medical member of the new Board of Health appointed by Lunalilo, the government carried out an immediate and energetic effort to fully enforce the segregation and isolation plan previously adopted in 1865. Before the year ended, over five hundred new victims of the disease were discovered and sent to the settlement, doubling its population. Included in this group was Peter Y. Kaeo, a cousin of Queen Emma and a member of the House of Nobles. Friends and relatives of the afflicted were no longer allowed to go to the settlement. This policy reversal caused bitter resentment among the Hawaiian people toward the government and also their king.

In mid-April of 1873, the editor of the bilingual newspaper *Nuhou* suggested that King Lunalilo pay a royal visit to the settlement at Kalawao in a good-will gesture to inspire and console his exiled subjects. The editor further suggested that "if a noble Christian priest, preacher or sister should be inspired to

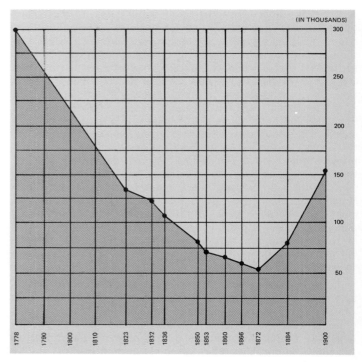

(IN THOUSANDS)

**Population of Hawaii —
1778 to 1900**

**Compiled From Various
Official Sources[1]**

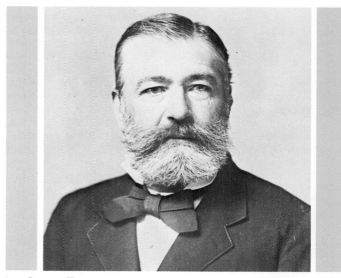

Dr. George Trousseau   **State Archives**

go and sacrifice a life to console these poor wretches, that would be a royal soul to shine forever on a throne reared by human love." Lunalilo did not go, sending instead two members from the Board of Health. But a Catholic priest named Father Damien[2] went to the settlement carrying only his prayer book. Bishop Maigret had intended for Damien to remain only about two weeks. But the public response to this singular act in the wake of the tightening segregation and isolation laws was overwhelming. The Honolulu press praised his actions and a surge of charitable feelings spread among many well-meaning citizens.

---

[1] Two of these sources are "Demographic Statistics of Hawaii, 1778-1965" by Robert C. Schmitt and "Atlas of Hawaii," by the University of Hawaii, Dept. of Geography. See bibliography at the end of this publication for publication data.

[2] Father Damien's original name was Joseph De Veuster. He took the name Brother Damien on February 2, 1859 when he took the religious habit with the Sacred Hearts Fathers. He arrived in Honolulu on March 19, 1864.

The Protestants were embarrassed by all the notoriety heaped upon Damien. They quickly pointed to the fact that a Protestant church had been built at the settlement several years prior to the Catholics constructing their church there. They also pointed to the fact that a Protestant deacon, a native Hawaiian who had contracted the disease, was now living at the settlement. In addition, they mentioned the fact that a healthy Mormon elder lived at the settlement with his diseased wife and held services there. But these and other evidences of good-will toward the patients including previous visits by other Sacred Hearts Fathers, had all taken place without fanfare. Father Damien alone excited the press and the people. The people believed that Damien went to the settlement at Kalawao voluntarily and that he would stay permanently to live and work among the patients. Bishop Maigret had planned to assign four priests to serve the settlement on a rotating basis. But the public response made this plan infeasible — almost anticlimatic. Not knowing how long he would be permitted to stay, Damien set to work comforting the poor souls of the sufferers, unaware that the decision to leave him there had already been made.

Lunalilo escaped leprosy, but in the middle of August, 1873, he was taken seriously ill with chest pains and a severe cold. He retired to his summer palace at Waikiki with his ministers, physicians and close friends. Avoiding public contact, his health improved, but he never returned to a normal state of health. Lunalilo's doctors called for complete abstention from intoxicating drinks, but the king would not hear of it. Recovering from pneumonia, he contracted pulmonary tuberculosis in his weakened condition.

In September, the sick and weary monarch faced a mutiny by the Household Troops. This group of approximately sixty men comprised the entire standing army of the kingdom! The mutiny revolved around the troops' bitter dislike for their drillmaster, a Hungarian named Captain Joseph Jajczay, and their resentment for the adjutant general, Charles H. Judd. Demanding the removal of the two officers, the mutineers occupied their barracks across from the palace, refused to leave, and then sent a delegation of three soldiers to the king, pleading their cause and attempting to get the king's personal assurance that they would not be punished. While the king pondered the situation, a court of inquiry was held but little resulted. Two companies of volunteers were called out, but they didn't do much except serve as guards while a push and shove situation took place for several days. The king finally agreed to protect the mutineers from injury and then abruptly disbanded the Household Troops except for the royal band. The kingdom was left without any regular, organized military protection.

The government was humiliated. Rumors circulated that David Kalakaua, a former candidate for the throne, had used the barracks mutiny for his own personal advantage. Lunalilo attempted to sidetrack the crisis by returning to the palace in Honolulu. In November, the king's health began to deteriorate again, and Dr. Trousseau suggested the king attempt recuperation in the warmer sunshine and clear sea air at Kailua on the island of Hawaii. But this change didn't help and the king's condition grew steadily worse. In mid-January, 1874, Lunalilo returned to Honolulu as an invalid, having had to be carried ashore.

Lunalilo clung to life for about two more weeks, dying on February 3, 1874 barely passing his thirty-ninth birthday. His reign was the shortest of any monarch—one year and twenty-five days. Often called the "people's king," Lunalilo left all of his estate for the establishment of a home for "poor, destitute and infirm people of Hawaiian blood or extraction, giving preference to old people." The Lunalilo Home later became an enduring monument to his memory.

Like his predecessor Kamehameha V, Lunalilo died a bachelor and consequently had no direct heirs to the throne. Likewise, he failed to appoint a successor, saying repeatedly that he had

Father Damien State Archives

Last Photograph of King Lunalilo State Archives

The Lunalilo Mausoleum State Archives

not made up his mind. Having felt slighted by the clannish Kamehameha family, Lunalilo's last wish was to be buried away from them. So instead of being entombed in the Royal Mausoleum in Nuuanu Valley, Lunalilo was buried in a separate mausoleum constructed after his death. Located in a corner of the cemetery at the entrance to Kawaiahao Church, the Lunalilo Mausoleum, with the remains of his family nearby, stands aloof to the remnants of the other reigning monarchs in the Royal Mausoleum.[1]

---

[1] The Royal Mausoleum, completed in 1865, houses the bodies of the descendants of the Kamehameha and Kalakaua families with the exception of Kamehameha the Great. His body, hidden in a cave on the island of Hawaii, was never recovered.

Pomp and Circumstance

Chapter 9

David Kalakaua[1]   State Archives

Queen Emma   State Archives

Once again, the Hawaiian Kingdom was thrown into disarray over the matter of succession. Once again, the names of the same small group of native alii came up for consideration to replace the deceased king. But of this group, only three were considered serious contenders: David Kalakaua, Queen Emma and Bernice Pauahi. Kalakaua, known to his friends and associates as "Taffy," became the most active contender. Having accepted his earlier defeat to Lunalilo with dignity, Kalakaua had been rewarded with an appointment to the king's military staff with the rank of colonel. During Lunalilo's brief reign, Kalakaua actively worked at achieving his ambition of becoming king someday. He took part in public discussions, formed a military company of young Hawaiians and became their leader, and he openly supported the popular slogan of the time - "Hawaii for the Hawaiians." On February 4, 1874, the day after Lunalilo's death, Kalakaua announced his candidacy in a straight-forward manner, expressing his desire to preserve the crown and the independence of the kingdom and its people.

The following day, Queen Emma who had not been a serious candidate in the past because of her support for Lunalilo,

announced her candidacy for the throne and asserted that the late king had intended her to become his successor. Since Kalakaua had the support of nearly all the local newspapers, Queen Emma and her followers resorted to distributing placards and handbills, both in English and Hawaiian, throughout the city causing a propaganda war to take place. Bernice Pauahi, handicapped by an American husband, displayed little desire to seek the throne.

While a number of Americans in Honolulu distrusted Kalakaua, their only other alternative was Queen Emma who displayed a distinct partiality for the British. So the politically active Americans concluded that their interests would be better protected by Kalakaua and they gave him their support. Much of this support can be traced to a letter which Kalakaua had written to the *Pacific Commercial Advertiser* the previous December. Dated December 9, 1873, the letter was published December 13. It reviewed recent occurrences in a conciliatory and conservative tone, expressed Kalakaua's confidence in the good faith of the United States government and flatly denied that Hawaiians were hostile to foreigners. Kalakaua had hoped that the letter would bring about a reconciliation between himself and the Americans and indeed it did!

---

[1] Kalakaua is wearing the uniform of a Scottish Rite Mason.

Within hours after Lunalilo had died, the king's cabinet scheduled a special meeting of the legislature for February 12 to take up the matter of royal succession. This nine-day period allowed the legislators from the outer islands sufficient time to journey to Honolulu. It also allowed the two candidates sufficient time to wage a furious campaign for the vacant throne. With three warships in Honolulu Harbor (two American and one British), the American Minister, Henry A. Peirce, arranged a shore-to-ship signal with the senior American naval officer to land troops should violence erupt. At noon on February 12, the legislature convened in the court house and proceeded with the election of a new monarch for the kingdom. Each legislator received two ballots: a plain one for Queen Emma and one with a large black heart on it for Kalakaua. Many of these legislators were native Hawaiians and they had recently been elected. Influenced by the events of the previous year, most were favorable to the candidacy of Kalakaua. When the ballots were counted, Kalakaua emerged victorious receiving thirty-nine of the forty-five votes cast.

The legislature appointed a committee of five to notify Kalakaua of his victory. As the committee members left the court house to enter a waiting carriage, they were attacked by Queen Emma's supporters who had just heard of the election results. Several committee members were wounded before they managed to get back inside the court house. The angry supporters demolished the carriage and used the pieces as clubs. They stormed the court house, throwing sticks and rocks and breaking windows. They managed to get inside through an unguarded rear door, and once inside, they smashed furniture, tore books and scattered papers, and attacked members of the legislature who were desperately trying to escape. More than a dozen legislators were wounded, and one member who was tossed out of a second-story window later died from his injuries.

While the number of rioters was small in comparison to the large crowd outside, little was done to restrain the attackers. The police were totally ineffective; many simply took off their badges and mingled with the crowd. The standing army had been disbanded the year before and although the militia companies were still in existence, many of their troops were new and white or part-white and evidently no one wanted to turn them loose on a rioting native mob. So with the riot in full swing, the new king along with minister Charles Bishop and the Governor of Oahu, John O. Dominis, asked American Minister Peirce to have the American warships send an armed force to put down the riot. Peirce sent his pre-arranged signal and within ten minutes 150 armed marines and bluejackets came ashore. Shortly thereafter, approximately 70 British troops joined the Americans. Thinking the British troops would help their cause, the rioters cheered the arrival of the British. Much to the rioters' dismay, the British troops aided the Americans in dispersing the crowd and restoring order. The troops arrested a large number of people and remained ashore eight days guarding government buildings until tensions eased.

On the following morning, February 13, Kalakaua took the oath of office in a simple ceremony held inside the disordered court house. The diplomatic representatives of the United States, Great Britain and France recognized Kalakaua as the new sovereign, thereby giving credibility to Kalakaua's election as king. Later that same day, Queen Emma, at the urgings of these diplomatic representatives, sent a message to the new king acknowledging him as sovereign. She also addressed her supporters asking them to accept the new king and to avoid any more acts of violence. The next day, Kalakaua personally called on Queen Emma to establish peaceful relations. While peace existed between the two rivals, there was no friendship between them.

One of the first important acts performed by Kalakaua was appointing his younger brother, Prince William Pitt Leleiohoku, as his successor, thereby restoring to the throne the function of selecting kings. Next, Kalakaua appointed his cabinet recognizing the cosmopolitan nature of the community:

Warships in Honolulu Harbor[1]   **State Archives**

William Pitt Leleiohoku   **State Archives**

as minister of finance a Hawaiian, Governor Paul Nahaolelua of Maui; as attorney general an American, Alfred S. Hartwell; as minister of foreign affairs an Englishman, William L. Green; and as minister of the interior a German, Hermann A. Widemann. Since Hartwell and Widemann were members of the Supreme Court, Kalakaua appointed Charles C. Harris and A. Francis Judd, both lawyers, to replace them.

Another early act performed by Kalakaua was the creation of a new military organization to replace the previously disbanded Household Troops. This new organization consisted of one regular company known as the "Royal Guards" and three volunteer companies: "The Leleiohoku Guard" (calvary); "The Prince's Own" (artillery); and "The Hawaiian Guards" (infantry). In addition, "Articles of War" were drafted and officially announced. Kalakaua had a special fondness for military matters and he took great pride in wearing elaborate military uniforms.

---

[1] This photograph was taken March 9, 1874 and shows an additional warship on the far right which wasn't in port at the time of the February 12 riot. Left to right, the ships are: *USS Tuscarora, USS Portsmouth, HMS Tenedos,* and *USS Benicia.* The *Benicia* arrived at the end of February.

Kalakaua did not ascend the throne a bachelor like his two predecessors. Instead, he had a wife, Julia Kapiolani, whom he had married in 1863. Kapiolani was the grand-daughter of Kaumualii, the last king of Kauai, and the widow of a chief named Benjamin Namakeha. But despite their many years of marriage, the couple remained childless.

Queen Kapiolani accompanied her husband, his staff and other attendants on a royal procession through the kingdom shortly after the king organized his new administration. Everywhere they went, they received enthusiastic welcomes. In fact, the king's support was better on the outer islands than on the island of Oahu. In speaking to his people, Kalakaua projected a fatherly image and always dwelt on the same problem that had been plaguing the kingdom for years - the decline in the native population. He hoped to restore new life and new vigor into the nation by increasing the population and by advancing agriculture and commerce.

As they had done in the past with each new reigning monarch, the sugar planters and other business interests lost no time in attempting to revive the movement to secure a reciprocity treaty with the United States. While Kalakaua opposed surrendering Pearl Harbor or any other Hawaiian territory to affect a treaty, he was not opposed to a simple reciprocity treaty, and in fact he recognized that it would be a great victory for his administration to get one. In addition, he saw the treaty negotiations as a means for him to visit the United States and possibly Europe.

Two treaty negotiators, Elisha Allen and Henry A.P. Carter, left Honolulu on October 18, 1874 and arrived in Washington in mid-November after making a brief stop in San Francisco. But their efforts soon bogged down in the same old objections that had been voiced in the past. On November 17, Kalakaua and his royal party boarded the *USS Benicia* as guests of the American government and were conveyed to San Francisco. On arrival, they received gun salutes, ceremonious honors and other demonstrations of high honor from General Schofield representing the United States and Mayor James Otis on behalf of the city of San Francisco. Kalakaua and his party spent a week in California and then traveled by train to Washington, arriving on December 12 to an official welcoming party. Kalakaua thus became the first monarch of any country to visit the United States.

Queen Kapiolani   State Archives

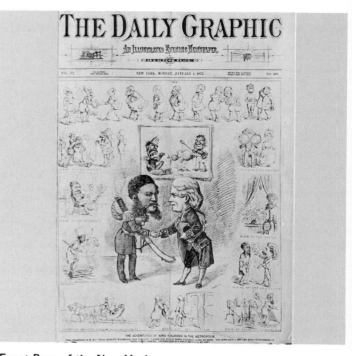

Front Page of the New York
Daily Graphic, January 4, 1875[2]   State Archives

Kalakaua spent the next ten days in an almost continuous round of official and unofficial entertainment highlighted by a state dinner hosted by President Grant. He also attended a reception by Congress in joint session. Not involved in the direct negotiations for reciprocity, Kalakaua's visit focused attention on relations between the two countries and greatly increased interest in the reciprocity discussions. Leaving Washington, Kalakaua then spent a week in New York making the rounds as depicted on the front page of *The Daily Graphic* shown above. Later, he visited New Bedford, Boston, and other New England cities before returning to San Francisco via stops in Niagara, Chicago, St. Louis, and Omaha. The *USS Pensacola* then conveyed Kalakaua and his party back to Honolulu where they arrived on February 15, 1875.

The Reciprocity Commission[1]   State Archives

---

[1]Members of the commission are left to right: (seated) Governor John O. Dominis of Oahu, King Kalakaua and Governor John M. Kapena of Maui; (standing) United States Minister to Hawaii Henry A. Peirce and Luther Severance.

[2]In addition to lampooning various phases of Kalakaua's visit to New York, the newspaper portrays Kalakaua meeting Father Knickerbocker, the legendary greeter of the city, and also ridicules the king's homeland by depicting the inhabitants as savage and pagan cannibals.

After the king's departure from Washington, the Hawaiian negotiators, Allen and Carter, resumed their discussions with Secretary of State Hamilton Fish. In early January, 1875, the rough draft of a treaty reached President Grant and his cabinet. Minister Peirce, who stayed behind when Kalakaua left, spoke favorably for the treaty, saying to the Senate's committee on foreign relations "If reciprocity of commerce is established between the two countries, there cannot be a doubt that the effect will be to hold those islands with hooks of steel in the interests of the United States, and to result finally in their annexation to the United States." His speech also stressed the importance of the islands in guarding the Pacific states, and he explained that failure to affect a treaty would force the Hawaiian government to seek closer relations with the British colonies.

The treaty reached the full Senate, and in the course of further discussions and a few heated debates, several amendments were added which bound the Hawaiian government from disposing of any territory to other foreign powers and also from allowing any other countries the privileges of reciprocity. On March 18, the Senate voted and the necessary two-thirds majority approved the treaty. But before it could take effect, it had to be ratified by both countries and then special enabling legislation had to be passed. The enabling legislation was introduced in the House in early January, 1876. Hearings were held and the bill was debated numerous times during March, April and May. Finally on May 8, the bill passed and was then sent to the Senate where it lingered in hearings and more debates. At last clearing the Senate, the bill putting the treaty into effect was signed by President Grant on August 15 and the treaty took effect on September 9, 1876.

The long delay in passing the enabling legislation to enact the reciprocity treaty caused much uneasiness in Honolulu and brought forth the prospect that it might fail. The treaty became one of the major issues in Hawaii's legislative elections held in early February, 1876. While several seats were lost to the opposition, a majority of legislators remained loyal to the king and to the treaty. The legislative session between April 29 and September 30 proved a trying time for Kalakaua's government. His ministry was criticized for its handling of the treaty, and other policies dealing with immigration and labor were likewise attacked. Twice during this legislative session, attempts were made to force the king's cabinet out of office for lack of confidence, but both attempts failed.

Word of the treaty's enactment greatly relieved tensions in Honolulu and gave Kalakaua's government a new sense of security. It also put an end to rumors that a conspiracy existed to assassinate the king, members of his household and several key government officials. A side effect of the treaty was a diplomatic dispute between Great Britain and Hawaii involving the most favored nation clause in their treaty of 1851. Henry A. P. Carter was sent to England and Germany in an attempt to persuade those governments to accept the Hawaiian view. After several years of negotiations, a change of government leaders in England, and the Hawaiian legislature of 1878 restoring tariffs to their former levels, the dispute was finally resolved.

After nearly twenty-five years of persistence, American planters and merchants in Hawaii had a reciprocity treaty which gave Hawaiian sugar preferential treatment over all other foreign sugar. Having a definite term of seven years, the treaty could be terminated by either side giving one year's notice. But since notice couldn't be given until at least the end of the seventh year, the treaty in reality ran for a minimum of eight years. Prices for sugar on the west coast of the United States did not drop as a result of the treaty. Rather, nearly all the benefits of the tariff's elimination accrued to the planters in the islands and a much smaller fraction to the refiners on the west coast.

Feverish activity took place in the expansion of the sugar industry. The number of business units active in its production nearly tripled from 32 in 1875 to 90 in the peak year of

Henry A. P. Carter   State Archives

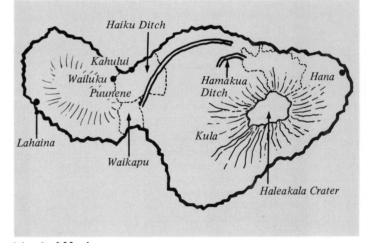

Island of Maui

1883. While many small independent planters and mills sprung up in the beginning, the long-term trend was for large, complete plantations that handled all phases of sugar production. Acreage devoted to sugar cane increased ten fold within twenty-five years and sugar production increased twenty fold during the same period. Since it required almost a ton of water to produce a pound of refined sugar, great improvements in irrigation, including aqueducts and artesian wells, enabled the rapid increase in acreage under cultivation. Aqueducts such as the Hamakua Ditch on Maui, a seventeen mile system of open ditches, tunnels and iron pipes, carried millions of gallons of water a day from mountainous streams down to the arid plains below. Soil analysis, commerical fertilizers, special varieties of cane and improvements in cultivation, transportation and methods of extraction all combined to vastly increase the yields from the cane fields.

This rapid expansion of the sugar industry required huge sums of capital. Ironically, most of the money came from reinvested profits, advances on future crops and loans from San Francisco banks. Few American capitalists took advantage of the opportunities opening up in Hawaii. Stringent financial conditions prevailed during the years 1879 and 1880 as local money was loaned or advanced to the plantations. No return could be realized for two years until the new cane matured and could then be harvested. The Hawaiian government even loaned money to Bishop's bank so that it could continue to make loans to the plantations.

One American capitalist who took advantage of opportunities in Hawaii was Claus Spreckels, a rich and ruthless California beet-sugar magnate. He foresaw the positive effect that the reciprocity treaty would have on Hawaii's economy and he came to Honolulu aboard the same ship that brought the news of the treaty's final approval. During his visit in 1876, he made contracts to purchase more than half of the total sugar crop coming up for harvest in the succeeding twelve months. Spreckels also made a shrewd investigation of business opportunities in the islands, and on Maui he got an idea for a grand project. His son, John D., purchased a part interest in a sugar plantation on Maui which opened the door for the father.

Spreckels returned to Hawaii in 1878 with his engineer, Hermann Schussler, and set in motion the first of his many enterprises that would make him an important individual in the political and economic history of the kingdom. Through purchase and lease, Spreckels acquired thousands of acres of land in central Maui. But to make it productive, an enormous water supply had to be provided. He applied to the government for a permit to bring water from streams on the northern slope of Haleakala[1] to his plantations in central Maui. Impatient with the slow pace of the government, Spreckels held a small party for the king in early July in which he gained the royal favor by giving the king an outright gift of $10,000 plus loaning him an additional $40,000 at 7% interest to repay other notes bearing an interest rate of 12%. Shortly thereafter, Spreckels received the water permit he was seeking.

Spreckels' engineer then supervised the construction of their grand plan - the Haiku Ditch, a thirty mile long waterway which would deliver 50 million gallons of water a day to the canefields on his Hawaiian Commercial & Sugar Company plantation. Built at a cost of $250,000, it was completed in 1880. Between 1878 and 1882, Spreckels acquired approximately 40,000 acres of Maui land using various devices from outright purchase and lease to blackmail.[2] He built a village, Spreckelsville, named after himself. Spending almost $4,000,000, he created the biggest, most modern, and most efficient sugar factory in the world and a plantation to match it. He revolutionized the industry with his technical innovations such as a five-roller mill,[3] using steam power and electric lights, building railroads for hauling the cane, and utilizing controlled irrigation.

Near the end of 1881, Spreckels established a shipping line between San Francisco and the islands. Known as the Oceanic Steamship Company, its modern steam-powered ships became an important link in Hawaii's commerce. Spreckels also established a bank, and his shrewdly placed loans bought the services of many politicians including the king. By 1884, Spreckels controlled the entire output of Hawaiian sugar. His plantations produced approximately one-third of island sugar, and through a partnership in the firm of W. G. Irwin & Company, he purchased the remaining two-thirds, thereby completely monopolizing the market. By this time, he also controlled the government by being able to get just about anything he wanted in legislation and concessions.

---

[1] A large, extinct, volcano in east Maui. The name means "House of the Sun."

[2] In 1880, Spreckels purchased from Princess Ruth Keelikolani all her rights and interest in the crown lands of Hawaii for the sum of $10,000. While she had no clear interest in these lands, their legal status was not fully understood and the government in 1882 granted Spreckels fee-simple title to approximately 24,000 acres of Maui land in exchange for surrendering his claim to an interest in the crown lands. Princess Ruth had claimed a one-half interest.

[3] The five-roller mill added an additional set of two rollers which gave the cane stalks a second squeeze, thereby yielding more juice which could be turned into sugar.

Claus Spreckels   **State Archives**

Spreckels (First Row with Floral Leis and Cane) and Party Aboard a Steamer   **State Archives**

The growth in the sugar industry brought a corresponding growth in the business community as well as in the population of the kingdom. Since Honolulu was the capital of the sugar kingdom, it likewise became the center for business activity. Of particular importance was the establishment of the "agency system." These were companies, usually the leading merchants in Honolulu, who served simultaneously as purchasing agents and sales agents for the plantations. They kept the plantations going by supplying laborers, arranging loans or providing funds or credit, cooperating with other agents, and representing the plantations in relations with the government. In addition, they sold the sugar and molasses that the plantations produced.

Samuel T. Alexander,
one of the founders of
Alexander & Baldwin, Inc.

Alexander & Baldwin, Inc.

Henry P. Baldwin,
one of the founders of
Alexander & Baldwin, Inc.

Alexander & Baldwin, Inc.

Samuel N. Castle,
one of the founders of Castle & Cooke, Inc.

State Archives

Theophilus H. Davies,
one of the founders of
Theo. H. Davies & Co., Ltd.

State Archives

The major agencies that served the plantations in 1878 in order of number of plantations served and extent of interests involved were:
1) H. Hackfeld & Company (German)
2) W. G. Irwin & Company (American: Spreckels involved)
3) Theo. H. Davies & Company (British)
4) C. Brewer & Company (American)
5) Castle & Cooke (American)
6) F. A. Schaefer & Company (German)
7) John Thomas Waterhouse (British)
8) M. S. Grinbaum & Company (German)[1]

While sugar dominated the agricultural market, other products were encouraged, including coffee, bananas, guava jelly and pineapples. Although the earliest recorded planting of pineapples dated back to 1813, they did not get a firm foothold in the Hawaiian economy until the end of the century. As an export item, their growth was hampered by the slow speed of ocean vessels at this period of time. Commercial canning of pineapples, first introduced in 1882 at Kona on the island of Hawaii, met with little market response and the venture was soon abandoned. Introduction of the Cayenna pineapple variety in 1885 gradually became the standard variety grown in Hawaii.

[1] Through acquisitions and consolidations, the top five companies emerged as "The Big Five" in Hawaii's business community. They acquired controlling interests, if not actual ownership, in many future businesses including railways, steamship companies, public utilities, banks, hotels and assorted retail establishments to name a few. Their influence spilled over into the political, educational and cultural life of the community. Alexander & Baldwin later replaced W. G. Irwin & Company, acquiring many of its agencies. American factors, Ltd. was created in 1918 to take over and Americanize the German controlled firm of H. Hackfeld & Company following America's entry into World War I.

The prosperity of the plantations created an almost insatiable demand for laborers. This situation, coupled with the continued decrease of the native population, created an urgent need for an increase in the permanent population of the kingdom. The government realized that both of these problems could be solved only by immigration from abroad. In 1874, the legislature appropriated $50,000 to be used for encouraging agriculture and immigration. By 1876, Chinese immigrants were flowing steadily into the kingdom, their passage partially subsidized by the Hawaiian government. But almost exclusively, only Chinese men could be induced to emigrate from China. Once their contracts were fulfilled, they abandoned the plantations and generally congregated in the towns, again adding to the labor shortages on the plantations. Other, more desirable labor sources had to be found, and the government actively sought out laborers in British India, the Portuguese Islands, Japan, and the islands of the Pacific.

After overcoming numerous difficulties, the pioneer group of Portuguese contract laborers arrived from the Madeira Islands in late September, 1878, joining approximately 400 other Portuguese who were already in the islands working as small farmers or dairymen, or working on the plantations and ranches. In the following ten year period, a total of just over 11,000 Portuguese were brought to Hawaii from Madeira and the Azores. Emmigration from British India, on the other hand, never materialized despite repeated attempts by the Hawaiian government.

In 1877, the Hawaiian government made another attempt to bring natives from the Pacific islands. In the course of approximately eight years, some 2,500 Pacific islanders, including a large proportion of women and children, were brought to Hawaii. Slightly more than 400 of these islanders came from the New Hebrides and other Melanesian islands; the balance came from the Gilbert Islands. But these islanders were not very enthusiastic laborers, and few stayed in Hawaii after their contracts expired. Private attempts to recruit immigrants from northern Europe were also not very successful.

So despite all efforts, both governmental and private, to encourage emigration from other nations, the Chinese continued to make up the largest share of imported laborers until 1885. In fact, once the human stream started, the government found it necessary to establish restrictions in an effort to control Chinese immigration. Between December 1, 1880 and April 2, 1881, over 4,400 Chinese were brought to Honolulu, creating a temporary labor surplus. Several ships, in addition to bringing laborers, also brought smallpox. Confined mostly to the island of Oahu, the disease spread rapidly striking mostly the native population.

Ever since 150 Japanese contract laborers had been brought to Hawaii in 1868, the Hawaiian government looked to Japan as a desirable source for large scale immigration. The Hawaiian-Japanese treaty of 1871 apparently opened the door for Japanese migration to Hawaii. But economic and political conditions in Japan, aggravated by tensions with China and Korea, plus the Japanese government's determination not to have its citizens labeled and treated as "coolies," prevented any emigration to Hawaii for nearly ten years.

Several significant events in the 1880's gradually reduced the reluctance of the Japanese government to allow its citizens to emigrate to Hawaii. In 1880, Robert W. Irwin, an American businessman, became Hawaii's consul general in Tokyo. Married to a Japanese, Irwin had been a long time resident in Japan and was well known and well liked in Japanese circles, both official and commercial. Also during 1880, Japan proposed a revision to the existing treaty between the two countries. In March, 1881, King David Kalakaua visited Japan during his world tour. He made a favorable impression with the Japanese and the following year he sent a diplomatic mission to Japan to discuss treaty provisions and also to touch on the question of immigration.

Portuguese Contract Laborers State Archives

Japanese Plantation Workers State Archives

While the Japanese government had softened its position on immigration, economic depression and discontent in Japan, especially among the agricultural workers, finally caused the government to change its position and allow a limited emigration to Hawaii. The first group of Japanese immigrants (943, including women and children) arrived in Honolulu in early February, 1885. The Japanese government monitored the treatment given this first group. The Hawaiian government, in an effort to make the immigrants' transition as smooth as possible established a bureau of inspection and interpretation. Assured that its subjects would receive fair treatment, Japan signed a treaty with Hawaii in late January, 1886 which paved the way for large scale emigration of Japanese contract laborers to Hawaii. Under this "convention system," a total of 28,691 Japanese immigrants, including women and children, came to the islands between February, 1885 and June of 1894.[1]

---

[1] The United States census of 1900 showed Hawaii's population at approximately 154,000, broken down as follows:

30,000	Hawaiians
10,000	Part-Hawaiians
27,000	Caucasians (Including 18,000 Portuguese)
87,000	Orientals (26,000 Chinese and 61,000 Japanese)
154,000	Total

Hawaiian Political Figures

Robert Hoapili Baker[1]

Curtis P. Iaukea

Simon K. Kaai

John M. Kapena

Edward K. Lilikalani

Robert W. Wilcox

Joseph O. Carter

William R. Castle

A. Francis Judd

Lorrin A. Thurston

Henry Waterhouse

Henry M. Whitney

Racial antagonism between native Hawaiians and foreigners had always existed, although serious confrontations were rare. The slogan "Hawaii for the Hawaiians" had been used to promote the political interests of several candidates during Hawaii's election for a new monarch in 1873 and again in 1874. An election for members to the House of Representatives had occurred on February 2, 1874, the day before Lunalilo died. The results of this election revealed the growing widespread prejudice of native Hawaiians against foreigners — only natives were elected. This was a positive factor in the election of Kalakaua to the throne. This racial antagonism intensified during Kalakaua's administration. New leaders in politics and business made their appearance during these and the preceding years, and many of these new leaders had been born in the islands and a number of them were children of missionary families. Being Hawaiian subjects, they actively participated in the political life of the kingdom.

While Hawaii had no organized political parties until late in Kalakaua's reign, two distinct groups emerged: native Hawaiians and part-Hawaiians in one group and haoles in the other.

Hawaiian Group

Robert Hoapili Baker
John E. Bush
Curtis P. Iaukea
Simon K. Kaai
John M. Kapena
Edward K. Lilikalani
William L. Moehonua
Joseph Nawahi
Samuel Parker
G.W. Pilipo
Robert W. Wilcox
(and others)

Haole Group

Henry A. P. Carter
Joseph O. Carter
*William R. Castle
*Sanford B. Dole
* A. Francis Judd
*Charles H. Judd
*William A. Kinney
*William O. Smith
*Lorrin A. Thurston
Henry Waterhouse
*Henry M. Whitney
(and others)

*Son of a missionary family

The rivalry between these two groups caused many of the political struggles during Kalakaua's reign. The Hawaiian group had the advantage of being more in touch with the major segment of the population. The haole group, on the otherhand, had some advantages in education and the practices of foreign governments since many of them had been educated in eastern schools.

---

[1]Baker is shown modeling for the Kamehameha I statue which will be discussed a little later in this chapter.

Walter Murray Gibson first appeared on the Hawaiian scene in July of 1861 when he arrived in Honolulu accompanied by his daughter Talula. His early life was filled with adventure, and his travels took him to New York, California, Mexico, Central America and finally to the East Indies where he narrowly escaped death at the hands of the Dutch authorities. Later, he became interested in the Mormons and their Utah settlement, and he was baptized in early 1860.

In Hawaii, Gibson kept his Mormon connections to himself as he quietly investigated the Mormon situation. He found the colony on the island of Lanai, called "The City of Joseph," literally abandoned due to the recall of its missionaries as a result of the Mormon War in Utah. Gibson quickly filled the void as a self-proclaimed representative of God and Brigham Young. Gibson's brilliant mind and ingratiating personality soon infused new life into the settlement. Under his careful guidance, substantial sums of money were amassed, and with this money, Gibson bought the valley of Palawai on Lani and began rehabilitating the settlement. Unbeknownst to the church members, Gibson had registered the land under his own name. Turning the settlement into his personal headquarters, Gibson found a rebirth and new beginnings in his valley "kingdom." His deviations from the practices of the founding elders ultimately led to his excommunication. But he steadfastly refused to give up title to the land and the settlement became his private estate which he developed primarily into a sheep ranch. Most of the native Mormons left the island for a new settlement on Oahu.

Having acquired a remarkable command of the Hawaiian language, Gibson later started a bilingual newspaper called the *Nuhou* which he published in Honolulu. In 1876, he took up residence in Lahaina, Maui after purchasing a business there. He got to know the Hawaiians better than most white men and soon became their champion against the businessmen of Honolulu and the planters of the outer islands, thereby setting himself apart from his fellow Americans. In 1878, he ran successfully for the legislature as a representative from Lahaina. During his first term, he kept a ferment of excitement in the air as he attempted to shine as a leader and protector of the remnants of the Hawaiian race. In the 1880 election, Gibson was again returned to the House of Representatives, this time by a large majority. During this second term, he was one of only three white men in that body.

Gibson ran for re-election again in 1882, this time as a representative from Honolulu. Despite heated attacks in the newspapers on his questionable past and his previous dealings with the Mormons, Gibson won his bid for re-election. These attacks on his past were useless as political weapons since most of his supporters were native Hawaiians who read only Hawaiian. Gibson was now a power to be reckoned with in any reconstruction of the executive branch. When the legislature convened in late April, 1882, the king's cabinet was shorthanded and disunited. The opposition, unofficially led by Gibson, strongly criticized the cabinet and demanded its ouster. On May 19, the entire cabinet resigned and the king immediately called upon Gibson to form a new ministry. The smooth-talking Gibson thus attained his goal to become administrative head of the government. He was now premier and minister of foreign affairs. Between 1882 and 1887, when Kalakaua kept changing his cabinet, Gibson remained, holding every ministerial post as well as many appointments of lower rank, often simultaneously.

Schemers and adventurers, by playing on Kalakaua's vanity or on his naive nature, could push the king into actions which invited political trouble. One such person was an Italian-American adventurer named Celso Caesar Moreno who arrived in Honolulu aboard a Chinese steamer in November of 1879. Because of his well-publicized exploits, which sounded similar to those of Walter Murray Gibson, Moreno received a favorable welcome in Honolulu. Having previously met Kalakaua in San Francisco in 1874, Moreno quickly became a close and confidential friend of the king, filling his head with grand ideas about

Walter Murray Gibson **State Archives**

Kalakaua in Uniform **State Archives**

trans-Pacific cables, trade with China, and enormous prosperity for Hawaii.

Moreno's lobbying activities, coupled with clashes between cabinet members and Kalakaua's alliance with Gibson[1] and Moreno against his own ministers, resulted in the king demanding the resignation of his entire cabinet on August 14, 1880. That same day, Kalakaua appointed a new cabinet with Moreno at its head. The announcement aroused indignation in the community to such an extent that a mass meeting was held by Honolulu's irate citizens on August 16 in an effort to get the king to change his mind. At the meeting, they adopted a resolution, introduced by Sanford B. Dole, which in part declared that the king's arbitrary "action therein is hostile to the permanence

---

[1] Gibson purchased the *Pacific Commercial Advertiser* during September, 1880. He now controlled two newspapers to publicize himself and his ideas: the Advertiser for English readers and the *Ka Elele Poaholu* for Hawaiian readers.

of Hawaiian independence, the perpetuity of the Hawaiian race and the security of life, liberty and property in the Hawaiian Islands." The resolution was forwarded to the king, but he did not respond. The diplomatic community, while maintaining its official policy of nonintervention, nevertheless refused to recognize Moreno's appointment. Two days later, American Minister J.M. Comly, after consulting with the British and French diplomatic representatives (James H. Wodehouse and J. L. Ratard, respectively), met with the king and tried to convince his majesty that Moreno was not only an unsafe advisor but was not even a fit associate. The king took the advice under consideration.

At another mass meeting called by Honolulu's leading businessmen and lawyers, word was received that the king had forced Moreno to resign. Not completely satisfied, the citizens continued the meeting in an effort to force the resignations of the other members of the cabinet and have more competent and suitable ministers appointed. To this end, they drew up a petition and sent it to the king. In the meantime, Moreno managed to stir up anti-foreign feelings among many natives who later held their own mass meeting to denounce the foreign element including the diplomatic corps.

Kalakaua remained under Moreno's influence right up to his departure on August 30. In late September, Kalakaua appointed several new members to his cabinet, including William L. Green a Honolulu businessman who served in the king's first cabinet. Claus Spreckels was in Honolulu at this time and he met with the king and remonstrated him for his foolish actions. Kalakaua then abruptly dismissed the entire cabinet and reappointed Green as minister of foreign affairs. Henry A. P. Carter was named minister of the interior and J. S. Walker was appointed minister of finance and acting attorney general until the expected arrival in late November of William N. Armstrong[1] from the United States.

For some time, Kalakaua had the desire to make a trip around the world. This topic was much on his mind during the closing months of 1880. Finally in January of the following year, Kalakaua announced to his cabinet that he planned to make a trip around the world, something no other king had dared. The official purpose of the voyage was to recuperate the king's health as well as search for new sources of immigration both for labor and repopulation. The king's ministers gave him a grand farewell banquet on January 14, and on January 20, 1881, the king and his party departed Honolulu for San Francisco on the steamship *City of Sydney*.

In California, Claus Spreckels wined and dined Kalakaua prior to his departure for the Orient. Sailing first to Japan, the royal party received a regal welcome and attended a series of receptions, dinners and other entertainment. The subjects of treaty revision and immigration were discussed, but no immediate decisions were made. Following his visit to Japan, Kalakaua visited China, Hong Kong, Siam, Malaysia, Burma, India and Egypt. Lavishly entertained in the splendid courts of these countries, Kalakaua and the other rulers exchanged decorations. After four months of travel in oriental lands, the royal party crossed the Mediterranean to Italy. Following an audience with Pope Leo XIII, Kalakaua and his party traveled to England where Queen Victoria and other members of the royal family entertained them. Returning again to the continent, they visited Belgium, Germany, Austria, France, Spain and Portugal. Returning again to England, the royal party sailed for the United States.

Kalakaua's European tour afforded him the opportunity to pursue two of his favorite personal passions: music and military

William L. Green   **State Archives**

King Kalakaua and Staff in Japan (March, 1881)[2]
                              State Archives

affairs. In writing to his sister, Princess Miriam Likelike, Kalakaua described Strauss's band in Vienna as "the best I have ever heard." In selecting the prettiest place he visited, Kalakaua wrote ". . . Paris seems to exceed all." In the United States, Kalakaua and his party visited New York, Philadelphia and Washington where he had an interview with President Chester A. Arthur. Traveling across the United States, they made stops at Chicago, Omaha and Ogden before arriving in San Francisco. In California, the king was again entertained and he spent several days at Spreckels' ranch where he was presented with several horses. The party finally arrived back in Honolulu on October 29, 1881. Their return was met by a large joyous crowd which had decorated the route from the dock to the palace. A celebration of music, feasting and dancing took place and lasted for several days.

---

[1] Armstrong was the island born son of Dr. Richard Armstrong who had served under previous monarchs. He also was a boyhood friend and former classmate of Kalakaua's.

[2] Seated, left to right, are: Lieutenant-General Prince Yoshiaki, King Kalakaua, and Minister of Finance Yoshii Amatami. Standing, left to right, are: Charles H. Judd, First Secretary of Finance Riyosuke Sugai, and William N. Armstrong.

On April 10, 1877, the heir-apparent, Prince William Pitt Leleiohoku, died of rheumatic fever. Kalakaua immediately proclaimed his sister, Princess Lydia Liliuokalani, as the new heir-apparent.[1] She was married to an American named John O. Dominis who served in the capacity as Governor of Oahu. The young prince's death was a serious blow to the Kalakaua dynasty since many feared a serious struggle would follow the death of the king. It was thought that Queen Emma's supporters might try to have her placed on the throne. But the passage of time and Kalakaua's continued good health soon eased tensions, and Queen Emma's attentions turned to church activities and works of charity.

Kalakaua restored the native hula to prominence and he and members of his family sparked and encouraged a revival in island music. Suppressed for many years, the expressive heritage of the Hawaiians emerged once again. Liliuokalani, like her brothers and sisters, possessed musical talent and she composed many songs, the best known being "Aloha Oe."[2] Prince Leleiohoku prior to his death had established an all male singing club and his sisters Liliuokalani and Likelike each formed clubs of mixed (male and female) singers. Performed in the old Hawaiian way, the songs were memorized and few were ever transcribed. During the Kalakaua reign, opera came to Honolulu as did visiting musical groups from other nations. Stringed instruments manufactured by enterprising Portuguese nationals became popular with many young native men. Bright uniforms and military trappings, splendid entertainment and glittering decorations became the order of the day.

Shortly after ascending the throne, Kalakaua let it be known that he wanted a new palace to match his new lofty position as king of the Hawaiian Islands. He considered the present palace "filthy and in poor condition," and he felt humiliated living in it. The legislative session of 1878 finally authorized $50,000 for a new palace. The design for the palace, prepared by Thomas J. Baker of Honolulu, was approved in July, 1879. The previous palace was razed and the cornerstone for the new palace was laid on December 31, Queen Kapiolani's birthday. An elaborate Masonic ceremony accompanied the cornerstone laying, since Kalakaua was a 33rd-degree Scottish Rite Mason and Knight Templar.

Completed in the latter part of 1882, the new palace was constructed of plastered brick and iron with concrete block trimmings. Its exterior was finished in a light-colored sanded paint. It consisted of two stories plus an attic and a cellar, and it was topped off by six towers. One tower occupied each corner of the building and a larger tower rose over each of the front and rear entrances. The corner towers prevented the lanai, or balcony, from surrounding the palace. A trench approximately six feet wide surrounded the palace to give light and ventilation to the basement.

A large hall with a staircase leading to the second floor greeted the visitor at the main entrance. To the right of the hall was the throne room, and on the left were the dining room and drawing room (later called the Blue Room). On the second floor were the queen's bedroom and two guest rooms to the right of the central hall and the king's bedroom, a library and a music room on the left. The basement contained the chamberlain's apartments, a workshop, billiard room and a kitchen.

The designer's initial estimate of $65,000 swelled to over $350,000 upon completion due in large part to Kalakaua's demands for regal splendor. The palace's interior, for example, was finished in various Hawaiian woods as well as American walnut and Oregon white cedar. An eight-foot-high wall of coral blocks surrounded the palace. Originally illuminated by gaslight

---

[1] Princess Liliuokalani served as regent in 1881 while Kalakaua circled the globe on his grand tour.

[2] Composed in 1878, this heart-rendering song spoke of a soft farewell.

Decorated Gate at Iolani Palace Honoring Kalakaua's Return From His Trip Around the World　　　State Archives

Princess Lydia Kamakaeha Liliuokalani　　　State Archives

New Iolani Palace　　　State Archives

in early November, 1882, the palace was later converted to electric light in mid-1888. A formal opening banquet was held for the Masonic fraternity of the capital on December 27, 1882 followed by a "Grand opening" and coronation ceremony in February, 1883.

One of the grandest events of the 1880's was the coronation of King Kalakaua and Queen Kapiolani on Monday, February 12, 1883 — the ninth anniversary of Kalakaua's inauguration. Funds to pay for the ceremony had been appropriated in the legislative sessions of 1880 and 1882. The total cost of the coronation celebration, which lasted two weeks, exceeded $50,000. While many local residents, most of foreign blood, objected to this extravagant waste of taxpayers' money catering to royal vanity, most native Hawaiians defended it. Preparations had taken months, and much of the clothing, jewelry and royal insignia, including two crowns, had been ordered from England and France.

A large pavilion[1] was built in front of the palace which connected to the palace itself by a bridge to the first-floor veranda. A covered amphitheater surrounded the pavilion on three sides and provided seating for several thousand spectators. The octagonal pavilion with its domed roof symbolized the crown, and its eight Grecian columned corners represented the eight inhabited islands of the Hawaiian kingdom. Other decorations included shields representing the insignia of some twenty nations plus Hawaii's coat of arms. Total cost: $4,850, a tidy sum in those days.

The formal investiture presented a mixture of ancient Hawaiian and modern European pageantry. The Hawaiian insignia included Kamehameha the Great's feather cloak (Royal Mantle), the tabu sticks (Puloulou), a whale's tooth necklace (Palaoa), and the royal feather standards (Kahili). The European regalia[2] consisted of jeweled crowns for the king and queen and a sword, ring and sceptre. After receiving his crown from the chancellor of the kingdom, Kalakaua placed it upon his own head and then proceeded to crown his queen. The warships in the harbor and the batteries on shore fired a salvo and the Royal Hawaiian Band played Meyerbeer's "Coronation March."

The king's crown was slightly larger than the queen's crown. Both had a gold Maltese cross at the apex and both were studded with diamonds, opals, rubies and emeralds. Custom-made in England, they cost $10,000. The rims, taro leaves and bars leading to the cross were gold. Each crown had eight bars which represented the eight inhabited islands of the kingdom. Velvet crimson caps lined the inside of the crowns.

The coronation celebration lasted two weeks and included a state dinner and coronation ball at the palace, a regatta, horse races at Kapiolani Park, hula dances, a luau and other entertainment. Also a part of the celebration was the unveiling of a statue of Kamehameha I in front of Aliiolani Hale across the street from the palace on February 14, 1883. Funds for the statue had been appropriated in the legislative session of 1878 to commemorate the centennial of Captain Cook's arrival in Hawaii. With nationalist tradition at a high state at the time of the centennial, the decision to erect the statue was one of the ways in which the emphasis of the centennial was shifted from the foreigner who arrived to the Hawaiian who met him. The statue would portray Kamehameha I as the warrior who united the islands under one kingdom and ushered in a new era of law and peace.

---

[1] Following the coronation, the pavilion was moved to another spot on the palace grounds where it still remains today. It has been used for a variety of purposes including a bandstand and a platform for public speaking and inaugurations.

[2] These items as well as several of the Hawaiian regalia are housed in the Bishop Museum in Honolulu.

Iolani Palace Main Entrance and Staircase   State Archives

Coronation Pavilion and Amphitheater   State Archives

King Kalakaua's Crown   State Archives

An American sculptor named Thomas R. Gould, who worked in Boston and Florence, was commissioned for the project. Gibson took a personal interest in the project and communicated frequently with the sculptor in Italy, supplying Gould with resource materials and criticisms on the various phases of the project. Working from a poor copy of Louis Choris' 1816 watercolor of Kamehameha I, Gould had to make him look as young as he had been in 1778. Numerous photographs of nude Hawaiians as well as several photographs of Hawaiians in full warrior dress were sent to Gould in an effort to have the statue show a true Hawaiian body. The pose and gesture of an outstretched arm were adapted from a classical statue of Augustus Caesar. The completed statue[1] welded the cultures of old Hawaii and the western world.

Kamehameha V ordered the formation of the Royal Hawaiian Band in 1870. Captain Heinrich (Henry) Berger, recently arrived from Germany, took charge of the band in June of 1872. Starting with a small group of young men, many from the Honolulu Boy's Reform School, Berger ruled with an iron hand and intimidated these would-be musicians until they played note-perfect. The band's size steadily grew as Berger added more members. Later in the century, a stringed instrument section was added to the brass and woodwinds sections pictured. Still later, native female singers were added bringing the band's total strength to approximately 48 members. The accomplished maestro remained in charge of the band for 43 years.

The band became a cultural institution in the city and King Kalakaua encouraged nearly everything musical and dramatic in order to bring gaiety and brightness to Honolulu. Berger mastered the Hawaiian language and transcribed countless melodies, chants and meles. Around 1880, Berger added music to Kalakaua's own composition of "Hawaii Ponoi" which became the Hawaiian national anthem at this time period. Seldom idle, the band played at coronations, inaugurations, funerals, steamship arrivals and departures, charity and military balls, state functions and holiday celebrations. The Royal Hawaiian Band also gave several weekly concerts at various squares and parks in the city. The band even accompanied royalty on state visits to the other Hawaiian Islands and in their spare time, its members played at private parties for many of Honolulu's leading citizens.

Because Hawaii's economic system was so closely tied to that of the United States, U. S. gold and silver coins gradually became the standard medium of exchange in the islands although coins of many other countries continued to have legal tender status at their current exchange value. Prior to 1884, Hawaii's money supply consisted of these gold and silver coins as well as paper certificates of deposit which represented coins on special deposit in the kingdom's treasury. These certificates of deposit were sometimes called "silver certificates" because the coins they represented were usually silver coins. First authorized in 1859, the certificates of deposit were issued around 1866 or 1867, but they didn't circulate freely until the late 1870's.

The earliest form of Hawaiian coinage was scrip issued by Ladd and Company in 1837 on the island of Kauai. The scrip's denomination was 12½¢, the value of a laborer's daily wage. The American Protestant missionaries also printed scrip in various denominations for use within their seminaries on Maui and Kauai in the 1840's. The Hawaiian government's first attempt at offi-

Statue of Kamehameha I   State Archives

Royal Hawaiian Band on
The Palace Stairs (1880's)[2]   State Archives

Hawaiian Paper Money
(Certificate of Deposit)   State Archives

cial coinage came in 1847 when it minted a small quantity of one-cent copper pieces with a bust of Kamehameha III on the obverse. But the coin's denomination was too small and it was not popular with merchants. It soon became a curiosity. The coin's failure to circulate freely discouraged the government, and plans for other denominations were abandoned.

---

[1] Enroute to Hawaii, the original statue was lost at sea in 1880 near the Falkland Islands along with the ship that carried it. A replica was ordered and it is this replica which was unveiled on February 14, 1883 and which still stands in Honolulu. The original statue later was recovered and erected in Kohala on the island of Hawaii, the birthplace of Kamehameha I. A third statue of Kamehameha is in the National Statuary Hall in the Rotunda of the Capitol in Washington, D.C. It was unveiled on April 15, 1969.

---

[2] Easily identified by his bushy beard, bandmaster Henry Berger stands in the forefront of this photograph.

Hawaiian Coin (The Kalakaua Dollar)

In 1880, the finance committee of the Hawaiian legislature, headed by Walter Murray Gibson, proposed a Hawaiian coinage in an effort to accommodate business, inspire confidence in the people, and add prestige to the kingdom. But nothing further transpired until the early part of 1883 when Gibson's ally, Claus Spreckels, was appointed the government's agent to procure a Hawaiian coinage for the kingdom. In exchange for interest bearing bonds backed by U. S. gold coins or their equivalent, Spreckels bought silver bullion and had it minted by the United States Mint into Hawaiian dollars, half-dollars, quarter-dollars and ten-cent pieces having a total face value of $1,000,000. Initially, a 12½ cent coin was to be minted but the idea was dropped in favor of the ten-cent coin in order to have all the Hawaiian coins conform to U. S. coins.

The dies were designed by Charles Barber at the Philadelphia Mint where several proofs were struck. The actual coinage, the same weight and fineness as U. S. coins, was struck at the San Francisco Mint and consisted of 500,000 dollars, 700,000 half-dollars, 500,000 quarter-dollars, and 250,000 ten-cent pieces. Because the cost of production was less than the face value of the coins, Spreckels pocketed a windfall profit of approximately $150,000. The coins arrived in Honolulu in several installments beginning in December, 1883 and by the middle of June, 1884, all the coins had been received. Their introduction into the economy roughly doubled the supply of silver coins in the kingdom and caused much controversy and criticism. Coinciding with falling sugar prices, the introduction of so much silver into the kingdom was believed to be partially responsible for a sharp rise in the exchange rate. Since silver coins were being discounted, the government employed various measures in an attempt to maintain an equilibrium between gold and silver coins. This resulted in the gradual elimination of coins from other countries as legal tender so that after 1886, only U. S. gold coins, U. S. dimes and half-dimes, Hawaiian silver coins, and new issues of certificates of deposit backed by U. S. gold coins were recognized as legal tender in the kingdom.

Kalakaua loved the sea and he delighted in the traditions of both paddle and sail craft. He had his own personal boathouse named Healani, an impressive two-and-a-half-story structure with a covered balcony and roof lookout. Located near Honolulu Harbor off the foot of Richards Street, the boathouse was linked by telephone to the palace. Here Kalakaua escaped the cares of state, often hosting high-stakes poker games or extravagant parties for his tight circle of friends. Many of the parties were held behind closed doors giving rise to rumors of ancient hulas being performed by naked young beauties and of more serious pleasure pursuits. Tables overflowed with a large selection of delicacies, and a plentiful supply of beer, liquor and imported champagne assured guests that an empty glass would not be tolerated!

The boathouse housed the royal barge as well as highly polished koa-wood racing canoes manned by the king's own racing crew. Kalakaua spent many hours watching and coaching the men who manned his racing canoes. To be chosen a member of the king's personal rowing team was a very great honor. Annual regattas, held on the king's birthday (November 16), were gala affairs that brought out stiff competition from other boat clubs.

Kalakaua's Royal Boat House (1885)   **State Archives**

Lavish Luau at the King's Boathouse   State Archives

Kalakaua's Boat Crew   State Archives

Queen Emma, widow of Kamehameha IV, died on April 25, 1885. The Honolulu Rifles, shown in the photo at right, made up only a small portion of the more than two thousand mourners, cavalry and foot soldiers who moved in a steady three hour procession along the mile and a half funeral route along King Street and then up Nuuanu Valley to the Royal Mausoleum. In ceremonies suited to her rank and importance, Queen Emma's remains were interred alongside those of her husband and her son. Emma's death was preceded by the deaths of two other important alii: Princess Ruth Keelikolani on May 24, 1883 and Bernice Pauahi Bishop on October 15, 1884, the last two descendants of Kamehameha the Great. With Emma's death, the last link to the Kamehameha dynasty was severed and it removed any further threats to the Kalakaua dynasty. Native opposition to Kalakaua weakened, and many of Emma's supporters transferred their allegiance to Kalakaua, thereby strengthening his administration.

Princess Ruth's will bequeathed her entire estate, both real and personal, to her cousin Bernice. Ruth had acquired great holdings, partly from the land division of the late 1840's (The Great Mahele) and partly through inheritance from her step-sister (Victoria Kamamalu) and her father (Governor Kekuanaoa). This left Bernice with a ten-fold increase to the lands she already held. The total acreage amounted to 375,569 acres, one-ninth of all the land in the kingdom. In attempting to follow the benevolent examples set by Queen Emma and her husband (Queen's Hospital) and Lunalilo (Lunalilo Home for aged Hawaiians), Bernice's will established the Kamehameha Schools, one for boys and another for girls, which gave preference to Hawaiians and part-Hawaiians. Her will also created the Bernice P. Bishop Estate,[1] a foundation which administered the royal lands and maintained the schools with the revenues derived therefrom. Later Mr. Bishop set up the Bernice Pauahi Bishop Museum Trust in his wife's memory and established the Charles R. Bishop Trust with his own funds to maintain the Museum.

Between 1872 and 1896, Honolulu's population doubled from 15,000 to 30,000. Most of this population increase became concentrated in the older sections of the city, especially

---

[1] Prompted by her husband, Bernice's will contained a provision restricting the sale of lands in the estate except under certain conditions. This restriction later became widespread in Hawaii as land ownership became more concentrated and additional trusts were formed to administer these vast holdings. Even today, this system of leasing land is the rule rather than the exception, although it is coming under increasing attack particularly by residential users.

Funeral Procession for Dowager Queen Emma   State Archives

Devastation Caused by the Chinatown Fire of 1886   State Archives

"Chinatown." This area of the city had narrow streets and was covered with large blocks of wooden tenement-style buildings which had balconies protruding into the streets. Fire hazards abounded, and disaster finally struck on the quiet Sunday afternoon of April 18, 1886 leveling the entire area to smouldering ruins and leaving over 6,000 people homeless. The fire also claimed the old Bethel Church, a landmark in the city. While the total destruction allowed improvements in street plans and some building restrictions were implemented, the area soon turned into a slum again and another fire destroyed a large part of it fourteen years later.

**Jubilee Celebration in Front
of Iolani Palace** State Archives

Gifts Presented to Kalakaua at His Jubilee State Archives

In the grand style of his coronation, King Kalakaua celebrated the fiftieth anniversary of his birth on November 16, 1886. The legislature appropriated $15,000 for the joyous occasion which lasted two weeks. The festivities actually started the night before with huge bonfires atop Punchbowl crater, rocket displays and the firing of a twenty-one gun salute at midnight. The cele-

One of Honolulu's well-known local characters, referred to as "Dandy" Ioane, provided many of the hula dancers for King Kalakaua's coronation and jubilee celebrations. As a hula master, dance instructor, banjo strummer, jew's-harp virtuoso and dandy extraordinary, Ioane gave many interesting and varied command performances for Kalakua, members of the royal circle and other prominent residents of the community.

**Grand Regatta at Kalakaua's
Jubilee Celebration** State Archives

Government officials, diplomatic representatives, various Hawaiian societies and the general population, both natives and haoles paid homage to the king on his birthday. The photograph above shows the many gifts Kalakaua received from his admirers.

"Dandy" Ioane Ukeke and Hula Dancers State Archives

**Princess Liliuokalani and
Queen Kapiolani (seated) in England in 1887** State Archives

bration included many of the same types of entertainment that accompanied the coronation celebration: lavish receptions at the palace, parades, regattas and other aquatic sports, competitive games, military drills and competitions, hula dances, a grand luau, balls and many speeches praising the king and the prosperity that the islands were enjoying. The jubilee celebration culminated in a giant state dinner on November 29.

Another jubilee celebration took place the following year, this time in Great Britain in honor of Queen Victoria's fiftieth anniversary of her accession to the throne, June 20, 1887. Hawaii sent a delegation to this joyful commemoration. Headed by Queen Kapiolani, the group also included the heiress-apparent Princess Liliuokalani and her husband John O. Dominis, Colonel Curtis P. Iaukea the king's chamberlain, and Colonel James H. Boyd the queen's aide-de-camp. Prior to reaching England, the group spent some time touring the United States.

Chapter 10

Reform and Rebellion

Lack of harmony in Kalakaua's cabinet plus the king's inclination to dismiss his cabinet ministers at will and appoint new members led to frequent cabinet changes during Kalakaua's seventeen-year reign. A total of thirty-seven men received cabinet appointments, eleven of whom were Hawaiians or part-Hawaiians. These frequent changes in the top administrative posts made consistent and constructive policy very difficult. Gibson added still more confusion and discontent by his policy of dismissing old and faithful government officials and members of administrative boards and replacing them with people who were more in accord with his own views. Gibson even assumed the presidency of several important boards (health and education) during this time. Despite growing opposition, Kalakaua and Gibson maintained control through the king's power of appointing his cabinet and members of the House of Nobles.

The passage of a $2 million loan authorization in 1882 opened the door for gross extravagance and put the kingdom in debt to Claus Spreckels. While Spreckels was not a Hawaiian citizen and never held any official position in the government, he could and did get almost anything he wanted. He held more than half of the kingdom's national debt, he held the mortgage on Gibson's Lanai property, and Kalakaua had been personally indebted to Spreckels since 1878. Roads, harbors and other public-works projects were grossly neglected as funds were channeled into frivolous activities such as maintaining unnecessary agents in foreign countries, jubilee celebrations, excessive military expenditures and various other regal prerogatives previously mentioned.

The election of February, 1886 saw two complete tickets: the Independent or Opposition candidates, the majority of whom were haoles; and the National or Government candidates, all of whom were Hawaiians or part-Hawaiians except for one — Fred H. Hayselden, Gibson's son-in-law. The Independent ticket had gained strength in the 1884 election and they made a strong showing of candidates in the election of 1886. Among this group, Lorrin A. Thurston and Sanford B. Dole stood out as leaders, seizing every opportunity to point out the shortcomings and errors of the Gibson administration. To support the Government candidates, the king made two electioneering trips to Maui and Hawaii, bringing to bear upon the people his personal influence. Taking advantage of the king's exemption on import duties, the Government party distributed large quantities of liquor for election purposes. The election outcome proved victorious for the Government party, Hayselden topping the list with a record number of votes. In spite of growing opposition, it looked as though the Gibson administration was stronger than ever.

Encouraged by Spreckels, economy became the watchword in the Gibson administration. But this state of affairs didn't last long, and soon there was talk of floating a $10,000,000 loan, a good part of which was to be used to organize and equip an army as well as to establish a navy for the kingdom. Spreckels intervened again and caused several changes in the cabinet, one of which was the appointment of an attorney (John T. Dare) who had worked for Spreckels in California and had been in the islands only two months. Spreckels' dictatorial actions against Kalakaua finally reached the point where the king wondered if

Kalakaua and His Staff (About 1886)[1]   State Archives

Fred H. Hayselden   State Archives

he really was king. Embarrassed by Spreckels' dictates and open references by many people to "King Claus," Kalakaua managed to float a loan with a London syndicate represented in Hawaii by Henry R. Armstrong. While Spreckels was finally paid off and his hold on the Hawaiian government ended,[2] the government paid dearly. Administrative expenses were high since the bonds sold at a 2% discount and the syndicate took a 5% commission. In addition, a sum of approximately $75,000 somehow vanished and was never recovered. In all, the government paid almost a quarter of a million dollars to borrow one million.

---

[1] Left to right, the staff members are as follows: James H. Boyd, Curtis P. Iaukea, Charles H. Judd, Edward W. Purvis, King Kalakaua, George W. Macfarlane, John O. Dominis, A. B. Haley, John D. Ho t, Jr., and Antone Rosa.

[2] Threatening vengeance, Spreckels returned the royal orders that Kalakaua had bestowed upon him and he left the Hawaiian Islands on October 23, 1886. He returned to Hawaii in early 1889 and affected a reconciliation with the king.

During the 1880's, international rivalry intensified in the Pacific as Germany adopted an aggressive policy of colonization. Great Britain felt compelled to annex additional territory because of Germany's policy, and the United States, while not having colonial ambitions in the islands of Polynesia, nevertheless maintained an active interest so as to protect its position in the Hawaiian Islands as well as protecting trade routes across the Pacific. Samoa became a chief trouble spot in the mid-1880's as internal strife intensified between the conflicting interests of German, British and American nationals and between the consuls, special agents and naval officers of these great powers. It was against this background that Hawaii took an initiative against its neighbor Samoa, one of the few remaining independent island groups in the Pacific.

Gibson appointed John E. Bush, a part-Hawaiian who had previously served in Kalakaua's cabinet, as minister to Samoa and Tonga. Bush, his family, his secretary Henry F. Poor, and an artist named J. D. Strong departed Honolulu December 26, 1886 on their mission to assist the great powers in finding a solution to the civil strife in Samoa and, if possible, form an alliance between Hawaii and Samoa and perhaps Tonga as well. Shortly after arriving at Apia (Samoa) on January 3, 1887, Bush entertained King Malietoa,[1] his cabinet and other chiefs and officials at a magnificent dinner followed by toasts and speech-making which brokeup the following morning. On February 17, King Malietoa signed a confederation agreement linking him with Kalakaua in a "treaty of political alliance and confederation." Another all-night party celebrated the signing of this treaty which Kalakaua ratified in March.

The *Kaimiloa* ("the far seeker"), a former British steamer purchased by the Hawaiian government and repaired, refitted and armed as a naval training ship, sailed from Honolulu in May, 1887 to assist Bush in his travels among the islands of Samoa and also to make a favorable impression on the Samoan people with its visible, though modest, armament. Having suffered a mutiny two days prior to sailing, the ship was ill-prepared for its mission. The scandalous behavior of the crew on shore, in addition to its near total disregard for discipline, did little to impress the people of Samoa.

Bush's crude, sometimes comical, methods employed to bolster the Samoan king's position, plus his own personal conduct and excessive drinking habits combined with mounting pressure from the United States, Great Britain and Germany, forced the Hawaiian government to recall Bush and the *Kaimiloa* in June. But word of the recall didn't reach Samoa until the following month. After numerous delays and internal difficulties, the *Kaimiloa* departed Samoa on August 8 for its return voyage to Honolulu while Bush and his family remained behind. The arrival of four German warships linked with a declaration of war aimed personally at King Malietoa caused the Samoan king to surrender to the Germans in order to avoid bloodshed to his people.[2] Following the king's exile, Bush and his family returned to Hawaii, arriving in mid-November. If Hawaii had any additional notions on interfering in Samoa, they were quickly put to rest when the German government warned the American and British governments in August, 1877, that if Hawaii interfered in Samoa in favor of the deposed king, "the King of the Sandwich Islands would thereby enter into (a) state of war with us."

Opposition to Gibson's administration grew steadily during the latter part of 1886 and the early part of 1887 fueled by a growing list of government scandals and misadventures including the London Loan, the Samoa adventure and an opium licensing

The Hawaiian Legation to Samoa[3]   State Archives

Kalakaua Aboard the Hawaiian   State Archives
Naval Vessel *Kaimiloa*

scandal that personally involved the king. Newspapers, including the *Pacific Commercial Advertiser* which acquired a new-found independence following Gibson's break with Spreckels, lambasted the administration. Burlesque shows and printed pamphlets in ballad form also lampooned the administration, their main characters being easily identified with their real-life counterparts. As demands for reform grew louder and louder, the opposition forces began uniting to put an end to the extravagance, corruption and incompetence of the Gibson administration. This solidarity helped the rapid rise of a secret organization known as the Hawaiian League which, assisted by the Honolulu Rifles, contributed the most to the downfall of the Gibson administration.

Formed in the beginning of 1887, the Hawaiian League sought to secure reform in the government and to put a limitation on the powers of the king, allowing him to reign but not rule which in reality was what he had been doing the past few years. Prominent residents of Honolulu made up its early membership and included such names as Lorrin A. Thurston, William A. Kinney, Sanford B. Dole, Peter C. Jones, William R. Castle,

---

[1]King Malietoa at this time was struggling to maintain his position as the legitimate king of Samoa against a rebellious chief and former vice-king named Tamasese who the Germans supported.

[2]King Malietoa was restored as king two years later, although in a nominal capacity.

---

[3]Left to right, the members of the Hawaiian legation are as follows: unidentified man with top hat (may be artist J. D. Strong); Lieutenant Jerone Feary; Lieutenant Samuel K. Maikai; King Malietoa of Samoa, wearing a uniform sent by King Kalakaua; John E. Bush, Hawaiian Minister; and Henry F. Poor, legation secretary.

Clarence W. Ashford and others. Its active direction and management were directed by an executive committee commonly called the "Committee (or Council) of Thirteen." The league's early activity concentrated on recruiting members, and by the middle of the year, its enrollment numbered slightly over four hundred. While a few of its members were part-Hawaiians, it was strictly a haole organization composed of many respected citizens in the community. All members took an oath to advance the cause of the organization.

The Hawaiian League developed two inner factions: a radical wing which favored the abolition of the monarchy and the setting up of a republic, possibly even seeking annexation to the United States; and a conservative wing which favored retaining the monarchy, but wanted a change in the ministry and a drastic revision of the constitution. To this latter group, a republic was a last resort should the king refuse to agree to the reforms demanded. Thurston was an early advocate for establishing a "Republic of Hawaii."

Believing that Kalakaua would not willingly agree to its reforms, the Hawaiian League felt that a show of force would be necessary. To this end, the League provided its members with guns and ammunition, and formed an alliance with the Honolulu Rifles — an all-haole volunteer component of the armed forces of the kingdom. Organized in the spring of 1884[1] under authority granted by King Kalakaua, the Honolulu Rifles attained little importance until Volney V. Ashford was elected captain in late July of 1886. He had extensive and varied military experience both in the Union Army during the Civil War and in the Canadian Army. Being an excellent drillmaster, Volney Ashford brought the small group up to a state of great proficiency. By the end of June, 1887 when the political crisis came to a head, the Honolulu Rifles consisted of a battalion of three companies numbering about two hundred men.

In addition to the Honolulu Rifles, there were five other volunteer companies (King's Own, Queen's Own, Prince's Own, Leleiohoku Guard and Mamalohoa Guard) composed of Hawaiians and part-Hawaiians. These volunteer companies, in addition to the regular troops of the kingdom (King's Household Guard), formed the military force of the kingdom. John O. Dominis had been appointed commander in chief with the rank of lieutenant general.[2]

During this critical period, Gibson, who had burdened himself with nearly every important aspect of his administration, suffered from ill health and his condition worsened. Yet despite alarming rumors and the large importation of arms and ammunition into Honolulu, Gibson and Kalakaua felt that they could ride out the storm. However, they took steps to prepare the palace and other government buildings to withstand an attack. Kalakaua, after meeting with American Minister G. W. Merrill who impressed upon the king the seriousness of the present situation and advised him to listen to the voice of the people who were paying the taxes, summoned his ministers at 1 A.M. on June 28 and forced their resignations in the hope of quieting the mounting opposition.

But the resignation of the ministry failed to quiet the clamor for reform. On June 29, the *Daily Bulletin* demanded "A real, complete, thorough change . . . The king must be prepared to take his own proper place, and be content to *reign* without ruling. We want capable, *responsible* Ministers, not *irresponsible* clerks." On June 30, the Honolulu Rifles were called out to protect government buildings and to keep the peace. While the Honolulu Rifles had been called out by the government, they were also under secret orders from the Hawaiian League.

Lorrin A. Thurston   State Archives

Three Members of the Honolulu Rifles[3]   State Archives

Cartoon from *The Gynberg Ballads* (1887)   Bishop Museum
Depicting the Ouster of Gibson[4]

---

[3] Seated, left to right: Lt. C. J. McCarthy and Lt. A. W. Carter. Standing: Captain Clarence W. Ashford.

[4] Gibson was charged with embezzling public funds, but at his trial no evidence could be found to substantiate the charge and it was dropped. Gibson sailed for San Francisco on July 12. Suffering from tuberculosis, his health deteriorated and he died on January 21, 1888. His remains were returned to Honolulu for burial.

---

[1] An earlier volunteer company bearing the same name had been disbanded after Kalakaua's election as king in 1874.

[2] Kalakaua held the position of supreme commander with the title of Generalissimo. The act of 1886 which created this position was later declared unconstitutional.

During the afternoon, the Hawaiian League held a public meeting and drafted a list of five demands that they presented to the king. Basically, they demanded the dismissal of Gibson and the present cabinet and the formation of a new one headed by a person on their recommended list as well as extracting certain other concessions from the king.

Taking the demands under advisement, Kalakaua met with the diplomatic representatives of the United States, Great Britain, France, Portugal and Japan in an attempt to place the affairs of the kingdom in their hands rather than submit to the Hawaiian League. They refused, suggesting instead that the king authorize William L. Green to form a new cabinet. Following this conference, Kalakaua agreed in writing to the demands placed upon him. During the afternoon of July 1, Green put together a new cabinet with himself as head and minister of finance, Godfrey Brown as minister of foreign affairs, Lorrin A. Thurston as minister of the interior and Clarence W. Ashford as attorney general. All except Thurston were of British origin.

The Reform Cabinet, as the new Kalakaua cabinet was often called, set about its first important task to which it had committed itself — securing a new constitution. The actual drafting of the new constitution was done by members of the Hawaiian League. Rushed to completion in a matter of days, it was presented to Kalakaua on July 6, 1887. Sanford B. Dole, in writing to his brother on Kauai, expressed the mood of the times when he wrote "If he (the king) doesn't accept it, he will be promptly attacked, and a republic probably declared." After several hours of heated discussion and open argument with his cabinet, Kalakaua yielded to the pressures placed against him and signed the new constitution. Thereupon the chief justice of the supreme court was summoned and the king and his cabinet swore an oath to support the new constitution.

Dubbed the "Bayonet Constitution" because of the manner in which it came into existence, the constitution of 1887 revised the constitution of 1864, taking away from the king the greater part of his power and transferring that power to the cabinet thereby making the Hawaiian monarch in effect a ceremonial figure much like the sovereign of Great Britain. Some of the more important constitutional changes that took place were as follows:

- While the king could still appoint cabinet ministers, he could no longer arbitrarily dismiss them without a want of confidence vote by the legislature.

- The king's veto power no longer was absolute; it could be overridden by a 2/3 vote of the legislature.

- The House of Nobles became an elective office similar to the House of Representatives.

- The king's authority as commander-in-chief was modified, giving the legislature the authority to organize military and naval forces.

- Future amendments to the constitution were exclusively the prerogative of the legislature; the king's approval no longer was needed.

- The voting privilege was extended to all male residents at least twenty-one years old who had paid their taxes, had taken an oath to support the constitution and the laws of the kingdom, and who could read and write Hawaiian, English, or some other European language. In addition, residency and property requirements for voting were also imposed.

The Reform Cabinet now turned its attention to administering the government. While attempting to avoid an excess application of the "spoils system" in making appointments to government positions, the Reform Cabinet nevertheless gave preferential treatment to members of the Hawaiian League provided they were available and competent for the job. One persistent and demanding patronage seeker was Lieutenant Colonel

Sanford B. Dole   State Archives

Colonel Volney V. Ashford   State Archives

Volney V. Ashford, the commander of the Honolulu Rifles. Supported by a group of his personal friends, Ashford sought to get himself appointed as lieutenant general and commander in chief of all the armed forces of the kingdom, a position that would have made him the equivalent of a military dictator. Fortunately, cabinet disagreement and a distrust over Ashford's military ambitions prevented his appointment to the position he sought. But Colonel Ashford remained in charge of the Honolulu Rifles, thereby continuing to provide potential military support for the reform administration.

The constitution of 1887 required a new election for nobles and representatives within ninety days. Held on September 12, 1887, the election proved to be an overwhelming victory for the Reform Party. They considered their triumph as a ratification of the new constitution. While many native Hawaiians on the outer islands supported the Reform Party, the foreign vote (including the Portuguese) on Oahu gave the party its decisive victory.

Within weeks after the special September election, the subject of the reciprocity treaty came before the cabinet and the legislature. Although the treaty had expired in 1883, it continued in effect on a year-to-year basis until either side gave a year's notice to cancel. One of the main reasons that the treaty managed to continue in effect between 1883 and 1887 was Washington's fear over increased British and German activities in the Pacific.

In 1883, a commission appointed by the Secretary of the Treasury of the United States investigated alleged fraud charges against Hawaii's sugar planters, and their report refuted the charges. But the report portrayed the United States as the loser, financially, in the reciprocity treaty due to the sugar monopoly created by Claus Spreckels on the Pacific coast and the economic advantages enjoyed by Hawaii. Consequently, various proposals were presented during the numerous Congressional debates involving the treaty's renewal in an attempt to make it more advantageous to the United States. One proposal which gained momentum in 1886 was the Pearl Harbor amendment. This amendment called for the United States to have "the exclusive right to enter the harbor of Pearl River in the island of Oahu, and to establish and maintain there a coaling and repair station for the use of vessels of the United States . . . ."

The Hawaiian government had been steadfastly opposed to any action which would relinquish control of its territory and threaten its independence. But the events that had taken place in Hawaii during 1887, especially the Samoa adventure and the recent political struggle, had all served to darken Hawaii's relations with the United States. Fearing loss of benefits from the reciprocity treaty, the Hawaiian government took preliminary steps to open negotiations with Canada, but this idea never went very far due to a change in Canada's government in the summer of 1887. Finally after much discussion back and forth between Washington and Honolulu, notes were exchanged which clarified the Pearl Harbor amendment, stating in effect that Hawaii's sovereignty and jurisdiction over the area would not be impaired, that the Hawaiian government was not bound to furnish land for any purpose, and that the privilege to use Pearl Harbor would terminate simultaneously with the termination of the treaty.[1] This clarification received the approval of the Reform Cabinet. Kalakaua, though opposed and feeling powerless, reluctantly signed the revised treaty with the Pearl Harbor amendment in late November, 1887, thereby extending it for seven years.

With firm control of the legislature in the 1887 special session and the 1888 regular session, the Reform Party set about repealing a number of laws in an effort to reduce government costs as well as to undo some of the legislation passed in 1886. Several of the king's pet projects, including the board of genealogists which perpetuated the genealogy of Hawaiian chiefs and the native Hawaiian board of health, were subsequently abolished. Acts were passed to ease the naturalization process for foreigners and to regulate Chinese immigration. Also, other acts were passed which further curtailed the king's power or influence and tended to concentrate more power in the cabinet ministers. Kalakaua responded by vetoing those acts which eroded his powers. Yet even this power came under attack because the king disregarded the cabinet's advice and refused to consult with them. The legislature sent the bills back to Kalakaua for reconsideration, and after a second veto, considered them law anyway! The supreme court in early February, 1888 finally settled the matter, deciding in favor of the king's right to veto legislation without the advice and consent of the cabinet. This decision invalidated the acts which the legislature had put into effect.

During this time, relations between the king and his cabinet became severely strained, partly as a result of normal disagreements and partly because of the cabinet's desire to go its own way against the wishes of Kalakaua. As a result of this in-fighting, Kalakaua avoided meeting his ministers as much as possible, and he took a personal dislike to attorney general Clarence W. Ashford. To escape these and other embarrassments, Kalakaua spent a great deal of time on the island of Hawaii planning extensive agricultural operations if he could find a way to finance them.

---

[1] The United States did not take advantage of its right to use Pearl Harbor at this time, although a naval vessel had made a survey of the harbor in the spring of 1888.

Pearl Harbor (in 1890)   Bishop Museum

Kalakaua and Company Visiting a   State Archives
Monument Erected in Memory of Captain
Cook at Kealakekua on the Island of
Hawaii (February, 1883)

Waikiki Beach and Diamond Head   State Archives
in the 1880's

During the 1880's, numerous island residents began to recognize the tourist as a potential factor in Hawaii's future economy. While small numbers of visitors had been coming to the islands for many years, recent improvements in transportation to and among the islands had caused their numbers to increase to as many as 750 per year. As early as 1875, trans-ocean and inter-island transportation companies were distributing advertising material in an effort to attract visitors. During the late 1880's, several guide books and travel pamphlets as well as a monthly journal were being published specifically to promote tourist travel to Hawaii. In addition, several travel agents representing agencies in the United States visited the islands with the intention of promoting tourist travel to Hawaii. Much attention was given to the volcano of Kilauea on the island of Hawaii.

While Honolulu rose in prominence as the commercial and political capital of the kingdom, Waikiki remained a favorite recreational area for Hawaii's kings and higher chiefs. Many of their seaside homes were interspersed among a large coconut grove along the beach. Foreigners slowly filtered into the area, first to enjoy the beach and later to become residents. Many Honolulu citizens built beach residences next to a park adjoining Diamond Head which had a race track and landscaped drives. Improved public transportation to Waikiki, first by omnibus in the late 1860's and then by tramcar in 1889, led to a steady increase in visitors to the small number of bathhouses and seaside cottages in the area. Several attempts in the 1880's to convert private residences into hotels or resorts failed. Other attempts made in 1889 ("Waikiki Villa") and 1893 ("Sans Souci") were more successful. An early distinguished guest at the "Sans Souci" was Robert Louis Stevenson who stayed there during his second trip to Hawaii in 1893. But the only large, first-class hotel during this entire period continued to be the Hawaiian Hotel in Honolulu.

Tramcars came to Honolulu after the telephone and electric lights. Organized in England, the Hawaiian Tramways Company, Limited began track-laying in May, 1888. The first cars began service on New Year's Day of 1889 along King Street. By July, the system consisted of twelve miles of track. Authorized to use electric traction the following year, the company nevertheless preferred to use mule and horse power.

The discovery of artesian water sparked interest in the development of leeward Oahu. Much of it was a wasteland of unclaimed marshland, ponds and taro fields. A former Yankee seafarer named Benjamin F. Dillingham had envisioned a great land colonization scheme which included a railroad along the western and northern coasts of Oahu. With the support of several local businessmen, Dillingham persuaded the legislature of 1888 to allow his company, the Oahu Railway and Land Company, to construct and operate a steam railroad for carrying passengers and freight. Construction began in March of the following year, and by September, a short trial run had been made. Several months later on Kalakaua's birthday (November 16, 1889), the railroad officially opened to the public. Offering free passage on an eighteen mile round trip between Honolulu and Aiea, the railroad carried more than 4,000 passengers that day. The line eventually expanded to a total of seventy-two miles of track. "Dillingham's Folly" became a successful reality.

During the summer of 1888, Robert Louis Stevenson sailed from San Francisco bound for the South Seas in a rented ninety-five foot luxury yacht named *The Casco*. Suffering from tuberculosis, Stevenson thought that the warm climate and healthful beauty of Polynesia would help him regain his failing health and add several years to his limited life. Following visits to the Marquesas and the Society Islands (Tahiti), Stevenson arrived in Honolulu in late January of 1889. His reputation as a writer[1] had preceded him and he was greeted as a celebrity. Stevenson's friendly nature enabled him to strike up a close friendship with King Kalakaua and Princess Liliuokalani. Settling in Waikiki with his wife, children and mother, Stevenson proceeded to finish his latest novel, "The Master of Ballantrae." He often spent the whole day writing, many times wearing only his pajamas. A number of these writing days were interrupted by a constant flow of friends, well-wishers and curiosity seekers. Since the king spent a considerable amount of time in Waikiki at his beach house, Kalakaua and Stevenson frequently hosted luaus and informal parties for one another, the king having the decided advantage in consuming alcoholic beverages.

---

[1] In addition to being a regular contributor to leading magazines, Stevenson had already published "Treasure Island," "The Strange Case of Doctor Jekyll and Mr. Hyde," and "Kidnapped."

Tramcar on King Street   State Archives

Honolulu Terminal of the Oahu   State Archives
Railway and Land Company

Robert Louis Stevenson at King   State Archives
Kalakaua's Waikiki Beach House

Stevenson stayed in the Hawaiian Islands a total of six months, departing in late June still searching for the proper climate in the South Seas that would prolong his life. Weighing less than a hundred pounds, Stevenson had caught several colds in Hawaii and he therefore considered the climate too cold! He eventually settled in Samoa. In 1893, Stevenson returned to Honolulu intending to stay only one week. But he became ill and was forced to spend five weeks in Honolulu, residing again in Waikiki. After recovering, Stevenson returned to Samoa which he considered home. He died there a year later, a happy prisoner of the Pacific's climate and beauty.

Father Damien always felt that he would contract leprosy, but he put the patients' welfare ahead of his own health. Early on, he sensed that leprosy had invaded his system, and he traced the disease back positively to 1876 when he noticed skin lesions that did not show perspiration. These lesions subsided, but additional symptoms appeared several years later. In the fall of 1881, Damien experienced severe pains in his feet. By the beginning of 1883, he had experienced complete insensibility on one side of his left foot. In 1884, several doctors suspected that he had leprosy, and an examination in January of 1885 officially confirmed these suspicions. Damien's notoriety greatly increased when the public learned of his leprosy because many people felt that he had made the ultimate sacrifice.

Father Damien accepted his fate calmly. Although his physical suffering increased as the disease spread, feelings of loneliness and delusions of being unworthy of heaven tormented him the most. The years 1885 to 1888 were probably his years of greatest hardship. They saw Damien have increased conflicts with his superiors, and his praiseworthy accomplishments tested his humility and often put the government, some Protestant clergymen, and his superiors in a bad light, or no light at all.

Following the ouster of the Gibson regime, the new president of the Board of Health tightened the segregation laws dealing with leprosy. As a result of this crackdown, the size of the settlement grew rapidly, rising past 1,000 patients for the first time. But donations continued to pour in and Damien persisted in his work. In mid-November of 1888, a contingent of Franciscan Sisters arrived and set up a girl's home. Other volunteers also arrived, and the settlement now had a total of five churches: two Protestant, two Catholic and one Mormon. In February of the following year, Damien's condition worsened, and toward the end of March he became bedridden. Prepared for death, he died peacefully during the early morning of April 15, 1889. The following day, the forty-nine-year-old priest was buried under the same pandanus tree next to St. Philomena Church where he had spent his first nights at Kalawao.[1]

Believing that the king yielded too easily to pressures put upon him by the reform movement, several groups of Hawaiians sought to have Princess Liliuokalani replace her brother on the throne. While she encouraged these natives to put pressure on the king to abdicate, she did not advocate the use of force to compel him to do so. Also, abdication talk among cabinet members and several legislators arose briefly near the end of 1888.

Robert W. Wilcox[2] was the prime agitator among the Hawaiians. In 1880, Wilcox and several other young Hawaiians had been sent to a military school in Italy where they remained until the fall of 1887 when they were recalled by the Reform Cabinet as a cost cutting measure. Wilcox returned to Honolulu in early October, 1887 with his new wife, an Italian Countess. He resumed his political activity, easily attracting followers with this magnetic personality. Having been a friend of Gibson, Wilcox could not find employment in any area where he could apply his military skills. He finally found a job as a surveyor in the waterworks department, but soon tired of it and quit. Unable to find other suitable employment, Wilcox and his wife were be-

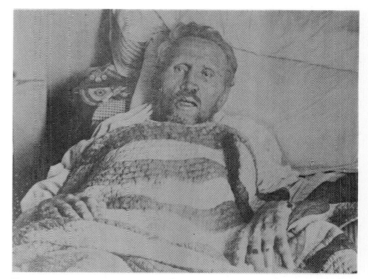

Father Damien on His Deathbed   **State Archives**

Robert W. Wilcox   **State Archives**

friended by Liliuokalani and lived for a while at her Palama residence. But Wilcox's political involvements combined with his unemployment, financial and marital problems, caused him to leave Honolulu for San Francisco with financial help furnished by the Italian consul, Liliuokalani and others. He arrived in San Francisco in mid-February, 1888, found employment as a civil engineer and stayed until the following spring.

Returning to Hawaii on April 7, 1889, Wilcox took up residence again at Liliuokalani's Palama dwelling which was unoccupied.[3] He opened a civil engineering office in Honolulu and later organized the Kamehameha Rifle Association. In June, he met with a small group of haoles and part-Hawaiians and formed a secret society known as the "Liberal Patriotic Association," of which Wilcox became president. The society's purpose was to restore the government and the king to their former positions and to get rid of the Reform Cabinet.

---

[1] All of Damien's belongings were fumigated and sent to Belgium where most of them were put on display in a museum attached to his family's home in Tremeloo. Some of these possessions can be seen today at the Damien Museum in Honolulu. At the request of the Belgian government, Damien's remains were exhumed in January of 1936 and returned to his native country where they were buried in the city of Louvain. On July 7, 1977, the Catholic church bestowed upon Damien the designation "venerable," the first step toward canonization.

[2] Born on Maui in 1855, Wilcox was a part-Hawaiian, the product of a Hawaiian mother and an American father.

[3] At some time during this period, Wilcox's wife returned to Italy and obtained an annulment.

Wilcox and his party held a final meeting on the evening of July 29, 1889, and very early the following morning (about 3 a.m.) they armed themselves with rifles, pistols and bird guns and marched toward Iolani Palace. Dressed in his Italian uniform, Wilcox and about eighty of his followers easily gained access to the palace grounds, but were prevented from occupying the palace by a contingent of the King's Guard. Occupying the palace grounds and several nearby government buildings, the insurgents positioned a small cannon at each of the palace's four gates. Kalakaua was not in the palace at this time,[1] but was nearby at one of the queen's residences. Wilcox sent the royal carriage there with a message inviting the king to return to the palace. Instead, Kalakaua, some of his staff and about a dozen guards proceeded to the king's boathouse and remained there for the balance of the day.

Informed of Wilcox's actions, government authorities positioned sharpshooters in buildings surrounding the palace yard and encircled the area with members of the volunteer forces. During the late morning, someone fired a shot and the fighting started. The insurgents managed to fire several rounds with their cannons, but they were quickly driven back by the sharpshooters. Shortly after noon, government forces rushed the occupied buildings, forcing Wilcox and his followers to take shelter in the Bungalow on the palace grounds. By this time, nearly a third of Wilcox's men had surrendered. Concentrated rifle fire peppered the Bungalow, and later in the afternoon several home-made bombs blasted the roof and second floor allowing several insurgents to escape. The rest, including Wilcox, soon surrendered and the rebellion came to an abrupt end. The insurgents suffered a total of seven killed and about a dozen wounded.

When the fighting started, a squad of marines from the USS Adams had come ashore to guard the American diplomatic compound. Also, the Adams furnished the government with about 10,000 rounds of ammunition, and later in the day sent a larger detachment ashore to assist government forces in preserving the peace during the night. But quiet prevailed, and the entire marine force returned to the Adams in the morning.

About seventy men were arrested for their involvement in the July 30 insurrection and they were indicted on various charges. Several escaped indictment by becoming witnesses for the prosecution. But of all those indicted, only three ultimately stood trial. A Belgian named Albert Loomens, who had been the vice-president of the insurgent organization, was found guilty by a foreign jury and was sentenced to be hung. However, his sentence was commuted to one year in prison on the condition that he leave the country. Another person, a young Chinese, received a fine of $250. Wilcox was the third person to be tried. The original treason charge was dropped when it became obvious that no native jury would convict him of treason. Wilcox had become a hero by the time he came to trial, and a native jury by a vote of nine to three found him "not guilty" even though sufficient evidence supported the conspiracy charge.

Following the July 30 uprising, the cabinet drew up a brief statement of principles in which they declared that the cabinet had the sole and absolute responsibility for conducting all departments of the government. Other actions were taken to lessen the danger of a repeat performance of the July 30 insurrection. All arms and other military equipment, except those used by the King's Guard, were removed from the palace and the barracks and taken to police headquarters. The size of the King's Guard was reduced. In addition, one of the native volunteer battalions was disbanded since few of its members responded to the July 30 call-up and in fact several of its members

Hale Akala, Backyard Bungalow on the   State Archives
Grounds of Iolani Palace[2]

Workmen Tearing Down the Palace Walls   State Archives
After the Revolution of 1889

had been involved in the Wilcox revolt. Finally, the high masonry wall surrounding the palace was reduced to a height of approximately three and a half feet, and an open iron fence was installed on top of the remaining wall the following year.

While Kalakaua did not agree with his ministers and their concept of government, he had no other alternative at the time. Being in sympathy with Wilcox's objectives of getting rid of the Reform Cabinet and obtaining a new constitution, Kalakaua bided his time, hoping for a political opportunity to arise. The upcoming general election in February, 1890, offered that hope. So did the growing dissension in the cabinet during the closing months of 1889.

A strong alliance of two political organizations emerged to challenge the Reform Party in the general election of 1890. Known as the National Reform Party, it consisted of the Hawaiian Political Association (called Hui Kalaiaina in Hawaiian) and the Mechanics' and Workingmen's Political Protective Union. The Hawaiian Political Association, dominated by native Hawaiians, sought to revise the constitution so as to maintain the Hawaiian people and their sovereign as the dominant force in the government. The other group, consisting mostly of haoles, sought to advance the interests of mechanics and workingmen,

---

[1] Several writers have theorized that Kalakaua knew of Wilcox's plan and was prepared to cooperate with him until the king learned that Wilcox also planned to depose him and put Liliuokalani on the throne. The exact intentions of some of the parties involved never surfaced, and in fact were sometimes contradictory.

---

[2] Built in 1844, the Bungalow served as the royal abode until the completion of Iolani Palace. King Kalakaua and Queen Kapiolani frequently fled the palace for the privacy of the Bungalow. The structure was razed in 1919.

and partly represented a defection from the Hawaiian League and the Reform Party. Opposition to the Reform Party and its administration served as the adhesive which kept these two groups together as the National Reform Party. Robert W. Wilcox, riding his wave of popularity among the native Hawaiians, rose to a position of leadership in the organization and represented its reactionary wing.

While the two political parties agreed on a number of issues involving domestic policies (such as efficiency and economy in government and promoting internal improvements), they differed widely on issues dealing with constitutional changes and foreign policy. In addition to seeking constitutional changes, the National Reform Party also pledged to maintain the "absolute independence" of the kingdom and opposed any treaties "which might lead to the practical annexation or absorption of our country by any other power . . ." As a result of the major differences on foreign policy, many British and German residents withdrew from the Reform Party and switched to the opposition party. This political in-fighting brought new hope to British Commissioner James H. Wodehouse who never abandoned the notion that Hawaii might somehow pull itself out of its close ties to the United States and become a link (but not necessarily a colony) in the British chain extending from Canada down across the Pacific to Australia. Also, during this period, Wodehouse became in effect a confidential advisor to Kalakaua who frequently sought out Wodehouse's advice, especially on matters dealing with foreign policy.

As the campaign gained momentum, the candidates carried out bitter verbal attacks against their opponents. The election, held on February 5, 1890, took place peacefully under the calming influence of British and American warships anchored in Honolulu Harbor. The Reform Party suffered a major setback, especially on Oahu where the National Reform Party had its greatest strength.

Following the election, a major disagreement took place between attorney general Clarence Ashford and the other ministers (Jonathan Austin, minister of foreign affairs; Lorrin A. Thurston, minister of the interior; and Samuel M. Damon, minister of finance). In fairly rapid succession, three areas of disagreement arose which ultimately led to a legislative investigation in June and caused the ouster of the Reform Cabinet. On June 17, Kalakaua happily appointed a new cabinet consisting of John A. Cummins as minister of foreign affairs, Godfrey Brown as minister of finance, Charles N. Spencer as minister of the interior and Arthur P. Peterson as attorney general. Cummins (a part-Hawaiian) and Spencer (an American) were personal friends of the king. Brown was British and Peterson was an American. This cabinet represented a compromise between the Reform Party and the conservative faction of the National Reform Party.

Having ousted the Reform Cabinet, Kalakaua and his followers turned their attention to replacing the constitution of 1887 with one similar to the constitution of 1864. In July, Wilcox and Bush organized a committee which oversaw the movement to call a constitutional convention. But the convention scheme eventually failed in the legislature where its opponents successfully argued that a number of amendments pending in that body of government would correct all the major objections to the existing constitution. By November, 1890, all of these amendments had passed and then they were scheduled into the 1892 legislative session for final action. Other actions by the legislature and the new cabinet during this time reversed many of the policies of the previous administration. Some of these actions included disbanding the Honolulu Rifles and repealing the Military Act of 1888 which also eliminated the office of colonel of the Hawaiian Volunteers.

When the Hawaiian legislature ended its 1890 session in November, King Kalakaua, whose health had been steadily deteriorating during the year, decided to spend several months on the West Coast of the United States in an effort to restore his

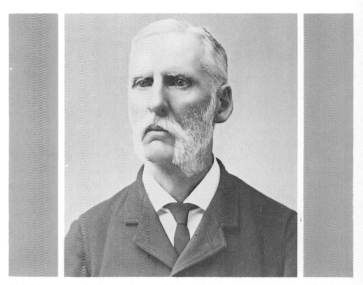

British Commissioner James H. Wodehouse State Archives

Samuel M. Damon State Archives

King Kalakaua and Rear Admiral George Brown State Archives
(Hand in His Coat) Aboard the USS Charleston

health. Rear Admiral George Brown, commander of the United States naval force in the Pacific, offered his flagship, the *USS Charleston*, to escort his majesty to San Francisco. Accepting the admiral's invitation, Kalakaua appointed his sister, Princess Liliuokalani, regent during his absence. Without fanfare and wearing a straw hat, black civilian coat and white trousers, Kalakaua and his small party[1] departed Honolulu on November 25.

---

[1] Initially, the royal party included the king's chamberlain, Colonel George W. Macfarlane, and an aide-de-camp, Major Robert Hoapili Baker.

Arriving in San Francisco on December 4, Kalakaua received a warm welcome from a large, cheering crowd. Having many friends in the area whom he had previously entertained in Honolulu, Kalakaua attended a barrage of receptions, balls and dinners. Several weeks later, the king journeyed to southern California in a private car furnished by the Southern Pacific Railway. The king's southern excursion extended into San Diego and briefly into Mexico. More banquets and receptions followed, and Kalakaua attended several operas. On the return trip, he suffered a mild stroke in early January while stopping in Santa Barbara. A local physician, Dr. McNulty, was called in and he accompanied the king back to the Palace Hotel in San Francisco. Several days later, Dr. George W. Woods, a fleet surgeon of the United States Pacific Fleet, took charge of the king's case under directions from Admiral Brown who had joined the royal party in Los Angeles. But despite the best efforts of Dr. Woods and other physicians consulted, Kalakaua's condition worsened and he lapsed into unconsciousness on January 18. The final moment came during the afternoon of January 20 when Kalakaua died of Bright's disease at the age of fifty-four.

Admiral Brown and the *Charleston* received the sorrowful task of returning the king's remains to Honolulu. A memorial service was held on January 22 and the king's casket was then escorted with full military honors to the waterfront and placed aboard the *Charleston.* Shortly thereafter, the American warship set sail for Honolulu. Early in the morning of January 29, the *Charleston* rounded Diamond Head with both the American and Hawaiian flags flying at half mast and with the ship's hull and spars draped in black. Unaware of the king's death, the residents of Honolulu had been erecting festive decorations in anticipation of the king's arrival in a few days. But as the news of the king's death spread around Honolulu, these decorations were quickly removed or covered with black cloth. Later in the afternoon, a naval escort from the American and British ships in the harbor delivered Kalakaua's remains to Hawaiian authorities at the palace. Placed in the throne room, the king lay in state, surrounded by tall kahilis which testified to his royal lineage. Earlier that afternoon, the chief justice of the supreme court, Albert Francis Judd, hastily administered the oath of office to Liliuokalani who then became the new monarch of the Hawaiian kingdom.

Kalakaua's funeral took place on Sunday, February 15, 1891. Prior to that date, the king's body had been transferred to a new casket fashioned from native Hawaiian woods and adorned with silver and gold decorations. The ceremonies were very elaborate, giving all segments of the population ample time to pay their last respects to the deceased sovereign. Following a religious service in the throne room, a long procession escorted the king's coffin through the city streets and up Nuuanu Avenue to the Royal Mausoleum as minute guns were fired by the American

Queen Kapiolani Kneeling Beside Kalakaua's Casket in the Throne Room of Iolani Palace　　**State Archives**

Kalakaua's Interment at the Royal Mausoleum　　**State Archives**

warships in the harbor and by the battery on Punchbowl.1 The Anglican Church read the committal service and members of the Masonic fraternity conducted the burial service. Thus the founder of the Kalakaua dynasty was laid to rest in grand ceremonial style, reminiscent of the manner in which he lived.

---

1 The funeral procession lasted one hour and fifty-nine minutes. During this entire time period, minute guns were fired continuously; the *USS Mohican* firing the first 30 rounds and the *Charleston* firing the remaining 89 rounds.

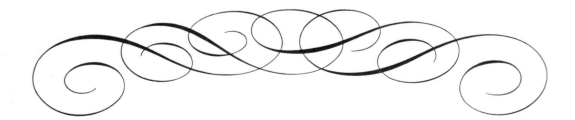

The Overthrow of the Monarchy

Liliuokalani became queen at the age of fifty-two. Having received her formal education at the Chiefs' Children's School, the new Hawaiian monarch spoke English fluently. During her lifetime, Liliuokalani adhered to the fundamental principles of the Christian religion, much more so than her late brother, Kalakaua. She attended church services regularly, and she had a long list of worthy charitable causes. Following her accession to the throne, a special koa wood pew was installed in Kawaiahao Church for her personal use. Married since September 16, 1862 to a childhood friend and long-time acquaintance named John Owen Dominis, the queen had no children. Her husband was the son of a prosperous Boston sea captain who had made Hawaii his home. John O. Dominis had received an appointment as a full general on the staff of Kamehameha IV, and he later became Governor of Oahu under Kamehameha V. The new queen conferred upon her husband the rank and dignity of "His Royal Highness the Prince Consort."

Liliuokalani had visited California in 1878, and in 1887 she toured the United States and England with Queen Kapiolani. Having been designated as heir apparent by Kalakaua in 1874 and having served as regent on two occasions during the late king's absence, Liliuokalani had prepared herself to someday assume the duties of sovereign of the Hawaiian kingdom. Proud of her alii lineage and aware of her new authority, the new queen believed in the divine right of an absolute monarch. Spirited and stubborn, yet warm-hearted toward her subjects, Liliuokalani was determined to maintain the traditional prerogatives of the ruling class, prerogatives that her late brother had been forced to relinquish by the "Bayonet Constitution" of 1887. While the native Hawaiians were filled with hope for change, the haoles were fearful that the new queen would attempt to restore the old constitution and regain for the crown the power that it had lost during Kalakaua's reign.

Pressured by the deceased king's cabinet ministers, Liliuokalani had been hastily sworn into office on January 29, 1891. While she showed some reluctance to support a constitution that she despised, Liliuokalani nevertheless took the oath of office, perhaps not fully realizing its significance at the time. Immediately thereafter, the question arose concerning the status of Kalakaua's cabinet ministers, but the new queen showed her independence by refusing to discuss the matter until after the king's funeral (February 15).

On February 16, 1891, Liliuokalani requested the hold-over cabinet ministers to resign. The queen took the position that their appointments had expired upon the death of the sovereign who had appointed them. But the ministers refused to resign, reasoning that only the legislature could remove them. The dispute quickly became public, and a lively legal debate ensued. The supreme court was asked to intervene, and after some deliberation, it handed down an opinion on February 25 which supported the queen's position. The ministers accepted the opinion and promptly resigned.

The following day, the queen appointed a new cabinet more to her choosing. It consisted of Samuel Parker as minister of foreign affairs, Charles N. Spencer as minister of the interior, Hermann A. Widemann as minister of finance, and William A. Whiting as attorney general. Parker, a rancher on the island of

Queen Liliuokalani on the Day She Became Queen State Archives

Queen Liliuokalani's Personal Staff[1] State Archives

---

[1] Standing, left to right, are Col. James H. Boyd, Col. Henry F. Bertelman, and chamberlain James W. Robertson. Seated is Col. John D. Holt.

Hawaii, was of mixed blood, though mostly Hawaiian. He had some legislative experience and was popular among both natives and foreigners. Spencer was reappointed to the same post he held in the previous cabinet. Widemann, a German married to a Hawaiian, had been a member of Kalakaua's first cabinet, had served a number of years in the legislature, and had plantation interests in the islands. Whiting, an American, was a Honolulu attorney. None of the queen's new cabinet ministers had any missionary connections.

During the early days of her reign, the queen made additional appointments, including appointing several new members to the privy council, naming a new chamberlain (James W. Robertson), and appointing a new marshal, Charles B. Wilson. Wilson, a close friend of the queen, was part-Tahitian and part-British, a combination that would focus much hostility on him and the queen.

Another important act performed early in Liliuokalani's reign involved the naming of her niece, Princess Kaiulani, as heir apparent. Kaiulani was the daughter of Princess Miriam Likelike, the queen's deceased sister, and Archibald S. Cleghorn, the inspector general of immigration and customs. The fifteen-year-old princess attended a girls school in England at this time under the guardianship of Theo. H. Davies, a family friend who had business interests both in England and in Hawaii. A special session of the House of Nobles, held on March 9, considered Kaiulani's appointment and gave it their unanimous approval.

The newspapers of this period, while describing the good points of the new queen, cautioned Liliuokalani to accept the modern constitution and reign but not rule. The editor of the *Friend,* Sereno E. Bishop writing in March, expressed his opinion of Hawaii's future: "It can hardly be doubted by any one that this Kingdom is advancing through a period of transition from Monarchy to government by the People. The nation is slowly ripening for the ultimate change." Voices of discord were already being heard from the more radical elements in the community, notably Bush and Wilcox who had split from the National Reform Party and had organized the Liberal Party. Finding themselves without any influence in the new administration, the leaders of the Liberal Party publicly vented their anger against the queen and her administration.

During the spring and summer of 1891, Queen Liliuokalani made an extensive tour of her kingdom, visiting all the inhabited islands. Throughout this tour, the queen's subjects demonstrated their loyalty and respect in the traditional Hawaiian ways. But the mood in Honolulu began to change. During the summer, rumors circulated that the queen's health was impaired and that she might die. Actually, the queen's husband, John O. Dominis, became ill. He died on August 27, leaving a vacuum in Liliuokalani's life during a critical period in her reign. Additional rumors circulated that the queen's personal feelings were strongly pro-British and anti-American. These rumors were taken seriously by many people, including government officials and diplomatic representatives. Partially as a result of these rumors, the United States warship *Pensacola* received orders to proceed to Honolulu in September in order to safeguard American interests.

The Reform Party's defeat in the 1890 election and the subsequent downfall of the Reform Cabinet caused many of the party's supporters to look for different ways to secure good stable government. One of these ways embraced annexation, and one of the individuals who had changed his mind on the subject was Lorrin A. Thurston. In the early 1880's, he openly favored independence for Hawaii. Later, from 1884 to 1890, he was one of the most active leaders of the reform government. But by 1892, Thurston had become an ardent annexationist. The growing importance of the radical faction in Hawaii, headed by Bush and Wilcox, and its growing influence on the native Hawaiians only served to undermine the stability of the queen, her cabinet, and the business leaders of the community. This latter group had begun to feel the effects of the growing economic depression caused by the enactment of the McKinley tariff act in the United States. To its supporters, annexation offered an alternative to the proposed free-trade

Princess Kaiulani   State Archives

Iolani Barracks and the Household   State Archives
Guards in 1892

treaty with the United States which had become bogged down in negotiations and political wrangling, including the upcoming elections in Washington.

The annexation issue did not become a major issue in the Hawaiian elections scheduled for February of 1892. Local issues dominated the campaign. The political arena had expanded from two to four political organizations. In addition to the Reform Party and the National Reform Party, the Liberal Party and the Native Sons of Hawaii made their appearance to vie for political power. But not all of these parties offered a complete slate of candidates, and in fact, some candidates' names appeared on more than one ticket. In addition, several independent candidates also ran for various offices. The Liberal Party, primed by Bush and Wilcox, became the most vocal, started campaigning earlier than the other parties, and drew their membership from the disgruntled ranks of the National Reform Party. In addition to adopting the battle cry "Hawaii for the Hawaiians," the Liberal Party advocated a new and more liberal constitution with a government "*of* the People, *by* the People and *for* the People." They also favored continued independence for the country as well as a revision of existing treaties, especially with the United States, to give Hawaii more advantages. The Native Sons of Hawaii, organized in the latter part of 1890, sought to preserve Hawaii's independence and its monarchial institutions. They also adopted the motto "Hawaii for the Hawaiians."

During the election campaign, the National Reform Party assumed the role of the government party since it had the approval of the queen who donated to its campaign fund. The Native Sons of Hawaii, and the Reform Party to a lesser extent, also supported the administration. While these three groups were not a coalition, they nevertheless became united in a common purpose to prevent the Liberal Party from acquiring control of the legislature. The election, which took place on February 3, 1892 without any disturbance, was considered a victory for the administration and its conservative allies. But no party held a majority in the legislature.

Following the election and prior to the opening session of the legislature on May 28, public and private discussions centered around the future of Hawaii, its relations with the United States, and possible changes in the government of the kingdom. With treaty negotiations at a standstill with the United States, three main topics received a great deal of attention. They were: 1) annexation of Hawaii to the United States; 2) the formation of an independent republic; and 3) the formation of a republic as a steppingstone to annexation.

Throughout the spring of 1892, the Liberal Party's leadership continued its attacks on the administration, called for the demise of the monarchy, and promoted a republican form of government. Near the end of March, insurrection rumors abounded and became so heavy and frequent that sandbags were placed around two entrances to the palace. While the government attempted to describe the sandbag incident as a military drill, the press ridiculed and embarrassed the government. The presence of the *USS SAN FRANCISCO* in Honolulu Harbor undoubtedly deterred the Liberal Party from taking any drastic action or employing the use of arms against the government. By this time, it had become United States policy to station a warship continually in Hawaiian waters to support the queen and to aid her government in preserving internal order. In this way, the United States reemphasized its "hands-off" warning to European powers, especially Great Britain and Germany.

Wilcox, in addition to attacking the monarchy and its cabinet, personally attacked the femininity of Queen Liliuokalani by using the following quotations in a May 5 speech: "I do not wish to be governed by dolls. I believe no woman ought to reign. They have no brains. They are generally weak." His cohort, Bush, directed racial slurs against Marshal Wilson and Minister Parker, calling them in a May 12 speech respectively "A half-Tahitian blacksmith and a half-caste cowboy (who) are running the Government . . ." Wilcox and Volney V. Ashford secretly formed an organization called the Hawaiian Patriotic League which sought to get equal rights, a new constitution, and a republic by the force of arms. Marshal Wilson soon learned of the secret organization and managed to have spies infiltrate it and supply him with information on the group's activities.

On May 9, 1892, warrants of arrest were issued, and on the following day, Wilcox, Ashford, and sixteen other members of the Hawaiian Patriotic League were arrested and charged with treason. But twelve of the defendants were subsequently released on grounds of insufficient evidence. Ashford, who had been released and who was considered the most dangerous of the group, made a hasty retreat to California. None of the other defendants were brought to trial since the attorney general (William A. Whiting) declined to prosecute, fearing such action would only incense the Hawaiian people. In the long run, this course of action caused the Hawaiian government to lose the respect of many of its citizens. Fearing anarchy and a possible annexation of Hawaii to the United States, British Commissioner Wodehouse requested the stationing of a British warship at Honolulu. The *H.B.M.S. Champion* arrived on June 27.

Another secret organization, formed in early 1892 by Lorrin A. Thurston, was the Annexation Club. Rather than promoting annexation outright, the Annexation Club prepared itself to act quickly to seek annexation to the United States should the queen precipitate a crisis by promulgating a new constitution or

Queen Liliuokalani and the Hawaiian Throne   **State Archives**

Marshal Charles B. Wilson   **State Archives**

performing some other absolutist act. Deeming such action inevitable, the club sought to determine the United States' attitude toward annexing Hawaii. Thurston, sent by the Hawaiian government to Chicago to arrange a Hawaiian exhibit for the 1893 World's Columbian Exposition, journeyed on to Washington in early May, 1892 to sound out official sentiment regarding annexation. He met with several influential members of Congress as well as with Secretary of State James G. Blaine and Secretary of the Navy B. G. Tracy. While Thurston did not meet personally with President Benjamin Harrison, he nevertheless received a report through Tracy that the administration would be "exceedingly sympathetic" to an annexation proposal if one were brought to Washington. However, by the time Thurston returned to Honolulu, the arrests of May 20 had significantly altered conditions in the islands, thereby putting a damper on his plans.

The legislative session of 1892 opened on May 28, and it proved to be the longest in the history of the kingdom. A major portion of this session was devoted to an appropriations bill and to measures to relieve the economic depression in the country. Credit had become tight and investment capital was being withheld, causing a general slowdown in industrial and commercial activities. Pay cuts hit every level of government, including the queen and her cabinet. But these cuts were not enough as the economic depression continued and the expected income never materialized. Other bills, including a national loan and increased duties on imported items, were passed in an effort to recover the lost revenues. In addition, several schemes at raising extra funds were also brought before the legislature and they caused heated debate and much controversy both in the legislature and in the community. Other major proposals which caused considerable debate included the licensing of opium (repealed in the legislative session of 1887-1888), limiting Chinese immigration, amending or replacing the constitution of 1887, and the adoption of amendments to the constitution which were passed by the legislature of 1890. Many of these amendments did not receive enough votes or simply died without ever being considered.

The fiercest and longest battle in the 1892 legislative session centered around control of the queen's cabinet. Seven resolutions for "want of confidence" against the cabinet were introduced during this session. Four of these resolutions were adopted, forcing the resignations of four separate cabinets appointed by the queen. While Liliuokalani exercised her constitutional right to appoint her cabinet ministers, the legislature, determined to have a cabinet favorable to the majority of its members, kept exercising its constitutional right to reject the ministers that the queen appointed. The underlying cause of this legislative power struggle was the fact that no party had a majority. In addition, Liliuokalani tended to appoint ministers who happened to have the least representation in the legislature. Other factors also entered into the power struggle. They included the demand for the dismissal of Marshal Wilson, the supposed lack of leadership skills of the individual cabinet members and their inability to deal with the economic depression gripping the nation, the ministers' positions on trade relations with the United States, and finally a desire by some legislators for a cabinet favorable to their own way of political thought.

This persistent jockeying for power caused rumors to circulate concerning a possible coup d'etat or of an intervention by United States troops through the action of American Minister Stevens and the commander of the current warship in the harbor. Finally on November 8, Liliuokalani, after consulting with British Minister Wodehouse, appointed a cabinet whose members belonged to the Reform Party. This new cabinet consisted of George N. Wilcox (no relation to Robert W. Wilcox) as minister of the interior and head of the cabinet, Mark P. Robinson as minister of foreign affairs, Peter C. Jones as minister of finance, and Cecil Brown as attorney general. All of these cabinet ministers were well-known and highly respected members of the community, and many people felt that this cabinet would remain in office until the next biennial legislative session in 1894.

Not committed to annexation, the Wilcox cabinet sought to continue Hawaii's independence and to administer the government in a business-like manner under the existing constitution. But as the new year approached, Queen Liliuokalani gradually turned against her cabinet. She had not been entirely pleased with their appointment, but under the circumstances she had reluctantly compromised with the legislature and accepted them. Rumors of their involvement in or knowledge of a coup attempt against the throne plus the cabinet's opposition to a lottery bill combined with a clash over the appointment of judges all served to deepen the rift between the queen and her cabinet.

On January 4, 1893, an attempt to oust the Wilcox cabinet failed. During the closing days of the legislature, the lottery bill was railroaded through the House and it passed several days later. Also at this time, the queen used her influence against her

Sanford B. Dole (left) and Lorrin A. Thurston in Dole's Private Office in His Home   State Archives

The Wilcox Cabinet[1]   State Archives

cabinet ministers and another "want of confidence" resolution was introduced in the legislature on January 12. After a short debate, it passed and the Wilcox cabinet promptly resigned. The following morning, Liliuokalani appointed a new cabinet more to her liking. It consisted of Samuel Parker as minister of foreign affairs, John F. Colburn as minister of the interior, William H. Cornwell as minister of finance, and Arthur P. Peterson as attorney general. On January 14, the queen signed the lottery and opium bills into law and at noon on the same day, Liliuokalani officiated at a colorful and impressive ceremony ending the legislative session.

---

[1] Standing, left to right: Cecil Brown and Peter C. Jones. Sitting, left to right: Mark P. Robinson and George N. Wilcox.

Samuel Parker   State Archives

John F. Colburn   State Archives

William H. Cornwell   State Archives

Arthur P. Peterson   State Archives

Prior to the closing of the legislature, Queen Liliuokalani had privately informed her cabinet ministers of her intention to proclaim a new constitution, and she requested their presence at the palace that afternoon to countersign the document after she had officially promulgated it. The head of the Household Guards, Captain Samuel Nowlein, and Marshal Wilson were also informed of the queen's intentions and they were instructed to be prepared to quell any violence initiated by the opposition. The faults in the present constitution and the continued petitions from her subjects would finally be alleviated. The new constitution would restore power to the crown and to the Hawaiian people. As witnesses to this historic event, Liliuokalani invited the diplomatic corps, the justices of the supreme court, members of the legislature, and a committee of the Hui Kalaiaina (the Hawaiian Political Association). Few individuals from among these diverse groups knew the true reason behind their royal invitations.

The cabinet ministers conferred privately. While they may have encouraged the queen in her endeavor or at least had knowledge of her desire to proclaim a new constitution, the ministers decided that they could not support Liliuokalani in such a revolutionary act. Colburn, later called a "traitor" by the queen, hastily informed several of his attorney friends about the queen's intentions. Soon Alfred A. Hartwell (a former supreme court judge), Lorrin A. Thurston, and William O. Smith knew of Liliuokalani's plans and they advised Colburn and Attorney General Peterson, who had joined the group, to stand firm against the queen and not resign lest she appoint new ministers favorable to her cause. The two cabinet ministers returned to the legislative building (Aliiolani Hale). Hartwell then sent word to Captain G. C. Wiltse, commander of the USS Boston, informing him of the queen's intentions. Fearing violence, Captain Wiltse made preliminary plans to land a military force should that action become necessary to safeguard American lives and property. Shortly thereafter, Hartwell proceeded to the United States legation and informed American Minister Stevens of the happenings and urged him to seek the cooperation of British Minister Wodehouse in persuading Liliuokalani to reverse her plans. While unable to meet with the queen, the two diplomatic representatives met with her cabinet and encouraged them to oppose the queen in her undertaking.

When Liliuokalani met with her cabinet at the appointed time in the palace, she again explained her desire to declare a new constitution and to have them join her in signing the document. But they refused, and a long and bitter debate ensued while the invited guests waited in the Throne Room. Liliuokalani was furious! She maintained that she had been encouraged to undertake this endeavor and now she had been abandoned! After several hours, the cabinet ministers, except Parker, adjourned for a time and consulted with all the foreign diplomats in the community. They strongly advised the cabinet ministers to persuade the queen to abandon her plans. Upon returning to the palace, the ministers read the new constitution and after more debate, pressured the queen into postponing her plans for two weeks. Reluctantly, the embarrassed queen announced to the people assembled in the Throne Room that she had yielded to her ministers, but that within the near future she would give them a new constitution.

News quickly spread of the queen's intended action, and groups of people began gathering to discuss the situation. William O. Smith's law office became the center for disgruntled residents. Faced with uncertainty and fearing danger to the community, these men decided to band together and adopt a course of action. Inspired by Thurston, who saw an opportunity to promote the views of the Annexation Club, a Committee of Safety was formed. Chaired by Henry E. Cooper who also appointed the other members, the Committee of Safety consisted of thirteen members including Cooper. All of the original members were also members of the Annexation Club. Smith served as the committee's secretary. Following the approval of the appointments, the room was cleared and the committee proceeded to formulate a course of action. They agreed with a suggestion made by Thurston that annexation to the United States was the solution to the dilemma confronting them. During the next two days, the committee took steps to establish and proclaim a Provisional Government which would establish law and order. They sought out and were encouraged by American Minister Stevens' views. While taking a somewhat neutral stand, he nevertheless stated that he would land American troops to prevent destruction of American lives and property and that he would recognize the existing government, whichever one controlled the government buildings. The committee also scheduled a mass public meeting for the afternoon of January 16.

By Sunday, January 15, the queen's government knew of the existence of the Committee of Safety and its intended purpose of dethroning the queen and forming a Provisional Government as a prelude to annexation. Yet no arrests were made. On the following morning, Marshal Wilson visited Thurston's office in an attempt to get him and the Committee of Safety to cease their plotting against the queen. But it was too late; the committee had decided to settle the matter once and for all. Also on Monday morning, the queen's followers distributed copies of a proclamation issued by Liliuokalani which explained that the queen had acted under stress and that she was giving her assurance "that any changes desired in the fundamental law of the land will be sought only by methods provided in the Constitution itself." But even this proclamation came too late to turn back the swelling tide of change that had descended upon the city. Before adjourning from Thurston's office, the Committee of Safety drafted a letter to Stevens asking him to land troops if the committee made a further request to him.

The January 16 mass public meeting drew a crowd estimated to be between 1200 and 1500 people. Nearly all of them were white males. Nearly all business establishments had closed.

Captain G. C. Wiltse of the *USS Boston*   **State Archives**

The Committee of Safety[1]   **State Archives**

Numerous speeches denounced the queen, her actions, and her supporters. By a unanimous vote, the Committee of Safety received the power to carry through its plans to secure law and order and the protection of the community. A similar royalist meeting, called by the "Committee of Law and Order," drew a much smaller crowd which displayed much less enthusiasm for fear of exciting the opposition.

[1] The original Committee of Safety consisted of Henry E. Cooper (chairman), Henry Waterhouse, Lorrin A. Thurston, H. F. Glade (replaced by Ed Suhr, pictured above), F. W. McChesney, Albert S. Wilcox (replaced by John Emmeluth, pictured above), William R. Castle, William O. Smith, John A. McCandless, C. Bolte, William C. Wilder, Andrew Brown, and Theodore F. Lansing. Within a day or two, Wilcox resigned to return to Kauai and Glade resigned because he was German consul. The majority of the members were either Americans, Hawaiian born of American parents, or naturalized Hawaiian citizens.

Besieged by nervous Americans throughout most of Monday (January 16), American Minister Stevens decided, just prior to the mass meetings held by both sides, to land American troops. He went aboard the *Boston* and handed Captain Wiltse a written request to land troops later that afternoon. But Wiltse was already prepared. He had been following the situation closely and he had been alerted to the various developments by Cooper, chairman of the Committee of Safety, and by American Consul General Severance. Instructed to remain neutral in any conflict, a fully equipped force of 162 Marines and bluejackets descended upon the city around five o'clock. After an accommodations hassle, the troops were finally quartered about ten o'clock that evening at Arion Hall, a small building alongside the government building (Aliiolani Hale) and out of sight from the palace. Caught somewhat by surprise, the queen's ministers protested to Stevens who in turn gave them an ambiguous answer and told them to put any complaints in writing. This action by Stevens may have led several of the cabinet ministers to conclude that Stevens supported the revolutionists.

Overwhelmed by exaggerated reports on the strength of the opposition and complacent because of the presence of the American troops, Liliuokalani's cabinet did nothing. In spite of continued activities by the Committee of Safety, Marshal Wilson could not get any authorization to act against them. The foreign diplomats advised the queen not to resist by force. During the evening hours, the Committee of Safety met and named an advisory and an executive council for the Provisional Government they were forming. They also selected a finance committee to procure arms and ammunition. Sanford B. Dole, an associate justice of the supreme court and a man who had the trust of many native Hawaiians, was asked to serve as president of the executive council. But he hesitated, proposing instead that Liliuokalani be deposed and Princess Kaiulani be installed as queen. He also suggested that a regency be established during her minority. But the supporters of the movement were adamant in their desire to overthrow the Kalakaua dynasty and its surviving members. Dole then decided to ponder the presidency overnight and give the committee his answer the following morning.

The following morning (Tuesday, January 17), Dole sought out several friends for their advice. Nearly all of them, including Thurston, encouraged him to accept the presidency. By mid-morning, Dole had decided to accept the position. On his way downtown to Smith's law office, Dole stopped by American Minister Stevens' home to drop off a letter that Thurston had given him earlier. The letter detailed the movement's plans and asked for Stevens' recognition. Dole recounted in his memoirs that they had a brief conversation and then Stevens said: "I think you have a great opportunity."[1] Upon arriving at Smith's office, Dole formally accepted the presidency of the executive council. The Committee of Safety then transacted other business including the appointment of John H. Soper as military chief with the rank of colonel, naming John Good as ordnance officer, speeding up the procurement of weapons, and making plans to halt all inter-island transportation for one day.

While the queen's ministers were in the police station drafting a letter to Stevens requesting his assistance, the Committee of Safety took over the government building without any resistance. Once in control of the government building, the Committee of Safety issued a long proclamation denouncing the excesses and unkept promises of the Kalakaua regime and the attempts of his successor, Queen Liliuokalani, "to follow the tactics of her late brother" in attempting to restore royal prerogatives and

Troops from the *USS Boston*   **State Archives**

American Minister John L. Stevens   **State Archives**

reduce popular rights. Stating that responsible government was impossible under the monarchy, the proclamation abrogated the monarchy, deposed the queen, ousted her ministers and Marshal Wilson, and established a Provisional Government to remain in force until a union with the United States could be affected. The proclamation also named the members of the executive and advisory councils.[2] With a strong armed force now surrounding the government building, the Provisional Government declared martial law, suspended the right of writ of habeas corpus on the island of Oahu, and demanded the surrender of the police station. By five o'clock that afternoon, Stevens had recognized the Provisional Government as the *"de facto* Government of the Hawaiian Islands."

---

[1] Stevens consistently encouraged close ties between Hawaii and the United States. By November, 1892, he openly favored annexation after Great Britain had declared a protectorate over the Gilbert Islands and had taken possession of Johnston Island. His sympathies were strongly with the Reform Party, and he developed a rapport with the annexationists, including Thurston.

[2] The members of the executive council were: Sanford B. Dole, president and chairman of the council and minister of foreign affairs; James A. King, minister of the interior; Peter C. Jones, minister of finance; and William O. Smith, attorney general. The fourteen members of the advisory council were Samuel M. Damon, Andrew Brown, Lorrin A. Thurston, J. F. Morgan, John Emmeluth, Henry Waterhouse, John A. McCandless, E. D. Tenney, F. W. McChesney, F. Wilhelm, William R. Castle, W. G. Ashley, William C. Wilder, and C. Bolte.

Informed of their ouster, the four ex-cabinet ministers returned to the palace and advised Queen Liliuokalani to surrender to the superior force of the opposition and not risk bloodshed. Under "protest," Liliuokalani yielded instead "to the superior force of the United States . . . to avoid any collision of armed forces and perhaps loss of life . . . until such time as the Government of the United States shall, upon the facts being presented to it, undo the action of its representatives and reinstate me in the authority which I claim as the constitutional sovereign of the Hawaiian Islands."[1]

Around seven in the evening, under direct written orders from Liliuokalani, Marshal Wilson surrendered the police station and its "army" of 272 men.[2] The final business conducted by the new Provisional Government was the approving of a motion to send a delegation to Washington to negotiate a treaty uniting Hawaii with the United States. By midnight, nearly all of the foreign diplomats had recognized the new government. The following morning, Colonel Soper (pictured here wearing a derby hat) assembled the Royal Household Guards, paid them to the end of the month, and then mustered them out of service. By this time, Liliuokalani had already retired to her private residence to await a favorable decision from the United States.

By disbanding the Royal Household Guards and taking possession of the barracks, more and more recruits were added to Soper's command. The opium and lottery laws were promptly repealed and the Hawaii National Guard was activated until a new police force could be created and a new military force recruited and drilled. In effect, the Provisional Government acted quickly to defend itself until the government of the United States made its desires known.

The new government lost no time in having itself recognized. By Janaury 19, all of the seventeen diplomatic or consular representatives of foreign governments had formally recognized the new regime. The Provisional Government outlawed the royal standard, ordered the gold crown insignia removed from the caps of various government officials, and required all government officials still in office to swear an oath of allegiance to the Provisional Government within twenty days. Saloons that were ordered closed on the evening of January 17, reopened three days later — a clear indication that business activities were returning to normal. Several major newspapers openingly supported the new government and assured its readers that the changes taking place offered security for all classes of the population. Other matters that received prompt attention included several appropriation bills, the authorization of a national loan, and the elimination of the position of governor for each of the major islands.

Events proceeded smoothly until the end of January when the rumor mills ground out fresh rumors concerning threats against the new government. Fearing unrest, the government placed its forces on alert, and on January 27, the troops from the *Boston* were also placed on alert. In an attempt to avoid civil disorder, the government asked American Minister Stevens to temporarily raise the American flag in a show of support. Stevens promptly agreed. On February 1, the American flag was raised over the government building and Stevens formally placed the "Government of Hawaii under the United States protection during negotiations, not interfering with the execution of public affairs." A company of marines remained on station

---

[1] Liliuokalani undoubtedly followed the example of Kamehameha III who surrendered his kingdom under protest to Queen Victoria of Great Britain under pressure from Lord George Paulet in 1843. His kingdom was restored several months later.

[2] This last surrender marked the official end of the Hawaiian kingdom. However, the events that occurred after this surrender were so closely related to the overthrow and its participants that it is necessary to continue this historical account until 1900.

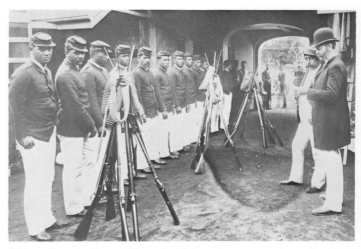

Disbanding the Royal Household Guards   **State Archives**

The Executive Council of the   **State Archives**
Provisional Government [3]

in the govenment building after the flag raising ceremony. This protectorate arrangement had a quieting effect on the community so that by February 5, martial law and its accompanying curfew were abolished. The writ of habeas corpus was also restored.

Two days after the overthrow of the monarchy (January 19), a five-man commission left Honolulu for Washington, D. C. to negotiate a treaty of union with the United States. The commission carried instructions to incorporate Hawaii as a Territory of the United States, or as a last resort, as a protectorate. Hoping to retain the rights and prerogatives assumed from the monarchy as well as continuing Hawaii's immigration and contract labor laws, the commission sought modifications to the customary territorial status granted by the United States. It also sought financial benefits such as a share in the bounty system on sugar, the improvement and use of Pearl Harbor, the assumption of Hawaii's national debt, the laying of a cable between the west coast and Hawaii, maintaining possession of all public lands, and financial support for ex-Queen Liliuokalani and Princess Kaiulani.

When the annexation commission arrived in Washington on February 3, they were joined by Hawaii's minister to the United States, Dr. John Mott Smith and several other Hawaiian citizens

---

[3] Left to right, the members of the executive council are: James A. King, Sanford B. Dole, William O. Smith, and Peter C. Jones.

who happened to be in the capital city. Overall sentiment appeared to favor annexing Hawaii. Secretary of State John W. Foster met with the commission and substantially modified their demands so that there would be no controversial items lingering to prevent the Senate from passing the treaty quickly. These modifications eliminated nearly all of the financial benefits that the commission had hoped to acquire. In addition, Foster proposed that the Provisional Government exist for a fixed or indefinite period until Congress decided on a form of government for the islands. While these terms went against their instructions, the annexation commission nevertheless accepted them as the best they could hope to obtain prior to the upcoming change in administration. The treaty was completed on February 14, and President Harrison sent it to the Senate the following day.

None of the queen's envoys were allowed to leave Honolulu on the same vessel that carried the annexation commission to the west coast of the United States. This gave the Provisional Government a head start in the negotiations. They did, however, allow the queen to send a written appeal to President Harrison asking that no conclusions be reached until her envoys arrived. The queen's envoys, Paul Neumann and Prince David Kawananakoa, left on the next available ship which departed Honolulu on February 2. Sailing on the same ship was E. C. Macfarlane who, acting privately, sought to protect the interests of Princess Kaiulani.[1] But by the time the queen's envoys reached Washington, the treaty had already been submitted to the Senate. Furthermore, the queen's envoys went completely against Liliuokalani's instructions and talked freely of annexation, provided that the queen and Princess Kaiulani received financial compensation. Macfarlane managed to get the royalist version of the revolution published in numerous newspapers in an attempt to delay any further Senate action until the Cleveland administration took office in early March.

Within days after the Cleveland administration came into power, President Cleveland withdrew the Hawaiian treaty from the Senate (on March 9) supposedly for "re-examination." The Hawaiian commissioners blamed the new Secretary of State, Walter Q. Gresham, for undoing the accomplishment of former President Harrison. Cleveland, suspicious by nature, refused to meet with any of the representatives of the Provisional Government. Instead, he appointed James H. Blount of Georgia, the former chairman of the House committee on foreign affairs, as a special commissioner to investigate the Hawaiian question. Having received secret instructions and given a wide latitude in dealing with Americans and with American military and civilian representatives in Hawaii, he received the nickname "Paramount Blount" from those people who were fearful of him. Blount's main objectives were to report on the causes of the Hawaiian revolution, the part played by American Minister Stevens, and the attitude of the people in Hawaii toward the Provisional Government.

Blount, his ailing wife, and his secretary (Ellis Mills), arrived in Honolulu on March 29, 1893 for their fact-finding mission. Since his intentions were unknown, Blount was besieged by a multitude of individuals representing either themselves or their organizations. One of Blount's first actions was to restore the Hawaiian flag to its prominence atop the government building and to send the American troops back to their ship. This action caused many people to believe that he planned to restore Liliuokalani to her throne. But Blount denied any such plans, stating instead that this action showed his desire of not interfering in domestic affairs. To the jittery Provisional Government, he explained that this action made it more independent to

The Annexation Commission[2]   State Archives

Special Commissioner James H. Blount   State Archives
and His Wife

negotiate. But generally, Blount remained silent on his instructions and on his intentions, thereby giving rise to rumors and conjecture.

After slightly more than four months in Hawaii, Blount departed on August 9, still tight-lipped. He could have remained as minister to Hawaii, but he refused, leaving before a replacement arrived.[3] In his final summation to Secretary of State Gresham, Blount defended the queen and advocated restoring her to the Hawaiian throne. But Blount slanted his report and the interviews contained in it. He allowed only testimony that built a case for restoring the queen to power. He failed to interview any of the members of the Committee of Safety to get their views nor did he interview any of the officers from the *Boston.* Blount made a case against Stevens, sighting his desires to see Hawaii annexed and his overeager recognition of the Provisional Government. Finally, he failed to mention the declining nature of the monarchy and the fact that it had existed only because the great powers in the Pacific had allowed it to exist.

---

[1]Princess Kaiulani and her friend and guardian, Theo. H. Davies, journeyed from England to Washington to assist Macfarlane in protecting Kaiulani's interests. But Davies' British background and Kaiulani's British training and upbringing only served to work against her cause if she had one in the first place.

[2]The prominent members of the annexation commission were: (left to right) William C. Wilder, Joseph Marsden, Lorrin A. Thurston, Charles L. Carter (standing behind Thurston), Dr. John Mott Smith, and William R. Castle.

[3]Stevens left Hawaii on May 24, 1893.

Secretary of State Gresham did not make a report to President Cleveland until mid-October of 1893. In his report, he blamed Stevens directly for the revolution, advised against resubmitting the Hawaiian treaty to the Senate, and suggested that the United States consider undoing a great wrong by restoring the "legitimate Government." The administration's new minister to Hawaii, Albert S. Willis, received instructions to reinstate Liliuokalani on the conditions that she would grant full amnesty to all those who had participated in the revolution and that she would assume all of the obligations incurred by the interim government. If the queen agreed to these conditions, then Willis was to inform the Provisional Government of President Cleveland's firm intentions in this case and then ask the Provisional Government to restore the queen to power. If either side refused, Willis was to report the facts to Washington and await further instructions. Believing that force would not be necessary, the Cleveland administration grossly underestimated the determination of the annexationists.

Willis' arrival in Honolulu in November 4 generated so much excitement that he decided to seclude himself at Snow Cottage, the same quarters that Blount had occupied, until the clamor eased. This action only served to confuse both sides and ignited restoration rumors. Disregarding protocol, Willis invited Liliuokalani to meet with him at the American legation on November 13. He apologized for the unauthorized intervention of the United States and then attempted to ascertain the queen's views on amnesty for the revolutionists. According to Willis' account, the queen stated: "My decision would be, as the law directs, that such persons should be beheaded and their property confiscated to the Government." Taken aback, Willis repeated his question and the queen's answer, and he asked her if that was what she really meant. She replied: "It is."[1] Willis reported the incident to Washington and waited for further instructions.

On November 24, the local newspapers published Gresham's letter to President Cleveland, thereby adding strength to the rumors circulating that Cleveland intended to use force in restoring the queen to power. Willis, waiting instructions from Washington, said nothing to the Provisional Government and Liliuokalani kept her promise to say nothing of their previous conversation. Rear Admiral John Irwin, current commander in the Pacific, fully expected to receive orders to land American troops to oust the Provisional Government. The jittery executive council issued arms and ammunition for the formation of a Citizens' Guard, ordered the volunteer companies to be quartered in the executive building (one company each night on a rotating basis), increased the size of the regular company, and fortified the executive building with sandbags. Government soldiers, if attacked, would fight to the death. Any government officials who would not fight were dismissed.

After receiving new instructions from Washington, Willis again met with Liliuokalani in mid-December in an effort to resolve the amnesty issue. Aided by Joseph O. Carter, Willis managed to convince the queen to accept the president's terms on December 18. But Liliuokalani's unyielding attitude had caused Willis to change his mind on the political stability of the monarchy if it was restored; he felt that she would not last. On the following afternoon, Willis dutifully informed the Provisional Government of Cleveland's proposition.

At midnight on December 23, Dole personally delivered the Provisional Government's reply to Willis. Point by point, it repudiated the scheme which the Cleveland administration had attempted to force upon the government. The reply made

---

[1] Liliuokalani denied using the word "beheaded." Her diary entry for November 13 generally agrees with Willis' account. However, concerning the amnesty issue, she wrote: "I told him that our laws read that 'those who are guilty of treason shall suffer the penalty of death, and their property confiscated to the Government. If any amnesty was to be made, it was that they should leave the country forever . . .'"

Albert S. Willis, New Minister to Hawaii   State Archives

Defending the "Executive Building"   State Archives
(Iolani Palace)

the administration look ridiculous and unreasonable. It stated that the rejection of the annexation treaty was the policy of the current administration and not the final decision of the United States government. Letters filled with charges and countercharges sped back and forth between the two governments. The United States found itself in an awkward position. It could not use force against a government that it and other foreign governments had recognized as being the legitimate government of the Hawaiian Islands. In addition, the United States, through American Minister Stevens, had placed the new government under the temporary protection of the American flag. The United States Attorney General, Richard Olney, had expressed the opinion to the Cleveland administration back in September that the use of force would be an act of war which was beyond the constitutional powers of the president. When it became clear that diplomatic efforts had failed to alter the position of the Provisional Government, the administration dropped the entire matter in Congress' lap in January of 1894.

**Delegates to the Convention that Framed
the Constitution for the Republic of Hawaii**

Even before Congress formally received the Hawaiian problem, Senator John Tyler Morgan of Alabama, an annexationist who was chairman of the Senate committee on foreign relations, began hearings in late December, 1893 to determine what, if any, irregularities had occurred between the United States and Hawaii. After two months of hearings, the Morgan Report presented an effective case for Stevens and the Provisional Government. The hearings put on record the testimony of many people who were ignored by Blount and his investigation. But the Morgan Report was definitely slanted toward the Provisional Government since Morgan had the advice and guidance of Lorrin A. Thurston, Frank P. Hastings (the Hawaiian charge d'affaires), and William D. Alexander who had a remarkable insight of the whole affair. The majority of the Senate committee on foreign relations found everyone "not guilty" except for Queen Liliuokalani. The Hawaiian affair became a political issue which caused great embarrassment to the Cleveland administration. Because of the issue's partisan nature, it was debated on and off during the entire second session of the Fifty-third Congress which ended August 28, 1894. In the end, Stevens was censured by the House, but no further action was taken against the Provisional Government.

Still intent on annexation, the Provisional Government decided to hang on by forming a Republic. On March 15, 1894, the Provisional Government passed an act calling for a convention to draft a constitution for the Republic of Hawaii. The act set May 2 as the date for the election of delegates. To insure that the original revolutionary leaders maintained control, a majority of nineteen of the convention's thirty-seven members consisted of the members of the executive and advisory councils. The remaining eighteen members would be elected. But special conditions were imposed to restrict voters. In order to vote for a convention delegate, the voter had to possess a certain amount of wealth, take an oath of allegiance to the Provisional Government, and oppose any attempt to re-establish the monarchy. Needless to say, the voter turnout was light.

The constitutional convention began on May 30, consumed the entire month of June, and extended into the opening days of July. The finished constitution resembled the United States Constitution in that it provided for executive, legislative, and judicial branches. In addition, it contained the usual statements about freedom of religion, speech, press, meeting, etc., but a number of these freedoms had certain restrictions attached to them. However, on closer examination, the new Hawaiian constitution deviated significantly from its American counterpart. In order to keep the American minority in firm control of the new government, stringent controls were put on voting qualifications as well as on the qualifications for holding elective offices. In effect, the high property qualifications and the oath not to aid in restoring the monarchy, to name only a few of the qualifications, insured that few Hawaiians could or would vote, and fewer still would be eligible to serve in the newly created Senate and House of Representatives. Citizenship requirements further restricted the number of voters. Requirements such as being able to read, write, and speak English as well as being able to explain the constitution in English, effectively kept the entire Oriental population away from the polls.

The constitutional convention nominated Dole for the presidency, and during the evening of July 2, a large mass meeting ratified the new constitution and the endorsement of Dole as president with a six year term. The following day, the Provisional Government passed a bill handing the government over to the Republic. Actually, it handed the government over to itself since the executive and advisory councils would continue (the advisory council temporarily) with the same people, but with slightly different titles. On the fourth of July, 1894, Dole promulgated the new constitution and formally established the Republic of Hawaii with himself as president. The ceremony was a civil rather than a military one in order to show that the new constitution rested upon the people rather than upon bayonets. Within two days, all the foreign diplomatic representatives, including American Minister Willis, had recognized the new regime. While the United States failed to accept the Hawaiian plum offered to it, the American government nevertheless had given ample warning when the House (on February 7, 1894) and the Senate (on May 31, 1894) had passed similar resolutions warning foreign governments that "intervention in the political affairs of the islands would be considered an act unfriendly to the United States."

Sanford B. Dole Proclaiming the
Republic of Hawaii on July 4, 1894

Chapter 12

Counterrevolution and Annexation

The Republic of Hawaii was launched peacefully without much fanfare when compared to previous monarchial inaugurations. Dole sent an autographed letter to President Cleveland announcing the establishment of the Republic, and in turn, Cleveland sent a letter recognizing the new government. Several Honolulu newspapers reported that this recognition settled the monarchy question once and for all, and they suggested that the Royalists give up any further plans to restore the monarchy. But the Royalists had to find out for themselves. A delegation consisting of Herman A. Widemann, John A. Cummins, and Samuel Parker arrived in Washington in early August, 1894 to ascertain the administration's position on restoring Liliuokalani as the lawful sovereign of the Hawaiian Islands. While the delegation did not meet personally with President Cleveland because of his illness, they nevertheless received a memorandum from the president giving his views. The president stated that he had done everything in his power and had turned the entire affair over to the Congress which had refused to go any further. In addition, Cleveland declared that the new Republic had been duly recognized by his administration and that it was fulfilling its duties. Nothing else could be done. This response finally convinced the Royalists that they could not expect any help from the United States. They would have to proceed on their own to restore their queen to power.

In September, Judge Widemann sailed to Europe to petition the governments of Great Britain, France, and Germany to aid Hawaii's queen in recovering her crown.[2] But these European governments had already recognized the Republic of Hawaii, and they were in no mood to discuss the matter any further. Even before Widemann's European trip, several ardent Royalists began planning a surprise strike against the young Republic. Starting around September 1, the government noticed indications of increased Royalist activity such as threats of assassination against Attorney General Smith and President Dole as well as attacks in the newspaper *Holomua* which were primarily in the form of advertisements. Ironically, native Hawaiians were not the leaders behind this increased activity. Instead, it came from disgruntled whites and part-Hawaiians. The editors of several native Hawaiian newspapers published fiery editorials in an effort to stir up the natives. By October and early November, reports were reaching various government officials about a Royalist plot to overthrow the Republic. In response to these reports and the continuing street rumors, the government beefed up its military and police units.

---

[1]Washington Place, located across Beretania Street from the State Capitol, is the current residence of Hawaii's governor.

[2]Liliuokalani had good reason to attempt a recovery of her lost throne. When she was overthrown in 1893, the Provisional Government took possession of the crown lands — nearly one million acres of fertile farmland, pastures, forests, and lava-covered wastes scattered among the various islands. Long-term leases on these lands brought significant revenues to the ruling sovereign.

Liliuokalani at Her Private Residence   State Archives
(Washington Place)[1] in the Summer of 1895

Marshal Edward G. Hitchcock   State Archives

During the fall of 1894, wealthy Royalists contributed funds for arms and ammunition. Major W. T. Seward, a former Union officer in the Civil War, quietly left Honolulu bound for California on a secret arms buying mission. In November, the schooner *Wahlberg* departed San Francisco with a cargo of rifles and ammunition for the Royalists. Upon arriving in Hawaiian waters, the schooner stood off the windward coast of Oahu and began a long wait to deliver its cargo. In the meantime, Marshal Edward G. Hitchcock began piecing together the bits of information being sent to him by his secret agents who had infiltrated numerous Royalist strongholds. One of these leads resulted in the December 9 arrest of John E. Bush, a longtime instigator in the community, and several other men on charges of conspiracy and levying war against the Republic. A search of their residences turned up numerous rifles. In late December, the new British Commissioner, Captain Albert G. S. Hawes, offered the jittery government the use of British troops from the *Hyacinth,* but the government politely declined the offer.

On New Year's Day, the guns from the *Wahlberg* were finally transferred to a small steamer called the *Waimanalo.* The steamer waited off Diamond Head for further instructions. But the Royalist high command had been haphazardly organized, and they were not quite ready to launch a revolution. A plan to land a portion of the weapons at Kakaako, the entrance to Honolulu harbor, never materialized. Many natives, restless to start the revolution, gathered near the harbor entrance much earlier than they were supposed to. The large crowd soon attracted the attention of the police. As they started to investigate, the crowd dispersed. Thus ended the plan to land arms, take possession of the police station, and surprise the nearby garrison. During the night of January 3, the *Waimanalo,* now running out of coal, landed two boatloads of weapons near Diamond Head. One boat beached at Kahala where the rifles were buried in the sand. The other boat landed a distance away at Black Point and hid the rifles in a dry gulch.

The Diamond Head area of Honolulu in 1895 was a sparsely populated, often dry and deserted country section — a good place to assemble a rebel army. On Saturday night, January 5, a small band of Royalists dug up the concealed rifles and moved them closer to rebel headquarters. The following morning, they cleaned the rifles and distributed them to the newly arriving patriots. In small groups they kept coming throughout the day: carpenters, painters, tram drivers, stevedores, and former band members and clerks who had given up their jobs rather than sign an oath to a government they despised. Some came barefooted; others wore their Sunday best. Instead of drilling, they sat around eating poi, drinking gin, telling jokes, or instructing their comrades in the basic facts of firing a rifle. While their ranks did not swell as anticipated, their spirits remained high at the prospect of an estimated two thousand Royalists in town waiting to rise to their aid. To avoid detection, they had divided their slender ranks into two camps: one at H. F. Bertelmann's house and the other at Antone Rosa's residence. Yet their main leaders, Sam Nowlein and Robert W. Wilcox, still had not arrived.

The Royalists had planned to march into town at midnight and split into two groups; one to seize the police station and the other to surround the palace. Hopefully by this time, other Royalists in Honolulu would have joined their ranks, some assembling at strategic street intersections to prevent the government's volunteer companies from mustering while others would arrest helpless government officials caught unaware in their beds. Still others would help protect the queen at her private residence until the Republic collapsed and Liliuokalani was restored to her rightful throne.

But the Royalists had a spy in their midst, and in the afternoon he slipped away and informed Marshal Hitchcock of the Bertelmann camp. The marshal, after consulting with the attorney general, then sent police Captain Robert Waipa Parker, Lieutenant Holi and six other police officers with a search warrant to Bertelmann's home. Several members of the Citizens' Guard, including Charles Carter, lived in the area and they augmented the small police force. As they approached under a darkening sky, gunshots erupted and Carter slumped over mortally wounded.[1] Both sides let loose with a barrage of gunfire which finally ended when Bertelmann called a cease fire. The rebels scattered up the cliffs of Diamond Head while Bertelmann was arrested and taken into custody.

---

[1] Carter, a young lawyer on Dole's staff, died the following morning. His death was the only fatality suffered by the government in the revolution of 1895.

Charles L. Carter   State Archives

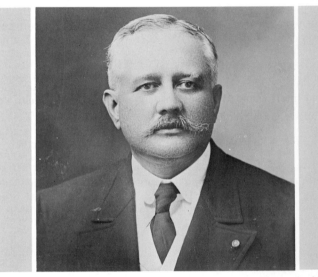

H. F. Bertelmann   State Archives

Horse-Drawn Cannon and Government   **State Archives**
Troops in Manoa Valley

News of the skirmish at Bertelmann's spread quickly. The hostilities had started before the insurgents were ready. With their plans thwarted, the Royalists had to take the defensive. Government troops arrived with artillery pieces and started shelling the rebel positions on the slopes of Diamond Head. The following morning, the government declared martial law and dispatched the tug *Eleu* to the battle area with a cannon and a detail of sharpshooters. Caught in a crossfire, the Royalists dispersed in small bands and headed for the safety of the adjacent valleys and hills. The disciplined government troops relentlessly pursued the rebels. Fleeing without food and other provisions, some of the insurgents surrendered while many others were soon captured. Wilcox led the decimated remnants of his rebel army far up into the Manoa Valley. The steep ascent made the going slow and rough. Government sharpshooters positioned themselves on the lower ridges, advanced boldly, and set up a crossfire. For the first time, the Royalists suffered heavy casualties. Many lost their will to fight and surrendered. The remaining rebels trickled over into the adjacent valleys and continued to elude their pursuers.

Within three days, the insurrection was over. But while the rebel leaders were still at large, apprehension and uncertainty prevailed in the community. Key intersections and important government buildings continued to be guarded and the curfew remained in effect. Additional insurgents were captured as they tried to return to the city. Oahu prison swelled not only with war prisoners, but with political prisoners as well. Some of the first political prisoners had been the editors and sponsors of *Holomua,* the newspaper that rallied the queen's followers. Others with known Royalist sympathies soon joined them. So did other citizens and foreigners whose open talk or covert behavior linked them to the Royalists. A clamor began building for the arrest of Queen Liliuokalani.

While the National Guard and mounted police patrolmen searched the valleys and guarded the passes, the marshal's men interrogated the prisoners for clues to the whereabouts of the movement's leaders. Native residents in the valleys were also being interrogated. Finally, on January 14, Sam Nowlein, Will Greig, Carl Widemann, and Louis Marshall were captured. But Wilcox and a few others still evaded the troops, and the government could not yet feel that the war was over. So they kept up the pressure, and a week later, Wilcox and most of the remaining rebels were captured.

Fearing a native uprising, the government hesitated in arresting Liliuokalani until it had the situation well in hand. On January 16, 1895, Liliuokalani was arrested and imprisoned in the executive building (the palace). The following day, Chief Justice Albert Francis Judd, commissioned by Dole to examine the queen's private papers for her upcoming trial, entered the queen's residence at Washington Place and carted off two grain sacks filled with the queen's personal papers. Later, Captain Parker, acting on a tip, dug up Liliuokalani's garden and unearthed a cache of weapons: twenty-one giant home-made bombs, thirty-four rifles, eleven large pistols, approximately one thousand rounds of ammunition, sixteen smaller bombs, and five swords.

Pressured by government officials and her supporters, Queen Liliuokalani signed an abdication document on January 24, 1895 forever renouncing her throne. Drafted by former supreme court justice Alfred S. Hartwell, the lengthy document contained six amply worded assertions. First, ". . . that the Government of the Republic of Hawaii is the only lawful Government of the Hawaiian Islands, and that the late Hawaiian Monarchy is finally and forever ended . . .". Second, "For myself, my heirs and successors, I do hereby and without any mental reservation or modification, and fully, finally, unequivocally and forever abdicate, renounce and release unto the Government of the Republic of Hawaii, and its legitimate successors forever, all claims or pretensions whatsoever to the late throne of Hawaii, or to the late Monarchy of Hawaii . . .". In the third part, Liliuokalani sought "Executive clemency" for all her subjects involved in the recent rebellion. Fourth, Liliuokalani vowed ". . . henceforth to live in absolute privacy and retirement from all publicity . . .". In the fifth part, she presented ". . . a certified oath of allegiance to the Republic of Hawaii." And lastly, "I have caused the foregoing statement to be prepared and drawn, and have signed the same, without having received the slightest suggestion from the President of Hawaii, or from any member or official of the Government of Hawaii . . .".

Six of Liliuokalani's supporters witnessed her signature

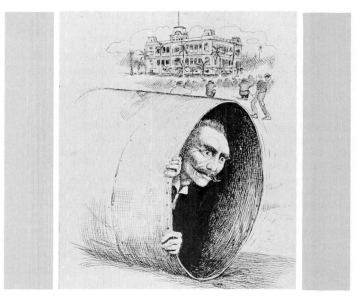

National Guard Officers at the   **State Archives**
Old Bungalow on the Palace Grounds

Cartoon by R. Yardley Depicting   **State Archives**
Robert W. Wilcox in Hiding

Portion of Liliuokalani's   **State Archives**
Abdication Declaration

and the document was duly notarized.[1] But in her book, *Hawaii's Story by Hawaii's Queen,* Liliuokalani flatly denied originating the idea of abdication. She stated that she did not have an opportunity to confer with any of her friends on the subject, and that she signed it only to prevent blood being shed by her subjects who were in jail. She further stated that it was represented to her that all of her people in jail "would be immediately released."

Sanford B. Dole, acting as commander in chief under martial law, appointed a military commission[2] to try the insurgents. The military court convened on January 17, and during the next thirty-five days, heard approximately one hundred and ninety cases. Hinting that the court would deal leniently with any prisoner who gave valuable information to the prosecution, many prisoners talked freely, implicating their friends and neighbors. The court learned that four of the Republic's most dangerous enemies had not even taken part in the January 6 insurrection. They were W. H. Rickard, Major W. T. Seward, Thomas B. Walker, and Charles T. Gulick. All of these white men had worked behind the scenes either raising money, purchasing arms and ammunition, making bombs, or drawing up plans for a new constitution and a new government.

The Republic of Hawaii did not consider Liliuokalani's abdication as being a sufficient reason for exempting her from personal liability for her complicity in the revolution. Accordingly, it kept the ex-queen under arrest, and in early February, the military court brought her to trial. The initial charge of treason was changed to misprision of treason, that is concealing knowledge of treason without actually participating in the act. In a trial that lasted several days, the prosecution presented damaging evidence including the ex-queen's personal diary and the discovery of the weapons cache in her flower garden. Liliuokalani's secretary, William Kaae, testified that he had prepared commissions appointing a new government and that he had engrossed a new constitution and several proclamations which would order martial law and rally the queen's subjects to support the restored monarchy. Several of the revolution's leaders told of meetings they had with the queen, strongly suggesting that she knew what was going on. The efforts of Liliuokalani's attorney, Paul Neumann, and her complete denials to nearly every allegation brought against her, failed to impress the military court. In the end, the court found Liliuokalani guilty and imposed the maximum sentence — a $5,000 fine and five years at hard labor. The humiliated ex-queen returned to her second floor "jail cell" in the palace. President Dole promptly remitted the hard labor portion of the sentence.

The sentences handed down by the military court varied, depending upon the evidence presented. Several of the leaders, including Wilcox, Nowlein, and Bertelmann, were sentenced to be hung. A majority of the other insurgents received fines of either $5,000 or $10,000 plus various prison terms ranging from five years to life in Oahu prison. The balance received suspended sentences or voluntarily exiled themselves from the islands rather than serve a prison term. Martial law ended on March 19, 1895, and the government returned to administering local affairs.

Several prisoners claimed foreign allegiance, thereby creating diplomatic complications. The intervention of the American and British diplomats plus a growing public opinion against severe punishments led Dole to mitigate the death sentences to

---

[1] The witnesses were William G. Irwin, Herman A. Widemann, Samuel Parker, J. Kalua Kahookano, Charles B. Wilson, and Paul Neumann. W. L. Stanley placed his notarial seal on the document.

[2] Judge W. A. Whiting headed the commission and received the rank of colonel. Captain W. A. Kinney served as judge advocate. The remaining members of the commission were Lieutenant Colonel J. H. Fisher, Captain C. W. Ziegler, Captain J. M. Camara, Captain J. W. Pratt, Captain W. C. Wilder, and First Lieutenant J. W. Jones.

Paul Neumann Speaking on Liliuokalani's Behalf at Her Trial in the Throne Room of Iolani Palace

State Archives/ San Francisco *Examiner,* February 6, 1895

Oahu Prison (Nicknamed "The Reef") [Insert — Prince Kuhio in Prison Attire]

State Archives (Both Photos)

fines and imprisonment. As time passed, the community felt intense relief, and Royalist supporters began petitioning the government for a general amnesty. On July 4, 1895, the five-year prisoners were released and the government reduced the sentences of the other prisoners. By early September, the government felt confident enough to grant conditional pardons to Liliuokalani, her nephew Prince Kuhio, and forty-seven other Royalists. On Thanksgiving Day, seven more Royalists received pardons, and by January 1, 1896, the last of the insurgents, including Wilcox,[3] was released. In addition, the government relieved Liliuokalani and the other Royalists from paying their fines, and the exiles were allowed to return to Hawaii.

Although Liliuokalani was freed from the palace on September 6, 1895, she could not change her residence wthout government approval. In October of the following year, she received a complete release, an absolute pardon, and complete restoration of her civil rights. In December, 1896, she sailed to the United States and remained there until the summer of 1898. During this time, Liliuokalani lobbied against annexation and wrote her memoirs with the help of Captain Julius A. Palmer, A Bostonian. The book, "Hawaii's Story by Hawaii's Queen," was published in 1898.

---

[3] Wilcox stayed out of trouble and later was elected as Hawaii's first Delegate to Congress. He served from December 15, 1900 to March 3, 1903. He died in October of 1903.

On April 26, 1895, several detachments of navy blue jackets and marines plus a band came ashore from the American warship *Philadelphia* ostensibly to conduct exercises in riot control and protecting American lives and property. The troops marched through downtown Honolulu, guarded important street intersections, scaled the seven-foot wall surrounding Kawaiahao Church, practiced bayonet exercises on a baseball field, and performed other infantry drills. While offering the citizens of Honolulu an impressive show, the military exercises unofficially demonstrated the United States' deep interest in the Hawaiian Islands and the strength of its forces should they be called upon to quell a civil disturbance.

With American influence increasing in the islands, the Hawaii annexationists patiently waited for President Cleveland's term to expire. During the United States' national elections held in November of 1896, the Democrats lost to the Republicans and their presidential candidate William McKinley who became the twenty-fifth president the following March. While McKinley was not a confirmed annexationist, he nevertheless warmed to the idea. Hawaii's annexation delegation met frequently with the senior men in the State Department, and on June 16, 1897, they signed a treaty of annexation similar to the one that had been withdrawn from the Senate in 1893. Both treaties called for the incorporation of the Hawaiian Islands into the American Union as a territory.

While the annexation treaty lingered in the Senate, new complications arose. The Japanese government formally protested that annexation would upset the status quo in the Pacific which was essential in maintaining peace in the area. In addition, Japan felt that annexation would seriously jeopardize the rights of Japanese subjects residing in Hawaii. The Hawaiian government had further complicated the issue by refusing to admit 1174 Japanese free laborers into the country in 1897. Previously, nearly all laborers had arrived under contract to the various sugar plantations. With annexation looming, the Republic of Hawaii took the position that too many Orientals would endanger Americanism in the islands.[1]

Japan, feeling her strength in the Pacific after a successful war with China, promptly sent a warship to Honolulu. Hawaii hurriedly appealed to the United States. The American Minister in Hawaii, Harold M. Sewall, received instructions stating that in the event the Japanese used force, he could, after consulting with the local authorities and the admiral in charge of naval forces in the area, land a suitable force and declare a provisional protectorate pending the conclusion of the annexation treaty. But diplomacy prevailed, and the Hawaiian and Japanese governments agreed to arbitrate the immigration dispute.

During the remainder of 1897 and into the beginning of 1898, Congress continued to drag its feet on the annexation treaty. The Senate debated the treaty in secret while the House, which had no ratification authority, publicly debated the pros and cons of annexing Hawaii. In an attempt to speed things up, the Hawaiian legislature appropriated $10,000 and sent President Dole and his wife to Washington in early 1898.

---

[1] In 1894, Congress repealed the McKinley tariff act, and through subsequent legislation, restored Hawaiian sugar to its privileged place in the American market while also eliminating the bounty system for domestically produced sugar. As sugar production rose sharply, the Hawaiian planters began importing more Oriental laborers, this time mostly Japanese. Thus business leaders, and the government which they supported, found themselves in a vicious circle; on the one hand, they needed cheap contract labor for the plantations and the economy to prosper, while on the other hand, they feared the growing Oriental influence on Western civilization. Many of these business and government leaders believed that annexation, without statehood, would enable Hawaii to be protected from Japan, and should cheap labor end, the wealth of the United States would help the islands avoid financial chaos.

Sailors Scaling the Wall Surrounding   **Official Navy Photo**
Kawaiahao Church During Riot Duty Training

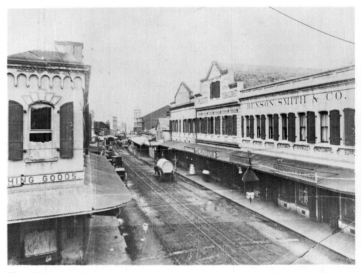

Fort Street in Downtown   **State Archives**
Honolulu in 1898

In spite of Dole's presence in Washington, it became clear to the McKinley administration that there were enough reluctant Democrats in the Senate to prevent the annexation treaty from receiving the necessary two-thirds majority. As the threat of war with Spain edged closer to reality as a result of the sinking of the battleship *Maine* in Havana harbor (February 15, 1898), the McKinley administration initiated another tactic to speed up annexation. Some fifty years before, Texas had been admitted to the Union by a joint resolution passed by a simple majority in both the House and the Senate. On March 16, the Senate Committee on Foreign Relations reported favorably on a similar resolution to annex Hawaii. By mid-May, the House Committee on Foreign Relations had done the same. But in the meantime, Congress had declared war on Spain in April, calling only for Cuba to be freed from Spanish control. On May 1, American warships, under the command of Captain George Dewey, sank the Spanish fleet in Manila Bay. American expansionists like Captain Alfred T. Mahan, Republican Senator Henry Cabot Lodge, and Assistant Secretary of the Navy Theodore Roosevelt quickly realized that in order to hold the Philippines, they would need a way station in the Pacific. Opposition to annexing Hawaii began to melt.

The defeat of the Spanish fleet at Manila Bay greatly relieved tensions in Hawaii. Even before war had been declared, the Republic of Hawaii had opened itself up for possible attack from

Spain by refusing to declare its neutrality, in effect becoming a silent partner with the United States. In addition, coal stockpiles were increased in anticipation of the arrival of American warships.

The first transports carrying American troops to the Philippines (the *City of Peking,* the *City of Sidney,* and the *Australia)* arrived in Honolulu on June 1. Huge crowds greeted the troops on shore. Schools closed, and elaborate decorations abounded. In two shifts, the approximately 2,500 American warriors were treated to an elaborate meal on the palace grounds. After taking on coal, the troop ships departed on June 4 bound for Manila. They were escorted by the *USS Charleston* which had arrived several days ahead of the transports. A second convoy of transports arrived in Honolulu on June 23. The islands were practically annexed. How could the United States permit the islands to get into trouble following such a display of good-will and generosity?

The Spanish-American War quickly brought the strategic importance of the Hawaiian Islands to the attention of the American public. The joint resolution for annexation passed the House on June 15 and the Senate on July 6. President McKinley signed the resolution into law on July 7, and the news reached Honolulu six days later. But final annexation was delayed by the immigration dispute still pending between Hawaii and Japan. The United States refused to inherit the controversy and therefore pressured the Hawaiian government for a quick settlement. The main stumbling block continued to be the amount of indemnity. As pressure mounted for a prompt settlement, the Hawaiian government finally agreed to pay the Japanese government an indemnity of $75,000 in return for Japan dropping all claims in the immigration dispute. This sum was paid on August 1.

While preparations were being made for the final transfer of the Hawaiian Islands to the United States, additional problems arose which further delayed the formal ceremony. Most of these delays involved procedures for the ceremony itself while the remaining ones centered around such matters as tariffs, filling vacancies, court procedures, and other administrative topics. The date was finally set for noon on Friday, August 12, 1898. The two American warships in Honolulu Harbor, the *Philadelphia* and the *Mohican,* sent several detachments of troops ashore to attend the ceremonies and to assure an orderly transition.

Before a large crowd assembled in front of the executive building (formerly known as the palace), United States Minister Harold M. Sewall read the annexation resolution. President Dole then made a short speech to Sewall in which he yielded ". . . up to you as the representative of the Government of the United States, the sovereignty and public property of the Hawaiian Islands."

American Troops Camped at Kapiolani Park Prior to Being Sent to the Philippines State Archives

Sailors and Marines From the *USS Mohican* Preparing to Attend Annexation Ceremonies State Archives

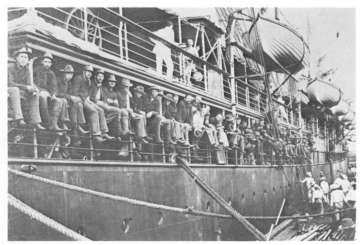

American Troops on the Steamer *Australia* in Honolulu Harbor State Archives

President Dole Transferring Hawaii's Sovereignty to United States Minister Sewall State Archives

Lowering the Hawaiian Flag at Annexation　　　　　　　　　　　　　　　　　**State Archives**

Following his short speech, Dole waved his hand and the Hawaiian National Guard battery and the warships in the harbor fired salutes to the Hawaiian flag. The Hawaiian national anthem, "Hawaii Ponoi," was played for the last time as the song of an independent nation. Taps were sounded, and the Hawaiian flag was hauled down.

Raising the American Flag at Annexation　　　　　　　　　　　　　　　　　**State Archives**

As the band played "The Star Spangled Banner," the American flag rose to its prominent position atop the executive building. Like it or not, the Hawaiians had become American citizens. Dole continued to lead Hawaii, only this time as governor designate of the Territory of Hawaii until Congress proclaimed a formal government. During this transition period, Sewall continued to reside in Honolulu, serving as Special Agent for the State Department which continued to supervise the island government until Congress legislated otherwise. With minor changes, the government of the Republic of Hawaii continued as the government for the annexed islands.

Many native Hawaiians avoided the annexation ceremonies. Liliuokalani, Kapiolani, Kaiulani, and other prominent alii had been invited to the ceremonies, but none of them accepted the invitations. Instead, most of them gathered at Liliuokalani's residence to console the deposed queen and the heir apparent, Princess Kaiulani. For them, it was the saddest day in memory. Their feeble attempts at resistance had failed in the past. Most of their leaders had withdrawn from politics, and the few that remained active found themselves at a disadvantage in the white man's political ways. Liliuokalani's immortal song "Aloha Oe" ("Farewell to Thee") would have seemed appropriate at this somber gathering of Hawaiian alii.[1]

Royalists[2] Consoling the Dethroned Queen   Bishop Museum

In December of 1899, stowaway rats from Asiatic seaports jumped ship in Honolulu and several outer island ports, spreading bubonic plague bacilli to local rats, fleas, and people. The first Honolulu victims were Orientals living in the squalid and crowded run-down tenements of Chinatown. As the death toll mounted, the Honolulu Fire Department, acting under orders from the Board of Health, set a number of controlled fires in an effort to eradicate the infested areas. On January 12, a strict quarantine was placed around the area and the Hawaii National Guard patrolled the area. Deceased victims were incinerated, and domestic workers could leave the area only after undergoing a thorough soap and shower disinfectant routine.

On January 20, 1900, one of these controlled fires went wild. A sudden gust of wind sent sparks spiralling into the air, and within minutes, one of the steeples of Kaumakapili Church (shown in the background of the photo at right) was engulfed in flames. The fire quickly spread to adjacent structures and soon roared out of control. Handicapped by low water pressure, the firemen watched in frustration. When it ended, the holocaust had consumed over thirty-five acres in the heart of the city. Miraculously, the great fire took no lives, but property damage ran into the millions and thousands of people were left homeless. The plague, considered over in April, claimed over sixty lives.

---

[1] Princess Kaiulani died on March 6, 1899. Following her death, Liliuokalani named Prince Kuhio and his brother Prince David Kawananakoa (David Laamea Kawananakoa Piikoi) heirs to the nonexistent Hawaiian throne. Queen Kapiolani, Kalakaua's widow, also died in 1899. Prince David lived until 1908. Queen Liliuokalani gradually mellowed in her later years and passed away on November 11, 1917. Prince Kuhio was elected as a Delegate to Congress in 1903 and he continued in that capacity until his death in 1922. These were the last great Hawaiian alii.

[2] Liliuokalani is seated in this photograph. Her nephew, Prince Kuhio (Jonah Kuhio Kalanianaole) is on the far left and Princess Kaiulani is standing between them.

Residents of Chinatown Being   State Archives
Evacuated During a Controlled Burning

Results of Controlled Burning in   State Archives
Plague Infested Chinatown

Shortly after annexation, President McKinley had appointed a commission to recommend legislation concerning a permanent form of government for the Hawaiian Islands. It consisted of Senator Shelby M. Cullom of Iowa as chairman, Senator John T. Morgan of Alabama,[3] Representative Robert R. Hitt, Dole, and Walter F. Frear, a justice of the Hawaiian supreme court. The three American commissioners journeyed to Honolulu to confer with Dole and Frear. In December, 1898, the commission issued a 560 page report, 395 pages of which were devoted to a digest of existing Hawaiian laws and recommendations on which ones should be repealed. The report further recommended a territorial frame of government in the form of a bill which Congress should enact.

But issues arising from the Spanish-American War delayed Congress for almost two years before it finally enacted a perma-

---

[3] Morgan, although a Democrat, was appointed in recognition of his long fight for annexation.

Dole's Inauguration as Governor of the Territory of Hawaii

nent form of government for Hawaii. Congress made some minor changes to the recommendations it had received, specifically dropping the property qualifications for voting and holding office. But the definition of citizenship remained more or less intact, thereby excluding Orientals.[1] The territorial frame of government was established with a bicameral legislature and a governor appointed by the president. Sanford B. Dole received the appointment as first governor of the Territory of Hawaii, and the new regime officially began on June 14, 1900. Thus began a new era in Hawaii's history.

---

[1] Citizens of the Republic of Hawaii in 1898 automatically became citizens of the Territory of Hawaii and hence also of the United States. Since the citizenship requirements of the Republic excluded nearly all Orientals, they likewise were excluded under territorial status.

Appendix A

RULERS OF THE HAWAIIAN ISLANDS

NATIVE RULERS OF THE HAWAIIAN KINGDOM

NAME	BIRTH	ACCESSION	DEATH
Kamehameha I	c. 1758	1795	May 8, 1819
Kamehameha II (Liholiho)	1797	May 20, 1819	July 14, 1824
Kamehameha III (Kauikeaouli)	Aug. 11, 1813	June 6, 1825*	Dec. 15, 1854
Kamehameha IV (Alexander Liholiho)	Feb. 9, 1834	Jan. 11, 1855	Nov. 30, 1863
Kamehameha V (Lot Kamehameha)	Dec. 11, 1830	Nov. 30, 1863	Dec. 11, 1872
William C. Lunalilo	Jan. 31, 1835	Jan. 8, 1873	Feb. 3, 1874
David Kalakaua	Nov. 16, 1836	Feb. 12, 1874	Jan. 20, 1891
Liliuokalani	Sept. 2, 1838	Jan. 29, 1891**	Nov. 11, 1917

* Kaahumanu served as regent from Nov. 27, 1823 until her death on June 5, 1832. This was during Liholiho's trip to England and the minority of Kamehameha III. Kinau succeeded Kaahumanu as regent until that position was abolished on March 15, 1833.

** Liliuokalani was overthrown on January 17, 1893, thereby ending the Hawaiian kingdom.

RULERS OF THE PROVISIONAL GOVERNMENT

NAME	TERM BEGAN	TERM ENDED
Sanford B. Dole#	Jan. 17, 1893	July 4, 1894

RULERS OF THE REPUBLIC OF HAWAII

Sanford B. Dole	July 4, 1894	June 14, 1900##

#Dole was born in Hawaii on April 23, 1844. The son of missionary parents, he died on June 9, 1926.

##Although the United States annexed Hawaii on August 12, 1898, the territorial government was not formally established until June 14, 1900. During that time, Dole served as governor-designate. On June 14, 1900, Dole became the first governor of the Territory of Hawaii. He ended his term on Nov. 23, 1903 to become Judge of the Federal District Court.

Appendix B

SELECTED BIBLIOGRAPHY

Alexander, William D. *A Brief History of the Hawaiian People.* New York: American Book Company, 1891.

Alexander, William D. *History of Later Years of the Hawaiian Monarchy and the Revolution of 1893.* Honolulu: Hawaiian Gazette Co., 1896.

Armstrong, William N. *Around the World with a King.* Rutland, Vt.: Charles E. Tuttle Co., 1977 (Reprint of the 1903 edition).

Bailey, Paul. *Those Kings and Queens of Old Hawaii.* Los Angeles: Westernlore Books, 1975.

Barrow, John. (Editor). *Captain Cook's Voyages of Discovery.* New York: Dutton, 1906.

Beaglehole, John C. *The Life of Captain James Cook.* Stanford: Stanford University Press, 1974.

Beevers, John. *A Man for Now; The Life of Damien de Veuster, Friend of Lepers.* Garden City, N.Y.: Doubleday and Co., Inc., 1973.

Bingham, Hiram. *A Residence of Twenty-One Years in the Sandwich Islands.* New York: Praeger Publishers, 1969 (Reprint of the 1855 third and final edition).

Black, Cobey & Mellen, Kathleen D. *Princess Pauahi Bishop and Her Legacy.* Honolulu: The Kamehameha Schools Press, 1965.

Blackman, William F. *The Making of Hawaii: A Study in Social Evolution.* New York: Ams Press, Inc., 1977 (Reprint of the 1906 edition).

Bradley, Harold W. *The American Frontier in Hawaii: The Pioneers, 1789-1843.* Gloucester, Mass.: Peter Smith, 1968 (Reprint of the 1942 edition).

Burns, Eugene. *The Last King of Paradise.* New York: Pellegrini & Cudahy, 1952.

Callahan, James M. *American Relations in the Pacific and the Far East, 1784-1900.* New York: Praeger Publishers, 1969.

Curtis, Caroline. *Builders of Hawaii.* Honolulu: The Kamehameha Schools Press, 1966.

Damon, Ethel M. *Sanford Ballard Dole and His Hawaii.* Palo Alto, Cal.: Pacific Books, 1957.

Dampier, Robert. *To the Sandwich Islands on the H.M.S. Blonde.* Honolulu: University Press of Hawaii, 1971 (Reprint of the original edition).

Daws, Gavan. *Holy Man; Father Damien of Molokai.* New York: Harper & Row, Publishers, Inc., 1973.

Daws, Gavan. *Shoal of Time; A History of the Hawaiian Islands.* New York: The MacMillan Co., 1968.

Day, A. Grove. *Hawaii and Its People.* New York: Meredith Press, 1968.

Day, A. Grove. *Kamehameha, First King of Hawaii.* Honolulu: Hogarth Press, 1974.

Dole, Sanford B. *Memoirs of the Hawaiian Revolution.* Honolulu: Advertiser Publishing Co., Ltd., 1936.

Dulles, Foster R. *America in the Pacific; A Century of Expansion.* New York: Da Capo Press, 1969.

Dutton, Meiric K. *Hawaii's Great Seal and Coat of Arms.* Honolulu: Loomis House Press, 1960.

Ellis, William. *Polynesian Researches: Hawaii.* Rutland, Vt.: Charles E. Tuttle Co., 1969 (Reprint of the original edition).

Farrow, John. *Damien the Leper.* New York: Sheed & Ward, Inc., 1937.

Feher, Joseph. *Hawaii: A Pictorial History.* Honolulu: Bishop Museum Press, 1969.

Frear, Walter F. *Mark Twain and Hawaii.* Chicago: The Lakeside Press, 1947.

Gillis, James A. *The Hawaiian Incident: An Examination of Mr. Cleveland's Attitude Toward the Revolution of 1893.* Freeport, N.Y.: Books For Libraries Press, 1970 (Reprint of the 1897 edition).

Hawaii, University of — College of Arts and Sciences, Dept. of Geography. *Atlas of Hawaii.* Honolulu: University Press of Hawaii, 1973.

Hawaiian Mission Children's Society. *Missionary Album; Portraits and Biographical Sketches of the American Protestant Missionaries to the Hawaiian Islands.* Honolulu: Hawaiian Mission Children's Society, 1969.

Hodge, Clarence L. *Building Honolulu.* Honolulu: Chamber of Commerce of Honolulu, 1950.

Honolulu Star-Bulletin. *Centenary Number, 1820-1920; Supplement to Honolulu Star-Bulletin, April 12, 1920.* Honolulu Star-Bulletin, 1920.

Ii, John Papa. *Fragments of Hawaiian History.* Honolulu: Bishop Museum Press, 1963 (Translated by Mary Kawena Pukui).

Joesting, Edward. *Hawaii; An Uncommon History.* New York: W. W. Norton & Co., Inc., 1972.

Judd, Gerrit P. IV. *Dr. Judd, Hawaii's Friend.* Honolulu: University of Hawaii Press, 1960.

Judd, Walter F. *Let Us Go: The Narrative of Kamehameha II, King of the Hawaiian Islands, 1819-1824.* Honolulu: Topgallant Publishing Co., Ltd., 1976.

Judd, Walter F. *Palaces and Forts of the Hawaiian Kingdom: From Thatch to Amercian Florentine.* Palo Alto, Cal.: Pacific Books, 1975.

Kamakau, Samuel M. *Ruling Chiefs of Hawaii.* Honolulu: The Kamehameha Schools Press, 1961.

Kent, Harold W. *Charles Reed Bishop, Man of Hawaii.* Palo Alto, Cal.: Pacific Books Publishers, 1965.

Kinney, W. A. *Hawaii's Capacity for Self-Government All But Destroyed.* Salt Lake City, Utah: Frank L. Jensen, 1927.

Kuykendall, Ralph S. *Hawaii: A History, From Polynesian Kingdom to American State.* Englewood Cliffs, N.J.: Prentice-Hall, Inc., 1961.

Kuykendall, Ralph S. *The Hawaiian Kingdom.* Vol. I, *1778-1854, Foundation and Transformation.* Honolulu: University of Hawaii Press, 1938.

Kuykendall, Ralph S. *The Hawaiian Kingdom.* Vol. II, *1854-1874, Twenty Critical Years.* Honolulu: University of Hawaii Press, 1953.

Kuykendall, Ralph S. *The Hawaiian Kingdom.* Vol. III, *1874-1893, The Kalakaua Dynasty.* Honolulu: University of Hawaii Press, 1967.

Lee, William S. *The Islands.* New York: Holt, Rinehart and Winston, 1966.

Liliuokalani. *Hawaii's Story by Hawaii's Queen.* Rutland, Vt.: Charles E. Tuttle Co., 1964 (Reprint of the 1898 edition).

Loomis, Albertine G. *For Whom are the Stars?* Honolulu: University Press of Hawaii, 1976.

Malo, David. *Hawaiian Antiquities (Moolelo Hawaii).* Honolulu: Bishop Museum Press, 1951.

McGaw, Sister Martha Mary, C.S.J. *Stevenson in Hawaii.* Honolulu: University of Hawaii Press, 1950.

Medcalf, Donald & Russell, Ronald. *Hawaiian Money; Standard Catalog.* Honolulu: Nani Stamp & Coin, Ltd., 1978.

Mehnert, Klaus. *The Russians in Hawaii, 1804-1819.* Honolulu: University of Hawaii, 1939.

Mellen, Kathleen D. *An Island Kingdom Passes.* New York: Hastings House, 1958.

Mellen, Kathleen D. *The Lonely Warrior: Kamehameha the Great of Hawaii.* New York: Hastings House, 1949.

Mellen, Kathleen D. *The Magnificent Matriarch, Kaahumanu, Queen of Hawaii.* New York: Hastings House 1952.

Mouritz, A. *Our Western Outpost Hawaii.* Honolulu: The Printshop Company, Ltd., 1935.

Mrantz, Maxine. *Women of Old Hawaii.* Honolulu: Aloha Graphics and Sales, 1975.

Nellist, George F. (Editor). *The Story of Hawaii and Its Builders.* Honolulu: Honolulu Star-Bulletin, Ltd., 1925.

Olmstead, Francis A. *Incidents of a Whaling Voyage.* Rutland, Vt.: Charles E. Tuttle Co., 1969 (Reprint of the original edition).

Potter, Norris W. *Hawaii, Our Island State.* Columbus, Ohio: Charles E. Merrill Books, Inc., 1964.

Price, A. Grenfell. (Editor). *The Explorations of Captain James Cook in the Pacific as Told by Selections of His Own Journals 1768-1779.* New York: Dover Publications, Inc., 1971.

Pukui, Mary K. *Place Names of Hawaii.* Honolulu: University of Hawaii Press, 1974.

Pukui, Mary K. & Elbert, Samuel H. & Mookini, Esther T. *The Pocket Hawaiian Dictionary.* Honolulu: University Press of Hawaii, 1975.

Russ, William A. *The Hawaiian Republic (1894-1898).* Selinsgrove, Pa.: Susquehana University Press, 1961.

Schmitt, Robert C. *Demographic Statistics of Hawaii, 1778-1965.* Honolulu: University of Hawaii Press, 1968.

Scott, Edward B. *The Saga of the Sandwich Islands (Volume I).* Crystal Bay, Lake Tahoe, Nev.: Sierra-Tahoe Publishing Co., 1968.

Smith, Bradford *Yankees in Paradise (The New England Impact on Hawaii).* Philadelphia/New York: J.B. Lippincott Co., 1956.

Stewart, Charles S. *Journal of a Residence in the Sandwich Islands, During the Years 1823, 1824, and 1825.* Honolulu: University of Hawaii Press, 1970 (Reprint of the 1830 edition).

Tate, Merze. *Hawaii: Reciprocity or Annexation.* East Lansing, Mich.: Michigan State University, 1968.

Tate, Merze. *The United States and the Hawaiian Kingdom (A Political History).* New Haven, Conn.: Yale University Press, 1965.

Thurston, Lorrin A. *Memoirs of the Hawaiian Revolution.* Honolulu: Advertiser Publishing Co., Ltd., 1936.

Towse, E. *The Rebellion of 1895.* Honolulu: Hawaiian Star, 1895.

Tregaskis, Richard W. *The Warrior King: Hawaii's Kamehameha the Great.* New York: MacMillan Publishing Co., Inc., 1973.

United States 91st Congress, 1st Session, 1969. *King Kamehameha I and Father Damien; Hawaii's Presentation to the National Statuary Collection.* Washington, D.C.: U.S. Government Printing Office, 1970.

Villiers, Alan J. *Captain James Cook.* New York: Charles Scribner's Sons, 1967.

Weaver, Samuel P. *Hawaii, USA.* New York: Pageant Press, Inc., 1959.

Webb, Nancy. *Kaiulani: Crown Princess of Hawaii.* New York: The Viking Press, 1962.

Williams, Edith B. *Ka Hae Hawaii (The Hawaiian Flag); The Story of the Hawaiian Flag.* Honolulu: South Seas Sales, 1963.

Wyndette, Olive. *Islands of Destiny; A History of Hawaii.* Rutland, Vt.: Charles E. Tuttle Co., 1968.

Young, Lucien. *The Real Hawaii; Its History and Present Condition.* New York: Arno Press and the New York Times, 1970.

Zambucka, Kristin. *The High Chiefess Ruth Keelikolani.* Honolulu: Mana Publishing Co., 1977.